THE JAPANESE
AND SUN YAT-SEN

THE JAPANESE

AND SUN YAT-SEN

Marius B. Jansen

Stanford University Press
Stanford, California

Stanford University Press
Stanford, California
Copyright 1954 by the President and Fellows of Harvard College
First published in 1954 by Harvard University Press
Paperback edition first published in 1970 by Stanford University Press
Printed in the United States of America
SBN 8047-0700-6
LC 70-108027
Last figure below indicates year of this printing:
79 78 77 76 75 74 73 72 71 70

FOR MY MOTHER AND FATHER

ACKNOWLEDGMENTS

It is a pleasant duty to thank the many friends whose advice, help, and encouragement have made this study possible. The topic was first suggested to me by Professor John K. Fairbank in 1946, and in the years that followed he and Professor Edwin O. Reischauer gave freely of their knowledge of China and Japan. To them both I owe a debt of gratitude for their generosity and interest.

Professor Serge Elisseeff, under whose kindly guidance I first began the study of Japanese and Japanese history, has also followed the project with interest and encouragement. I am grateful to him and to the Harvard-Yenching Institute, of which he is the Director, for sharing with the Department of History of Harvard University in making publication possible. Thanks are also due the Social Science Research Council for a research grant in 1949.

Many persons have helped in assembling and lending the books which I have used. The writings of the Japanese participants in the Chinese revolution are seldom found in the major libraries, and librarians have had to go out of their way to locate them. Dr. A. Kaiming Chiu of the Harvard-Yenching Institute Library and Dr. Mary Wright and Dr. Nobutaka Ike of the Hoover Library at Stanford were most helpful. Dr. Fang Chao-ying first lent me his copy of the memoirs of Miyazaki Torazō, and Dr. Charles B. Fahs and Professor Chitoshi Yanaga also provided volumes from their personal libraries. Dr. Edwin G. Beal, Jr., of the Library of Congress helped select the microfilm copies of the Tokyo Foreign Office files. A Rockefeller Foundation grant to the Far Eastern and Russian Institute of the University of Washington enabled me to visit Japan in the fall of 1951, and thereby to gather more material as well as to meet several of the participants in this story. Mr. Miyazaki Ryūsuke, Mr. Tokutomi Iichirō, and the late Kojima Kazuo were unfailingly gracious in extending their help, as were many of the Japanese authors mentioned in the text.

Of the many who have read all or part of the manuscript and contributed their suggestions, I should like to thank Dr. E. Herbert Norman, Dr. Nobutaka Ike, and my colleagues at the University of Washington, Professors George Taylor, Franz Michael, Hellmut Wilhelm, John M. Maki, and especially Richard N. McKinnon, who by his careful reading spared me many an egregious blunder. All of the above, and many others, have my hearty thanks. What merits this first work may possess derive largely from their help. I remain, of course, responsible for the errors which remain.

M. B. J.

Seattle, Washington
July 1954

CONTENTS

ILLUSTRATIONS

Following page 118

Rubbing of inscription composed by Sun Yat-sen to honor Yamada Yoshimasa.

Power of attorney given by Sun Yat-sen to Miyazaki Torazō.

Following page 166

Photograph taken on the occasion of a visit by Sun Yat-sen to the graveyard of the *Genyōsha* adventures in Fukuoka during Sun's visit to Japan in 1913.

INTRODUCTION

By the first of June 1929, the Northern Expedition of the Kuomintang armies had been brought to a successful conclusion. The Russian advisors had been welcomed, used, and then repudiated. Chiang Kai-shek, although humiliated by unexpected Japanese opposition to his forces as they advanced through Shantung in 1928, had emerged shortly after from a temporary retreat in Japan as the new strong man of the Nationalist Government. He had established a firm alliance with the financial and industrial forces of the treaty ports, and, secure in domestic force and foreign praise, seemed likely to give China the stability and consolidation of power it had lacked so long.

Ever since April of 1925, the remains of Sun Yat-sen had lain in a temple in the Western Hills outside Peking. From that eminence they awaited permanent committal near the capital whose central location Sun had believed as early as 1895 was an essential factor in national unity. And, now that the turbulence of the war lord era had been brought to an end, Sun Yat-sen was returning to Nanking. From a magnificent mausoleum on Purple Mountain outside the city he was to overlook the deliberations of the new government as it took up the tasks of internal reconstruction and abolition of the unequal treaties. In Sun's new role as patron saint of Chinese nationalism the inadequacies and inconsistencies of his efforts were forgotten, and he seemed sure to exert greater force and influence from his lofty resting place than he ever had through his activity in the valley below.

On this first of June, the boom of guns broke the dawn silence to announce to the thousands assembled along the Chung-shan Road that the last rites for Sun had begun. A procession over two miles long moved out of Nanking. It was made up of soldiers, Boy Scouts, representatives of many guilds, and Girl Guides. The thousands of simple mourners who lined the roadside were held back by a thin line of rope guarded by lines of soldiers. Conscious of the role they had played in making this day possible, the soldiers remained alert and vigilant and kept their fingers on the triggers of their Mausers. The throngs watched the varied elements of the procession pass quietly, until at last their patience was rewarded by seeing the large and elaborate casket on the funeral car. Behind the hearse followed Madame Sun, her brother T. V. Soong, her sister and Chiang Kai-shek, Sun Fo and his wife, Hu Han-min, and other comrades of the fallen leader. All were dressed simply and severely in white. From the hearse trailed ropes of blue and white, and to these members of the diplomatic colony and members of the Kuomintang Central Executive Committee attached themselves.

Over four hours later, at ten-thirty, the hearse had reached the base of the mountain that was to be Sun's resting place. The chief mourners, who had changed to automobiles outside Nanking, reformed to mount the steps. The bearers removed the casket to a massive catafalque of blue and white poles, and began the slow and laborious climb. This time the chief mourners led. The upward climb took over thirty minutes. Bands along the incline broke the silence playing the special dirge that had been composed for the ceremonies. The bearers, working in relays of sixteen, were helped at times by various of the mourners. Behind them came a group of civilian and unofficial mourners.

A group of Japanese were conspicuous among these mourners, and among them two venerable members stood out for their striking appearance. At the final ceremonies within the mausoleum one of the Japanese held a place of honor next to Chiang Kai-shek.[1]

Those two Japanese and their company of friends got little attention from observers at the funeral ceremonies, but they stood there as testimony to a very important part of the ideals for which Sun Yat-sen had lived and worked — Pan Asianism. The carnage of the war with China, which Japan waged under slogans of Asiatic brotherhood, has put those slogans in very bad repute. Nevertheless, for Sun Yat-sen those ideas were more than words; they were the integrating rationale that made possible his alliance with the Japanese who had come to do him honor. He himself never tried to slight the part which the Japanese aid had played in his work. "We must wait," he wrote, "for the official history of the Chinese Revolution to record in greater detail the invaluable work of our

Japanese friends." [2] Few of those friends had done more than the two kindly graybeards who now stood before his tomb.

Tōyama Mitsuru, seventy-four, had devoted over fifty years to a cherished project of Asian unity under Japanese leadership and inspiration. But the fiery nationalism which his spiritual followers espoused made an equal partnership with China out of the question, while Chinese students who had breathed in the same type of nationalism in Japan would accept nothing less than full equality. As a result, Tōyama had achieved little more than some close friendships. His help to Sun Yat-sen had not availed to keep the latter from accepting Soviet aid later, and in death Sun's legacy of opposition to imperialism had served chiefly to stiffen opposition to the desires of Tōyama's followers. Chiang Kai-shek too had been a recipient of Tōyama's favors, but he was already resentful of Japanese interruption of his northward progress a year before. Under the influence of his American-educated wife, Chiang seemingly made a poor candidate for Tōyama's type of Oriental leadership basing its strength on Asiatic virtues and goals.

Inukai Ki, also seventy-four, popular Parliamentarian, had devoted a lifetime to the struggle for representative government in Japan. He was as conscious of the necessity for Asiatic unity as Tōyama or Sun, and he never failed to attack the government if its policies seemed too pro-Western, too dominated by the Anglo-Japanese alliance. Inukai had found Sun a like-minded Asiatic, one who needed and appreciated Japanese aid, and one who usually accepted Japanese explanations that aggressive lapses in Japanese policy were due more to the unworthy Chinese government which was their mutual foe than they were due to fundamental Japanese expansionism. Inukai had been a staunch supporter of Sun Yat-sen. In times of depression for the revolutionary cause, he had been able to soften official displeasure against Sun, and he had often given him shelter. In times of prosperity, Inukai was a source of aid by his appointment of agents to investigate and help the revolutionary cause. In 1932, Inukai summed up his feelings toward Sun: "Few can be more genuinely sympathetic toward the Chinese nationalists and their aspirations than I have been. When Sun Yat-sen and his associates were exiles among us . . . I shielded them. For a time Sun Yat-sen lived with me. My home was a secret meeting place. . . Often they shared my food and clothes and my meager income. When Sun Yat-sen lived with me, I told him that the only sensible way China could follow was the way pursued by Japan." [3]

Once before, in 1911, Inukai and Tōyama had gone to China together. At that time there had been with them a third bearded figure, Miyazaki Torazō. He was represented at the tomb by his son and by a friend, Kayano Chōchi. Sun Yat-sen had found the closest *rapport* with Miyazaki and Kayano; they were men who used the words of John Stuart Mill and who sought the solutions of Henry George. Their presence had probably done more to atone for Japanese errors than all the rhetoric of the government officials.

However anomalous the coöperation of Chinese nationalists with Japanese expansionists, that of the disparate groups represented in that small group of Japanese was no less remarkable. Tōyama stood for the old Japanese virtues and the samurai spirit; he considered himself a modern equivalent of the anti-foreign theorists at the end of the Tokugawa era, and he professed to carry on the spirit of that last great feudal warrior, Saigō Takamori. Miyazaki had been nurtured in a different tradition of protest. The fear of Western imperialism, phrases of western liberalism, and the arguments of an embryonic agrarian socialism, had produced in him a singularly unstable mixture of agrarian radicalism and Oriental traditionalism. Inukai's represented a third path of opposition to the oligarchic government and the predatory West. He had chosen the way of parliamentarianism, and he was a veteran of the first organizations formed to agitate for an elective assembly. Because of the inherent weaknesses of Japanese "liberalism" of early Meiji days, his group had found it necessary to rely more and more upon nationalistic agitation in its fight against the government. Due to a dearth of political education and experience in Meiji Japan, his parties gradually came under increasingly direct control of the industrialist forces, who sought to use them to keep the government on a course of gradual commercial penetration of neighboring lands.

The collaboration of three such different groups was possible only so long as they could agree on mutual foreign and domestic opponents — Western imperialism and domestic repression. That collaboration was closest when the opponents were strongest, and it weakened with them. Sun Yat-sen's greatest intimacy with those Japanese groups came during the Meiji era. By 1929, although their individual representatives might continue as friends, the three Japanese groups could no longer work together.

Miyazaki's early death was symbolic of the passing of his group, whose position was least stable and soonest anachronistic. The early agrarian radicals had had to choose between a withdrawal from politics and conversion of their party into a Parliamentary foil to other groups by representing similar and competing commercial interests. Miyazaki, Ōi Kentarō, and most of their companions in Asian adventure had chosen the former course. The coöperation between Inukai's party men and Tōyama's nationalists also ended, for as Japanese power grew the foreign issue was no longer their main concern. Inukai and Tōyama thus found themselves on opposite sides in the fight for universal suffrage which had been waged for years before the adoption of the legislation in 1925. In 1932, Inukai, who had just won an election by promising to use his wide knowledge of China to administer a firm policy there, was cut down by young navy officers who objected to the entire machinery of parliamentarianism. To them, it seemed as much a usurpation of the Imperial prerogative as the old oligarchy had seemed to Inukai and Tōyama.

In other words, these groups were able to work together only because they had a common foe, for their solutions were not uniform. The same thing was true in their Asian interests; they could help Sun Yat-sen revolt, but, the revolution once accomplished, they could not combine to help him build.

*   *   *

The pages which follow will trace the coöperation of those Japanese with Sun Yat-sen. The close friendships which brought the Japanese to Nanking in 1929 turned out to be the only permanent result of that coöperation, but it remains a highly significant chapter in the relations between China and Japan. After the friendships between Japanese nationalists and Chinese nationalists changed to enmity, both sides regretted their former intimacy. Except for the

Miyazaki group, most Japanese decided that the Chinese had proven themselves unworthy ingrates. In turn, the Chinese came to read back into events at the turn of the century a consistent plan for eventual Japanese aggression.

Whether one accepts either of these interpretations or prefers a third, the story of the doings of the Chinese and Japanese friends deserves telling; its main characters were colorful and intriguing activists. Moreover, it is a story full of revealing sidelights on the better-known developments of Chinese republicanism and Japanese militarism. In the progression of Sun Yat-sen's friendship with the Japanese, from a warm partnership at the turn of the century, through a gradual disenchantment as Chinese nationalism and Japanese power grew, and, finally, into desperation as Sun tried to gain Japanese support against Yuan Shih-k'ai, one sees mirrored the effects of political and international strains on the fortunes and character of the Chinese leader and his Japanese friends.

Several important themes emerge from the details of the co-operation of Chinese republican nationalists with Japanese imperialists and parliamentarians.

In the first place, it becomes apparent that the idea of an Asiatic union under Japanese leadership to combat Western imperialism was not merely the contrivance of Japanese imagination. In re-creating the contemporary attitude and climate of opinion which Chinese revolutionaries and Japanese nationalists shared at the turn of the century, this story will show that for Chinese, as well as for Japanese, the overwhelming danger was Western imperialism. To meet this certain threat, less certain enemies could logically be used. For Sun and his friends, China and Japan had so much in common that there was no reason why they should not work together.

The main actors in this coöperation certainly had a great deal in common; they represented comparable adjustments to the West. Sun Yat-sen and his friends among the Japanese liberals subscribed to a rather poorly thought out and frequently contradictory set of political ideas. The Western impact had invalidated many of the tenets of their own tradition only to replace them with a jumble of ideas that seemed useful and attractive. Sun Yat-sen and Miyazaki Torazō put their faith in the single tax of Henry George, however poorly it applied to the problems of an Asiatic peasantry, and Ōi Kentarō could misread Western liberalism to stress chiefly its possibilities for greater national unity. Sun went on to put his faith in the initiative and referendum, as though the products of generations of self-rule would solve China's problems overnight. The friendship of such men could easily transcend national boundaries. Men like Sun, Miyazaki, Ōi, and their Korean and Filipino associates were on the fringe of political and intellectual respectability in their societies. They were also impatient with delay and with theories that threatened to retard Asia's rise to full equality with the West. They were activists and adventurers. The activities that will be described here constituted for them a way of life and, usually, a form of income as well. For several decades Sun and his Japanese friends pooled their resources and the contributions made by others toward their activities. Full time workers for the "new Asia," they were professional revolutionaries who lived by and for conspiracy and adventure.

It follows naturally that such individuals approached success only when their activities were useful for those who held political and economic power in their respective societies. Sun Yat-sen, despite his ties with the new commercial class of China, was a consistent loser in tilts with opponents whose support was better rooted in Chinese society. His Japanese colleagues had even less likelihood of success. Idealists like Miyazaki and Ōi Kentarō might become popular heroes, but they could never come through with promised help. Inukai and Tōyama, politician and nationalist, enjoyed more stable backing. Their industrial and military sponsors had fairly definite goals, however, and those goals proved inconsistent with the glowing promises held out to Sun Yat-sen. By the end of the Meiji period Miyazaki and Ōi were little in evidence, and Sun's bids for Japanese help took on the appearance of sordid deals for power.

Despite the ultimate failure of the elaborate plans and theories of men like Ōi and Miyazaki, however, this study suggests that previous estimates of Meiji Japan have been too sweeping and too severe. The Meiji period has become the victim of historical analysis which reads back into that period the tight totalitarian controls which prevailed in 1941. The Meiji environment was actually a vastly more stimulating and invigorating one than it is credited with having been. On the great issue of how to construct a modern state there was not a Japanese attitude, but there were attitudes. However general the goal of a strong state, the means advocated were so diversified that they could easily have resulted in ends as different from those originally contemplated as the Meiji government itself was different from the new Shōgunate envisaged by many samurai who struggled against the Tokugawa. To be sure, the Meiji government was authoritarian. But among the intellectuals, who were then an even more strategic group than they have been since, regimentation was far less pronounced; the haste of Western reforms made for a very different and a less self-centered atmosphere. The Japanese government itself has acknowledged this. The official *Kokutai no hongi* (Cardinal Principles of the National Entity of Japan) of 1937 [4] deplored the frequently uncritical acceptance of elements of individualism in the Meiji period. In early Meiji a *Kokutai no hongi* setting forth the proper philosophical, governmental, educational, and religious opinions, would have aroused spirited opposition. Even the Rescript on Education of 1890 drew the criticism that its virtues were outmoded, its ideas were Chinese, and its purpose reactionary.

Certainly this diversity of opinion in Japan helped make Sun Yat-sen's close friendships there possible. Sun's reputation has suffered along with that of Meiji Japan. If the Japan of 1898 was like that of 1941, Sun had no business finding friends there. For some representatives of the treaty ports, Sun's every act betrayed an egotism which allowed him to subscribe successively to Japanese aggression and Bolshevik terror.[5] On the other hand, doctrinaire Marxists find that Sun fits so few categories that he can be dismissed as a rather unimportant running dog of Japanese imperialism.[6] It is difficult to claim for Sun Yat-sen qualities of perception or discrimination as to Japanese motives, but the retention of any part of his claim to a leading role in Chinese nationalism requires the adoption of a contemporary and reasonable view of the Japanese society that he knew.

Finally, this study will make possible a new appraisal of Japanese policy and plans for Asia. When it has been seen that there were more often plans than a plan, and that the tortuous path of government policy in Tokyo represented diversity of opinion as often as it represented duplicity, the way will be open for an interpretation somewhat different from that which has been generally accepted. For most writers, the shifts and turns in Japanese policy toward China were motivated only by a desire to use dissident forces for eventual aggression.[7] Consistent adherence to such a plan would have required of Japan an undeviating policy as well as superhuman ingenuity. During the years Sun dealt with his Japanese friends, Japan never had both, and usually she had neither.

This is not to deny that most Japanese desired some degree of control over China for their country. Every logic of commerce, culture, and politics made this an obvious goal. But from 1895 to 1915, China was in constant ferment. Who was most likely to win? Which side would benefit Japan most? Which group would provide the best neighbor for Japanese cultural and political traditions? Considerations like these were the ultimate root of the Tokyo government's hesitation and indecision. Moreover, the Japanese government could not always act on its decisions. It was under constant pressure from organized and popular groups which favored opposing parties in China. As different groups won out for a time, their personnel and their Chinese friends would find temporary favor and funds. The checkered course of the relations between Miyazaki Torazō and his government absolves him of duplicity as thoroughly as it absolves his government of charges of consistency.

But Japan's many shifts of policy toward China derived from more than the pressure exerted on the Tokyo government by particular factions. Equally important was the changing power status of Japan and the consciousness of that status on the part of Japan's military and political leaders. After the Sino-Japanese War, Japan for the first time took an active, leading role in the various attempts at change in China. Through the Reform Movement of 1898 and the Boxer Rebellion of 1900, she moved cautiously, hoping that a change would prove possible before Western imperialist powers would divide the Chinese melon. Still unsure of her own power, Japan dreaded a possible division of China. Slogans like *Shina Hozen*

(Preservation of China) had a greater emotional impact in Japan than the "Open Door" in America. Yet, if division were to ensue, Japan must have her share. Both domestic politics and Japanese concepts of international justice required this. Thus 1900, the year of Japan's coöperation in the Allied Expedition in North China, was also very nearly the beginning of her active expansion on the mainland in South China. The same year saw Japanese support of a revolt led by Sun Yat-sen. Perhaps Tokyo thought Sun would prove a useful puppet. On the other hand, he might have been able to create the national state that would avert European division of the spoils, a national state that would naturally be grateful to Japan.

This hesitation gradually changed to a conservative policy after the Russo-Japanese War. Japan was now securely in control in Asia, and she need no longer tailor her policy cautiously to fit international politics and Chinese revolutionary movements. Now she could bully the decadent Manchu dynasty. With that dynasty apparently well under control, Japan could indulge in the luxury of reflecting that a neighboring constitutional monarchy would be more desirable than a friendly and grateful republic. As a result, Sun Yat-sen found less favor. His Japanese friends, once government agents, now became objects of surveillance by new government agents.

Yet public opinion in Japan forbade a clean break. Moreover, there was always the possibility of a successful revolution. Thus Sun was ejected from Japan, but he was set down gently with funds and apologies. His movement no longer carried the blessing of Tokyo, but it remained a constant concern of Tokyo. Any potential Chinese government was worth time and money.

After the Revolution of 1911 replaced the tottering Manchu dynasty with the comic "Republic" of Yuan Shih-k'ai, Japan had less to lose; Yuan would grant her less than his Manchu masters had. Once again Sun could be harbored. He was at least a convenient weapon with which to threaten Yuan. The failure of so many policies and hopes, the constant irritation of a public opinion definitely favorable to Sun, and the skillful evasion of Japanese demands by Yuan Shih-k'ai, finally led to the Twenty-One Demands in 1915. Far from solving Japan's problems, these but complicated them. Her neighbors in China were no more desirable or dependable than previously, and the critics at home were more scornful than ever.

Japan never really solved the problem she set herself of selecting desirable continental neighbors. The personalities in China changed from time to time, but the basic problem of selection between constitutional monarchy, conservative reformers, and revolutionary republicans was one which the Tokyo government was never able to resolve. As World War II neared its end, the Tokyo leaders had reached an ambiguous compromise whereby they found themselves supporting all three forms of government simultaneously in China. In Manchukuo the last Manchu Emperor headed a constitutional monarchy. In Peking, a delegation of venerable Confucian reformers held for moderation and conservatism. In Nanking, the "revolutionary" Kuomintang of Wang Ching-wei claimed the mantle of Sun Yat-sen. Each of these regimes, and all of the personalities involved, traced their origins to the two decades of revolutionary ferment with which this study is concerned.

Those decades cannot be considered without a grasp of the contemporary problems and attitudes of the individuals concerned. Since this is a story dominated by personalities, Inukai Ki, Tōyama Mitsuru, Miyazaki Torazō, and Sun Yat-sen must first be considered in relation to their backgrounds.

THE IDEOLOGICAL AND POLITICAL
CONTEXT OF MEIJI EXPANSIONISM

1

The Japanese adventurers who helped Sun Yat-sen considered themselves the heirs of an outstanding group of patriots who had opposed Tokugawa rule at the end of the feudal period. Before considering the manner of their involvement in the Chinese scene, it is desirable to survey briefly the tradition to which they laid claim. Each group of Japanese derived from a tradition of ideological and political protest which was historically related to Japanese thought about Asia in general and about China in particular.

Sun Yat-sen's friends shared many things with their Tokugawa predecessors. Their stress on character, on will, and on the merit of spectacular deeds of protest found them squarely in line with some of the most hallowed traditions of recent Japanese history. Their indignation with the "weak" and conciliatory policy of the Japanese government had been anticipated by the scorn of the Tokugawa patriots for the Shōgunate's hesitation after the arrival of Perry. Since the Tokugawa writers had held up the fate of China as an example of the dangers of appeasement of the West, it was natural for their Meiji followers to seize that point and develop it further. They despised the weakness, backwardness, and traditionalism of the recent past. They felt that all these conditions obtained in China. In fact, degeneration was so far advanced that China could not possibly save herself. Finally, many Tokugawa writers had felt it essential for Japan to protect China from the West. The Tokugawa parallel could thus be a useful one.

In the early years of the Meiji period these theoretical positions were buttressed by concrete social and economic grievances. The samurai class found itself pushed aside. A small privileged group had ensconced itself in power. Its cautious attitude in foreign affairs provided a perfect touchstone for political dissension. Militarists broke with their government over the issue of war with Korea. Others argued for the same war in hopes of achieving representative institutions. Long before Tōyama Mitsuru and Inukai Ki stood together at the tomb of Sun Yat-sen, Saigō Takamori and Itagaki Taisuke worked together for war in Asia.

1. Ideological Forerunners of Meiji Adventurers

The Japanese who worked with the Chinese revolutionaries were men who had a great interest in Chinese affairs and problems. Some sought in China a way to combat their own government. They wanted to overthrow that government by accusing it of neglecting the national interests in China and in Asia. Others, more idealistic, hoped for the establishment of a friendly government in China which would institute reforms that might prove beneficent to all Asia.

These men all justified their activity by comparing themselves to the opponents of the Tokugawa regime during its closing days. Like those men, they called themselves *shishi* (men of high purpose). Most of them added to this the title *rōnin* (unemployed samurai, lit. "wave men"). The Meiji *shishi* considered themselves homeless, self-denying idealists dedicated to the achievement of lofty national goals set a generation earlier.

The Tokugawa *shishi* had justified their desperate struggle against the Shōgunate by accusing it of usurping the rightful prerogatives of the Emperor. To this charge they added others; the Shōgunate had failed to prepare for the coming of the West, and it was subservient to the foreigners. The Meiji *shishi* transferred to their own government the charge once made against the Tokugawa — it constituted a barrier between Emperor and subjects. The oligarchy ruled selfishly. Worse, it hesitated to offend the foreigners; it was not struggling for revision of the unequal treaties.

At the same time, however, the Meiji adventurers felt that their government compared very favorably with those of other Asian countries. The Japanese had managed to overthrow the Tokugawa Shōgunate when the impact of foreign and superior technology had demonstrated the archaism and inadequacy of the entire national structure. The Tokugawa government had come to seem a selfish usurpation that was corrupt, archaic, inefficient, and, ultimately, immoral. In philosophy, in political techniques, and in foreign policy, the Shōgunate had come to typify everything that was backward, outmoded, and — in one word — Chinese.

This attitude toward feudalism, obscurantism, and political weakness that had compounded the Japanese opinion of Tokugawa rule was extended to governments and nations that still languished under those crushing burdens. They, too, were historically anachronistic, morally wrong, and politically doomed. Just as the Tokugawa *shishi* had struggled to end corruption, inefficiency, and cowardly weakness in Japan, his Meiji successor felt impelled to pursue similar ends in China and Korea. The benefits and reforms of the Restoration of 1868 might seem meager at home, but they would be invaluable abroad.

These general prejudices and beliefs centered around several slogans of the Tokugawa *shishi* which seemed particularly useful.

a. Exclusion and loyalism

Tōyama Mitsuru and his fellow nationalists lost no opportunity to assert that their only ideology was contained in the slogan under which the opponents of the Shōgunate had rallied — *Sonnō, jōi: Revere the Emperor, Drive out the Barbarians*. It would be superfluous to detail the broader political, economic, and intellectual context in which these slogans matured in Tokugawa days, for we are concerned chiefly with the emotional content of these shibboleths. That content was the legacy of the *shishi* who, in dramatic gestures of fidelity and protest, dared to flout the Tokugawa rules and laws. Such patriots, by their eagerness in courting almost certain death, became models for the Meiji extroverts who followed.

For the nationalists of modern Japan, examples like those of Hayashi Shihei (1754–1793), Gamō Kumpei (1768–1813), and Takayama Hikokurō (1747–1793) provided striking proof that a seemingly insignificant individual could inspire his contemporaries. All three men broke feudal barriers by travelling about Japan. They prized their loyalty to the Emperor above that due their lords and the

Shōgun, they brought home to their fellows the truth about Japan's disunity and weakness, and they challenged punishment and death for their beliefs. Historians have sometimes dated the decline of Tokugawa power from the time of these patriots.[1]

During the Meiji period such spectacular acts of patriotism were so respected that no government figure could afford to be indifferent to them. Of necessity, however, such measures were best suited to gestures of protest. Responsible public officials could only be the objects of protest. As a result, the Meiji oligarchs became the victims of the precedents set by their teachers.

b. Danger from the West

The Tokugawa *shishi* also warned against imminent aggression by England or Russia. At the same time, they denounced their government for not having prepared for this. The Tokugawa antiforeign agitators, like their Meiji successors, centered their censure not on the foreigners, who were insensible to their invective and usually safe on their gunboats, but on the government which had so dishonored its self-assumed responsibility as to bring Emperor and country to the brink of ruin.

Such writers were usually scholars who had learned of the English moves in China from Chinese books or through contacts with the small Dutch settlement at Deshima. Two such scholars were Watanabe Kazan (1793–1841) and Takano Chōei (1804–1850).[2] Watanabe was one of the first to insist on coastal defense and renewed intercourse with foreign countries. After he was arrested and reprimanded, he committed suicide to spare his lord difficulty. His friend, Takano Chōei, was a prominent student of Dutch medicine. Takano's crime came with the publication of a little volume entitled *Yume Monogatari* (The Story of a Dream) in 1838. In this, he described a dream in which the British missionary Dr. Morrison was about to come to repatriate some Japanese fishermen. The Shōgunate seemed likely to deny his ship entrance, and Takano was worried about the consequences. "Morrison has fixed his residence in Canton," he wrote, "and exercises control over many warships. Moreover there are many islands in the vicinity subject to

England. If we treat Morrison unlawfully what calamity may it not entail!"[3] The author was seriously mistaken, for Dr. Morrison had been dead several years, and the ship named for him had already been turned away. Nevertheless, the book showed a new interest in foreign problems. For the unorthodox solution he advocated, Takano was arrested. He escaped, only to be cut down later in a bloody fight with the police.

Most of the factual material such *shishi* used in their arguments against the government and its policies derived from the example of the plight of China. Writers warned of the identity of Chinese and Japanese interests, and pointed out that Japan would soon share the unhappy fate which was China's after the Opium War ended in 1842. Their advice, which ranged from suggestions for alliance with China to an ambitious plan for conquest of Asia to anticipate Western imperialism, made expansionism a logical corollary of loyalism and anti-foreignism.[4]

c. Western science, Eastern morals

The best informed and most responsible of the Tokugawa *shishi* realized that loyalism and anti-foreignism contained no adequate answer for the situation which Japan faced, and they knew that military adventures were unthinkable for years to come. They warned that Japan would have to learn Western techniques in order to maintain her independence. When the country was split between advocates of *kaikoku* (opening the country) and *jōi* (driving out the barbarians), such men counseled a temporary apprenticeship for Japan — a temporary *kaikoku* for an eventual *jōi* policy.

The leaders of this school were Dutch scholars who realized the futility of opposing Western weapons with effete samurai.[5] Sakuma Shōzan (1811–1864), the most important member of this school, showed the changes of *shishi* thought in his lifetime. Sakuma progressed from "official" to "heretical" Confucianism before he turned to Dutch learning because of its value in defense, war, medicine, and technology. After the Perry treaties had been signed, Sakuma decided that Japan stood to gain by trade with the West. For this reluctant acceptance of the *kaikoku* position, he was struck down by an anti-foreign fanatic. Nevertheless, he exerted tremendous influence through his students.[6] For Meiji nationalism, however, none of those students was as important as one who knew only failure and discouragement in his lifetime.[7]

Yoshida Shōin (Torajirō) (1830–1859) achieved fame by his celebrated attempt to leave Japan with Commodore Perry. While in prison, he wrote a book which outlined his plan for national expansion. Three years before his death he was released on parole; he then founded a small school in which he expounded to young samurai his doctrines of imperialism.

At first, Yoshida had been a student of things Chinese; he was an advocate of exclusion from Japan for all foreigners. By 1849 he had decided that England was bent on the conquest of Korea and Japan, and he called for military action to head off the crisis. The best bar to England, he felt, would be Japanese expansion on the mainland of Asia. Yoshida justified all this by his strong belief in the sacred character of the Emperor-state. His was a divinely ordained hierarchic order wherein the smaller should serve the larger as a servant his lord, and secondary countries should present their tribute to the sacred land. Yoshida wrote that Japanese had formerly been able to reconcile loyalty to the Emperor with service to the Shōgunate, but he felt that such loyalty would no longer suffice to bring about the military and inner unity that was needed. Gradually Yoshida came to advocate the opening of Japan in order to profit by Western knowledge. This done, he planned expansion to Manchuria, Korea, Formosa, and the Philippines. These areas, in turn, could serve as bases against England, Russia, and America. Yoshida was bitterly opposed to the Perry and Harris treaties, for he regarded them as humiliating. He was executed for his complicity in a plot to assassinate the official who had negotiated those treaties.[8]

Yoshida had a tremendous influence on the next generation of *shishi*. Among his pupils were such men as Kido Kōin, Itō Hirobumi, Yamagata Aritomo, and Shinagawa Yajirō.[9] Ironically enough, he was the particular patron saint of the men who fought against his pupils when those pupils came to power.

There were, of course, other figures and other themes among the

Tokugawa writers. But enough has been said to suggest the traditions of ultra-nationalist, emotional fervor which Meiji *shishi,* like Tōyama, inherited. The few personalities that have been named were, on the whole, those to which the Meiji figures felt most attracted. They were not slow in telling their Chinese friends about such heroes. When the Chinese reformer Liang Ch'i-ch'ao fled to Japan in 1898, he adopted the name Yoshida after one of the *shishi* explained to him the life story of Yoshida Shōin. Sun Yat-sen himself used the name of Nakayama Shū. When he was becoming too well known under that name, Sun changed to the name of that other medical student, Takano Chōei.[10]

2. Social Bases of Political Protest in Meiji Japan

The influence of the Tokugawa expansionist theorists whose lives and ideas have been mentioned would have remained insignificant if there had not been a sizeable body of discontented and embittered men in the new Meiji society. The fortunes of Sun Yat-sen and his cause were to be conditioned to a considerable degree by stresses and strains within Japan.

The burdens the Meiji regime carried were so heavy that it would have been remarkable indeed if all classes had been fully satisfied with the procedures that were followed. But since the change was engineered by a very small group of leading samurai from the western fiefs, their reforms inevitably aroused fierce opposition. The new government, like the earlier Shōgunate, failed to provide outlets for restless energies and ambitions. Instead, the Meiji oligarchy had to restrain the anti-foreign frenzy of the warrior class. In the race against time and foreign imperialism, it also had to strengthen the nation by speeding the industrialization and modernization that had begun in late Tokugawa days. A modern army and navy had to be created to guard against disaffected areas within Japan as well as to discourage foreign aggression. The dangers of Russian moves to the north, and the example of European domination of China, were more generally known and seemed more menacing than they ever had before.

In order to achieve the required strength and unity, feudalism fell by the wayside as the daimyō were offered governorships, pensions, pension commutations, and, finally, new titles of nobility. With such rapid changes, many felt victimized or neglected.

a. Economic and ideological complaints

The heaviest burden fell upon the peasantry. The costs of the new government were far greater than could be met by the old levies of rice. The new industries required substantial subsidies. Since most merchants of feudal days proved unable to make the shift to modern capitalism, for the most part the giants of the new Japanese industry were former samurai financed by their government. Government help was constantly needed to meet the unequal competition from foreign products which profited from low tariffs set up by the unequal treaties. The costs of the army and navy, and the pensions of the privileged classes, subjected the tax structure to tremendous strains. In the government's anxiety to avoid foreign control and foreign loans, the whole cost devolved upon the peasantry.[11] The new land laws, which permitted alienation, subjected peasants to new and increased usury, tenantry, and hardship. The peasants saw their sons called up for military service or attracted to the shifting proletariat of the new manufacturing towns, and they were constantly on the verge of mutiny. For the first decade of Meiji, in fact, peasant riots and uprisings took place at a greater rate than they had in the years of greatest Tokugawa unrest.

Along with the peasants, many conservative writers objected to the myriad reforms and changes. Foreign ideas, goods, and visitors centered attention anew on those things completely and typically Japanese. Such writers were concerned lest the essence of things Japanese, the kokusui, be lost, and they tried to wage with their books the same hopeless anti-foreign struggle of the die-hard warriors who constantly embarrassed the new government by murdering foreigners. The priest Sada Kaiseki (1818–1882), for instance, expressed the conviction of many who opposed the principles of the settlement with the West.[12] Sada fought for the retention of the principles of feudalism, and stressed the differences between Japan and the West. He felt that they were in fundamental opposition in human nature, customs, culture, government, economics, and thought. Moreover, Sada felt that it would be quite possible to drive the invaders from Japan thanks to the greater population and higher virtue of the Japanese.

b. The discontented samurai

The frustrated hopes of the former samurai posed a far more serious problem than conservative peasants or obscurantist writers. Most of the samurai involved in the Restoration struggles had little interest in westernization. Their only desire had been an upset of the rigid political framework in order to open up new opportunities for themselves. Many had little more in view than the establishment of a new Shōgunate under their leadership; they wanted opportunity, jobs, and adventure.

Instead, they were the first victims of the reforms that ended feudalism. Their social position was lost, their rice incomes were diverted to taxes imposed by the new government, and they were quietly let down with small and inadequate pensions. During the long years of Tokugawa peace, the warriors' income had dwindled steadily. Under the new regime, they received pensions which, in 1871, amounted to only half of their earlier salaries; in 1876, those pensions were paid off altogether. The new conscript army deprived them of their traditional occupation, and before long over half of the nearly two million members of samurai families were hardly able to provide for the necessities of life. The government did what it could to help. Samurai were set up in business, they were given land, and they were given jobs in the new army, bureaucracy, and police force. But there were always more who could not be accommodated and who could not adapt themselves to the new order.[13]

The warriors of the northern and Tokugawa clans caused little trouble. They had been defeated in battle, and indeed, many were no longer very warlike. Moreover, they were nearer the new centers of industry. The southern samurai, however, posed a more serious problem. They had led the Restoration movement, and they naturally had the highest hopes of all. The first difficulties of the new government were thus with the two lesser clans of the first coalition, Tosa and Hizen. When these had been defeated, there remained the warriors of Satsuma. And after it had been demonstrated that the discontented groups were no match for the armies at the government's disposal, leading samurai from southern clans tried a new variant of the old plan; they decided to use Western ideas to defeat the westernizers.

Disgruntled samurai dominated every movement of opposition to the Meiji government. Under Saigō Takamori, they tried first to direct that government into paths of military expansion that would ensure their primacy in state councils. When this failed, they led several great rebellions. Thereafter they formed political parties to agitate for representative government. At all times they held the foreign policy up to attack and ridicule; it was decried as weak and imitative. Because of that policy, Japan was rapidly losing her proper role in China and Asia.

The Japanese who stood at Sun Yat-sen's tomb in 1929 were all former samurai. Inukai had become an advocate of representative institutions. Tōyama, most Quixotic and most popular, had professedly modeled his life upon that of Saigō Takamori, a man whose contribution we must now consider.

3. EXPANSIONISM AND POLITICAL OPPOSITION

The first great conflict within the oligarchy came over the question of war or peace with Korea. During the absence of a mission led by Iwakura Tomomi in 1873, a war party led by Saigō Takamori decided that insulting replies from Korea to a Japanese request for formal diplomatic relations should be answered by the use of force. The *Seikanron* (Discussion about sending an expedition to Korea) was the first major attempt by the military minded to reassert their primacy. The episode marked a decisive milestone for modern Japan; it was the first, and remained the most celebrated, attempt to direct the government's plans by capitalizing on foreign insults. In the course of the debate, the coöperation of "liberals" with militarists was prophetic of the days to come. For this reason, the elements that made up the war party deserve brief mention.

Saigō Takamori wanted to be sent to Korea as ambassador in hopes that his murder would provoke war. He felt that war was necessary to reassert the traditional military values of Japan, to give the military their proper share in the new government, and to salvage the remnants of the samurai class who had failed to adjust to the new conditions. According to Torio Koyata, one of Saigō's followers, it was evident that Japan could not reform her martial and polite learning simultaneously. Since militarism, which could be reformed more quickly than polite learning, was the real root of Japan's strength, she should concentrate on restoring the samurai class as the core of an army that would receive two thirds of all revenue.[14]

A Foreign Office group, led by Soejima Taneomi, thought that the war would be an aid to national prestige as well as a solution for internal difficulties. In a conversation with the British Minister Harry Parkes, Soejima confidently predicted that two armies of 25,000 men could drive across the Korean peninsula and subjugate the country in one hundred days. He boasted that Korea could support 100,000 samurai; her resources in minerals and silk would prove valuable, and her government would be delegated to Saigō and to himself.[15] Soejima was not concerned with Korean independence; he felt that the peninsula was sure to be seized soon, and he wanted Japan to be first on the scene. He was furthermore convinced that Japanese independence required control of Shantung and of North China as well as control of Korea.[16]

The third element in the Korean war party is of particular interest, for it included the outstanding leaders of later Japanese liberalism. It is true that Itagaki Taisuke, Gotō Shōjirō, and Etō Shimpei were not advocates of a liberalism that would be recognized as such today, but in their opposition to the clan-dominated government and in their fight for a measure of popular participation they offered the most hopeful element in the Meiji political picture. They introduced a new ingredient into the argument: the idea that decisions of war and peace should be those of all the people. We are told that even Saigō shared this view.[17]

During the debate, the activities of adventurers and secret agents foreshadowed the role of the expansionist societies in the decades to come. Sada Hakubō (1832–1907), who had been an exponent of anti-foreignism in Tokugawa days, argued that Korea was necessary to Japan on historical and geopolitical grounds. In 1870 he went to Korea and tried, unsuccessfully, to act as the properly delegated Japanese representative. When he returned, his plan for the invasion of Korea met with agreement from Itagaki and others, but Ōkubo Toshimichi, a member of the Iwakura mission, disapproved.[18] Sada's plans were supplemented by those of many others. Etō Shimpei, for instance, at one time suggested sending Buddhist priests to China and following them with troops for their protection.[19] In 1872, Saigō, after consulting with Soejima and Itagaki, sent three personal followers to Manchuria. On their return, they were convinced of the weakness of the Chinese forces, and their reports contributed to the war fever.[20] Again in 1873, Saigō sent army and navy men as consuls to observe conditions in Formosa, Amoy, and South China. Among other things, they brought back a map of Formosa that was used by the Formosan Expedition of 1874.[21] Still another advocate of the Korean war, Maruyama Sakura (1840–1899), formed a scheme for a filibustering expedition to Korea. A German merchant was to lend the money, and Jardine, Matheson and Company were to provide a ship. When the plan was discovered, Maruyama was jailed. The general enthusiasm for war was both reflected and stimulated by such plans and planners.[22]

Despite the popularity of the war party, they lost the argument to Iwakura, who prevailed by stressing Japan's peril from Russia and the West.[23]

The advocates of war left the government, but the oligarchy's problems were far from solved. Discontent was rife, and the opposition was now sure of the support of some of the most popular leaders.

As a sop to the extremists, therefore, the government allowed a punitive expedition against Formosa to avenge maltreatment of some shipwrecked Ryūkyū Island fishermen by aborigines.[24] The expedition consisted of some 3600 samurai headed by Saigō Tsugumichi, the brother of Takamori. Since the expedition was so small and the negotiations which followed it were only partially successful, it solved few of the government's problems.[25]

In the years that followed, the foreign policy of the oligarchy was not calculated to satisfy the extremist nationalists who had left the government. Several unsuccessful attempts to make a treaty with Korea bore fruit in 1876 only because of Chinese mediation. The government's anxiety to win equality with the West in imperialist prestige was such that it did all it could to eliminate a mild mutual assistance clause from the first treaty with China in 1871.[26] The adventurers and extremists knew they could expect little from such reasonableness and subservience to the West, and treaty revision and domestic reforms were conducted with constant pressure and opposition from below. The samurai revolts that followed were waged under slogans calling for war with Korea, and not until all hope of such a war was past did political organization for representative government assume any considerable momentum. Asian expansion was thus from the first the most popular program to use in attacking the government, and Japanese parliamentarianism was chauvinistic from its very beginning.[27]

a. The samurai revolts

After the leaders of the war party left the government, their samurai followers were highly displeased with the government they had helped create. Not only had their hopes for glory and adventure proved misplaced, but they themselves were now objects of government suspicion. They ruminated bitterly on the ingratitude and cowardliness of the government. Feudal tradition and personal bonds were still strong with them, and regional affiliations resulted. The majority of the able men of Tosa followed Itagaki into his political parties, as those of Hizen followed Ōkuma Shigenobu. The Satsuma samurai who had not been included in the government structure followed Saigō, while other Satsuma men came to control the navy in the same way that their Chōshū allies controlled the army.

At first, political associations were not very different from the study groups set up for military purposes. Both sought to keep the expansionist issues alive. In January of 1874, Itagaki, Gotō Shōjirō, Soejima, Etō, and a few others enlarged an earlier, informal group to form the *Aikokukōtō* (Public Party of Patriots). In the statement of principles they drew up, the first three of four points stressed the preservation and protection of the universal rights of the people, patriotism, and national unity through popular participation in government. Their phrase for peoples' rights, *minken,* became the slogan of the political battles to come. The fourth point extended these concerns to the rest of Asia: "We, who seek to champion this universal right, of course regard it as a world task to champion throughout Asia."[28] Thus the first expressions of Japanese liberalism were directed toward broad, Asian goals.

Three months later Itagaki, Kataoka Kenkichi, and others founded in Tosa the *Risshisha* (Self Help Society). This was designed as a political training school for young samurai.[29] In February 1875, Itagaki set up another of these groups, the *Aikokusha* (Patriotic Society). The organization meeting in Osaka was attended by some forty samurai, the largest number connected with any of these groups to date. Once again, their manifesto proclaimed that the members, motivated by great love of Emperor and country, were going to press for inalienable individual rights.[30] These early samurai groups were forerunners of the later liberal parties, but to the government they seemed dangerous regional associations made up of restless malcontents.

The Saga Rebellion, led by the Restoration hero Etō Shimpei, showed that the government was not far wrong in identifying early liberalism with samurai discontent. Etō had been associated with the most progressive political circles in Japan. It seems clear that in his case, as with that of Saigō later, the immediate impulse to revolt was provided by the rural firebrands who constituted the membership of the early political groups. These youths thought that the nation would rally behind a war with Korea, and they felt that Japan should lose no time in taking advantage of this. The Saga men formed a *Seikantō,* or Korea Expedition Party. This was soon banned by an official proclamation which pointed out that Japan's real danger came from Russian aims, and not Korean snubs. The group nevertheless continued its activities, and it even explored the possibilities of obtaining foreign arms. The revolt broke out in February 1874, and it was fought under slogans which held that decisions for peace or war were properly those of all the people. The revolt thus had overtones of the *minken* struggle that was to come, and it used the foreign issue in order to put maximum pressure on the government.[31]

It remained for Saigō Takamori to lead the Satsuma samurai in the last and greatest movement of warrior protest against the new government. Saigō later became a hero of modern Japanese nationalism, and the expansionist societies generally dated their origin from his revolt.[32]

While Itagaki and the others had busied themselves with political associations, Saigō had organized private schools in Kagoshima. Those schools stressed loyalty to the Emperor, and they taught Chinese literature and military drill and organized political discussions. Students were taught to resent the Tokyo government's oppressive activities in restricting the Emperor's rule and the peoples' rights.[33]

Saigō wanted to postpone the revolt until the foreign situation became more threatening, but the rebellion broke out in February 1877, after a rumor spread that the central government had sent agents into Satsuma to assassinate Saigō. The suspicious samurai needed little prodding; they soon announced an expedition to Tokyo to remonstrate with the Emperor and to free him from his evil advisers. Bitter fighting raged until September when the last rebel band was wiped out after the leaders had committed harakiri. The government was so hard pressed in men and resources to put down this formidable movement that it even petitioned China for aid in the form of munitions.[34]

After his death, Saigō became the great symbol of patriotism and loyalty for Japanese nationalists. In pleading that the Emperor was ill informed, he had acted in the best tradition of Japanese history. In his life, Saigō exemplified those qualities of samurai and hero for which the nationalist societies later exalted him. He was a large, powerfully built man; a good swordsman, and an advocate of the simple life. Above all, his every act was announced as motivated by reverence for the Emperor. His popularity was not restricted to anti-government factions, for he was honored with a famous statue in central Tokyo.

Moreover, almost every political faction except the ruling oligarchy shared Saigō's opinion that war in Asia would head off European imperialism. During the rebellion, the government was continually fearful of the participation of Itagaki's Tosa samurai on Saigō's side.[35] This fear was not unfounded, for certain militant and radical elements of Itagaki's group, led by Hayashi Yūzō, were in frequent communication with Saigō's group. Another group of *minken* advocates led by Miyazaki Hachirō (elder brother of Torazō) actually joined in the battle in hopes of upsetting the government. Only the government's Kumamoto garrison's early success in avoiding capitulation kept many other sympathetic elements in army, bureaucracy, and samurai circles from joining Saigō. Within the liberal groups, a peace faction led by Itagaki and Kataoka Kenkichi finally won out as Saigō's fortunes ebbed. Nevertheless, the difference between the factions was almost purely one of means, for secret government reports quoted Itagaki as saying, "Saigō strikes the government with arms, we strike it with *minken*."[36]

After Saigō's failure, the only tools that suggested themselves for those who still sought power and adventure were political association and chauvinistic agitation.

b. The political parties

Political parties were perhaps the strangest fruit of the chauvinistic discontent of the samurai. From what has been said, it must be evident that whatever parties hoped to find popular support would have to criticize the government for its weak foreign policy. Chauvinism was the prerequisite of political success. Inukai Ki, who stood with Tōyama at Sun's tomb in 1929, was a good example of the political system he represented. That system and its history can be sketched in outline.

The first political party, the *Jiyūtō* (Liberal Party), was formed by Itagaki, Gotō, Kataoka, Hayashi, and their fellows in 1881.[37] The program they drew up did not express itself explicitly on the future role of Japan in Asia, but it pledged its members to strive for a constitution, liberty, peoples' rights, the reform of society, and a stronger, united Japan.[38] The strong emphasis on national unity shows that in domestic, as in foreign, issues, the conflict between such groups and their government was less concerned with ends than with means. The liberals' pledge to strive for rights and reforms, however, was to have considerable significance when extended to neighboring Asian societies. In membership, the party was restricted largely to samurai and rural landholders who resented the industrialization which they had been forced to support. They had at their disposal many adventurers and rowdies, men who could be expected to enter heartily into any scheme for Asian adventure that might develop.

The other important party was the *Kaishintō* (Progressive Party), led by Ōkuma Shigenobu. Ōkuma, who was a Hizen samurai leader in the early Restoration days, had sided with the peace party on the Korean issue. Later, he left the government in disgust at the autocratic behavior of the Satsuma-Chōshū clique. The *Kaishintō* was based largely on the new urban capitalist classes, and in ideology it made greater use of the English utilitarians than it did of the French school which the *Jiyūtō* leaders preferred.[39] Through the two private universities controlled by *Kaishintō* sentiment, Ōkuma's Waseda and Fukuzawa Yukichi's Keiō, competent young men were produced for the newspaper, political, and business worlds. The *Jiyūtō* could not appeal to these young men, for it was too impulsive, too radical, and too violent.[40] Although, in a sense, the two parties played complementary roles in rural and urban areas, from the beginning personal interests and differences prevented coöperation between them.

In Asiatic affairs, Ōkuma's group played, on the whole, a less active and adventurous role than the radical wing of the *Jiyūtō*. Nevertheless, it later gave the Japanese rationale for aiding Chinese revolutionaries its classical setting in the "Ōkuma Doctrine."[41]

Inukai Ki (1855–1932), who will figure prominently throughout this study, was a good representative of Ōkuma's domestic following and its Asian concerns. Inukai's early interest in politics led him to take up journalism. He became known as a reporter during the Satsuma Rebellion. Later, he worked with Fukuzawa, and, with Ozaki Yukio, he entered the *Kaishintō* fold.[42] Of all Japanese political figures, Inukai was closest to Sun Yat-sen. He also had numerous and close friendships with other Asian reformers and revolutionaries.

The official answer to these parties, the government-sponsored

Teiseitō (Imperial Party), was founded in 1882 by a group of newspaper editors which included Maruyama Sakura, the man who earlier had agitated for war with Korea.[43]

Government surveillance and repression prevented the liberal parties from attaining the national dimensions which would have been required for effective campaign organizations. Many smaller groups suffered the fate of the *Tōyō Shakaitō* (Eastern Socialist Party), which was founded in 1882 and banned almost immediately, despite the fact that its platform called for nothing more dangerous than virtue, equality, and happiness.[44] But even if the government had been less severe, it is likely that regionalism and factionalism would have prevented strong national parties. For example, the *Kyūshū Kaishintō* of 1882 illustrated the anomalous coalitions that could result from separatism. In that group were to be found representatives of many groups from Fukuoka, Kumamoto, and Nagasaki, the Kyushu centers of discontent, enrolled under the banners of constitutionalism. Among them was Tōyama Mitsuru as representative of the chauvinist *Genyōsha*,[45] which was to figure prominently in the early stages of Japanese imperialism.

In this manner the lines were drawn for the political battles of Meiji. In those contests, as in the battles of Japanese feudal lords centuries earlier, the victory was often won by treachery and knavery through the defection of key figures in the political scene to the opposition. The kaleidoscopic changes that resulted suggest that power generally loomed more important than consistency of ideals. Nevertheless, slogans and appeals for liberalism and peoples' rights filled the literature and the papers, and the government often found it necessary to repress these media for fear that ideas might lead to action.

Before very long, the political leaders had lost much of their prestige because of the bitterness and vituperation they used in exposing the corruption of their fellows. As students and money tended to go to the *Kaishintō*, the *Jiyūtō* was increasingly subjected to the local and violent leadership of youths who were intoxicated by the early success of the party movement.[46] The one issue on which the party leaders could be sure of good publicity and respectability was their insistence on a strong foreign policy. Several times they were able to stop treaty reform projects by assailing the government as spineless and traitorous.[47] The wisdom of their choice of issues was reflected in the popular literature of the day, for during the efflorescence of political novels the best sellers' happy endings pictured Japan in control of Asian destinies.[48]

The dependence of the party leaders on the foreign issue naturally brought them closer to the position taken by the chauvinist societies.[49] During periods when the party leaders were temporarily in the government or away from Japan, their constituency, especially that of the *Jiyūtō*, moved ever closer to the violence and direct action the chauvinists favored.

In such circumstances, it is apparent that the alliance between political "liberals" and expansionist leaders which made possible the Japanese aid to Sun Yat-sen reflected many common interests. Both invoked the same historical figures to justify Japanese expansion; both believed in the necessity for a strong, united Japan. They were agreed in their annoyance with the dilatory, hesitant policy the oligarchs followed in their relations with the West. Practical considerations and political exigencies thus made possible in 1929 the presence of Inukai Ki and Tōyama Mitsurù, apparent ideological opposites and yet political allies, at the tomb of Sun Yat-sen.

PERSONALITIES AND PRECEDENTS

2

In tracing the historical relationship between liberalism and chauvinism in the development of political parties, we have been dealing with the upper strata of Meiji leadership. Men like Itagaki, Ōkuma, and Inukai represented the path of respectable, recognized political procedure. Such prominent citizens could hardly risk discovery in political plots involving direct action at home or abroad. In fact, when the democratic movement in the 1880's seemed likely to result in adventurist coups at home and filibustering expeditions abroad, the party leaders hurried to disband their following for a time in order to salvage their own respectabilities.

An exiled Korean or Chinese revolutionary in Japan looking for help would therefore have to find men of a different type. His search could lead him in several directions. If he needed money and shelter primarily, influential leaders of patriotic societies could harbor him. Tōyama Mitsuru and his men, justifying their interest on grounds of chivalry and *bushidō,* could then mediate between a Sun Yat-sen and Japanese political or financial figures interested in him.

If, on the other hand, the Korean or Chinese refugee sought ideological support, the "Japanism" of a Tōyama had little to offer. The conservatism of the respectable leaders, should they prove available, would also mean little to a man bent on establishing a republic in China or Korea. He was likely to find a sympathetic hearing only among the radical wing of the democratic movement. There were, in Japan, a chosen few who did not restrict their concern to impoverished samurai and ousted politicians. Men like Ōi Kentarō and Miyazaki Torazō extended their interest to questions of economic justice, an oppressed peasantry, and civil rights. To be sure, they were also patriotic Japanese, and they offered no bar to the expansionist slogans of the patriotic societies. They had no independent sources of support, and so they had to coöperate with other groups. They might even be available for government sponsorship if it seemed likely to further their aims abroad.

Such figures were ideal channels of aid and friendship to Sun Yat-sen. Since they specialized in the irresponsible adventurism that had helped discredit the party movement in Japan, they could even take an active part in descents on the China coast. They lived on the borderline of political and social respectability, and their activity could pass almost unnoticed. It could merge with that of the patriotic society stalwarts of Tōyama, and it could, at times, fit in with government plans. Best of all, their intrigue, at home and abroad, provided an ideal emotional outlet for former samurai disturbed by the rapidity of the transition from the self-importance of Tokugawa days to the restless boredom of industrialization and westernization.

The Korean or Chinese refugee would soon discover that he shared at least one aim with each of these disparate groups in Japan. Political leaders, liberals, and professional patriots were united on the issue of an Asia free from the humiliating symbols of Western imperialism. This common hatred of treaty ports, extraterritoriality, and arbitrarily fixed customs constituted a bond of considerable strength. By 1900, however, Japan herself was benefitting from these imperialistic encroachments, and in her concessions the exiles could at times operate on their own soil. But it was long before the menace of Japanese imperialism could compare with that of the West. Since Japan had freed herself, she was the logical candidate to help her neighbors. This was a theme that lent itself equally well to idealism, opportunism, and chauvinism.

The Japanese who became Sun Yat-sen's patrons and associates, however, shared with the Chinese leader more than a dislike of Western imperialism. Almost without exception they were, like Sun, professional adventurers and full-time plotters. They had little real ideological and financial independence in their own society. Tōyama Mitsuru, whose patriotic societies will be considered next, was, to be sure, well rooted in the traditional tenets of "Japanism." But for economic support he had to rely on the mine owners who found his activities useful and desirable. Ōi Kentarō, whose interest in reform in Korea furnished important precedents for Japanese relations with Sun Yat-sen, advocated a program of social and economic reforms whose main points were often similar to the program of Sun Yat-sen. Unfortunately, sources of support for such a position were so few that Ōi's "radical liberals" were forced to resort to extra-legal measures. Failing in these, they not infrequently found themselves working with Tōyama's nationalists. These examples and precedents inevitably affected Miyazaki Torazō, who, as a follower in the tradition of Ōi Kentarō, sought to help Sun Yat-sen. A brief consideration of the nationalist groups and their relation to the "radical liberals" will thus explain the coöperation of the two parties in extending help to Sun Yat-sen.

1. TŌYAMA MITSURU AND THE PATRIOTIC SOCIETIES

The early patriotic societies constituted another expression of samurai discontent with the Meiji government. Like the political parties, they were regional in origin. But unlike the political parties, they never lost this regional character. Their key point was the city of Fukuoka on Kyushu. Fukuoka is the closest to the Asiatic mainland of any point in Japan. It was the target of the Mongol invasion of 1274, and Hideyoshi's Korean expeditions used it as a port of embarkation in the sixteenth century. During the Satsuma Rebellion, Fukuoka was a center for landing and a base of operations for government troops. The samurai of the city were evidently particularly embittered at that time, for at one point several hundred samurai almost succeeded in capturing the fortress.[1] The city remained in a backwash of the progress of the rest of Japan. The new industries and their benefits, as well as the new government posts, had little effect on the population. The Fukuoka area produced chiefly coal. From the first, the Japanese coal industry was noted for the barbarous manner in which its labor force was recruited and worked.[2] The Fukuoka mine owners, grateful for Tōyama's emphasis on traditional, conservative values at home and his militant expansionism abroad, contributed generously to his various ventures. Fukuoka became "the spiritual home of the most rabid brand of Japanese nationalism and imperialism."[3]

a. Origins and aims

After the fall of Saigō, the Fukuoka samurai organized to further his principles as they interpreted them. In 1881 several small discussion groups joined to form the *Genyōsha,* named for the gulf (*Genkainada*) which separates Kyushu from the mainland. The three principles of the organization called for reverence to the Emperor, love and respect for the nation, and defense of peoples' rights.[4] These were not unlike the announced aims of the liberal parties, but the *Genyōsha* leaders interpreted them to mean that their society, ever watchful for slights and insults from other powers, would consider itself the guardian of the nation's prestige. Although the liberal leaders were equally conscious of foreign insults, in the case of the *Genyōsha* insults tended to become means to an end, reverence for the Emperor became a full time job, and peoples' rights came to mean the rights of the recruit. Historically, the society had considerable significance. It affected, directly and indirectly, numerous Japanese leaders. Tōyama Mitsuru, its outstanding figure, became by all odds the outstanding nationalist of modern Japan.

The chief historical significance of the *Genyōsha* lay in the many patriotic groups that it spawned. Of these, the *Kokuryūkai* (Amur, *Heilung,* "Black Dragon" Society), which was founded in 1901, was the most important. Both the *Genyōsha* and *Kokuryūkai* were dominated by the same group of Fukuoka nationalists led by Tōyama Mitsuru. The *Genyōsha* was primarily committed to preservation and protection of Japanese ideals and values through an aggressive foreign policy, while the *Kokuryūkai* had a more concrete aim: containment of Russia, which seemed about to swallow Manchuria. The society advocated the Amur River as Japan's boundary, and thereby envisaged a comfortable zone for Japanese expansion.

The *Kokuryūkai* set forth a general five point program covering culture, government, foreign policy, national defense, and education which serves as a useful summary of the themes most emphasized by such groups. In *culture,* the society stood for a reconciliation of Western and Oriental civilizations in a synthesis which would retain Oriental values. This would give Japan a leading role in the revival of all Asian peoples. The platform declared that *government* should be strengthened by removing restrictions on peoples' rights and obstacles to leadership. In this way all could unite to further the Imperial Way. The declaration of policy also pointed to the necessity for *social reforms* which would promote internal welfare and solve social and labor problems. This would make possible a more active foreign policy for overseas development of Japanese interests. In *national defense,* the nation should be imbued with the spirit of the Imperial Rescript to soldiers. Japan might then become a nation in arms. Finally, the *Kokuryūkai* took a firm stand against the government's *educational policy*. It warned that Japan should imitate less of the West in this vital matter, and substitute a basic indoctrination in national polity (*kokutai*) in order to further the virtue of the Yamato race.[5]

The *Kokuryūkai* made little attempt at secrecy. Its official histories chronicled in elaborate detail projects such as language schools, research expeditions, pressure meetings to influence foreign policy, and, on occasion, help for foreign revolutionaries. In Meiji Japan, traditions of the feudal past were far from dead. Under those traditions, character and personal leadership counted for more than the programs and projects the histories describe. The nature and effect of the nationalist groups can therefore best be studied by looking at the backgrounds and character of their heroes. These men were supposedly the personification of virtues their followers fought to preserve.

b. Leadership

Tōyama Mitsuru furnishes a striking example of the power of charismatic leadership. But he was enough of a traditionalist to keep from assuming the formal leadership of his societies. Instead, he worked through two associates who merit brief notice.

The career of the *Genyōsha* head, Hiraoka Kōtarō (1851–1906), illustrates the cross currents of constitutionalism and nationalism which were described earlier. Hiraoka was a Fukuoka man with considerable military experience. He fought in the Restoration battles, and he served with the Satsuma forces under Saigō. For this, he was later imprisoned. One of his fellow prisoners had been incarcerated because of complicity in Maruyama's abortive plan for a Korean expedition, and together they studied the Chinese classics. After their release, Hiraoka, following a brief period of activity in the liberal movement, planned a descent on Korea with his fellow Sinophile. Their scheme called for Hiraoka and some Fukuoka friends to go to Korea. Saigō Tsugumichi was to help them get there. The plan matured too late, however; Japan's settlement of 1882, which ended any hope of provoking war with Korea, was signed before the conspirators could move.[6] Hiraoka then entered business. His family holdings resulted in sudden weath for him as a mine operator, so that he was able to support various parliamentary parties as well as the *Genyōsha* he headed. After 1894, he served in the Diet. On the whole, his affiliations in politics were with the Ōkuma groups. He campaigned for an active continental policy to combat Russia.[7] For a time, he also owned a newspaper in Fukuoka which, of course, took a strong nationalist line.[8] Besides all this, Hiraoka contributed such large sums to the coalition *Kenseitō* party formed by Ōkuma and Itagaki in 1898 that he almost went bankrupt.[9]

Uchida Ryōhei (1874–1937), head of the *Kokuryūkai,* belonged to the second generation of adventurers and plotters. He too was a native of Fukuoka. He entered the *Genyōsha* as a youth. He liked Chinese studies, and he busied himself in intrigues for action in Korea and China. In Japanese politics, Uchida was to be found to the far right on almost every issue. He led agitation against the Portsmouth Treaty in 1905, and in 1925 he was arrested for complicity in the attempt on Premier Katō's life. During the depression years of the 1930's, Uchida was the leading figure in the *Seisantō* (Production Society), one of the important fascist groups that agitated for rule by the military.[10]

Tōyama Mitsuru dominated both of these men. It is difficult to give an accurate picture of Tōyama, for in him legend and fact are so intertwined as to produce a paradigm of Japanese morality and virtue. Tōyama never held a formal post or a responsible position, but he exerted tremendous influence. To his followers his obscurity, his enigmatic silence, and his obvious prestige signified benign wisdom, inscrutable purpose, and pristine honesty.

Tōyama was often compared favorably with the outstanding figures of the Japanese political scene. For instance, a talk given at Ōkuma's Waseda University by Dr. Miyake Setsurei in 1916 was devoted to comparative evaluations of Ōkuma, Inukai, and Tōyama. According to the speaker, Ōkuma had the highest rank; Inukai had a third (Imperial) rank, and Tōyama had none. In the popular mind, however, those ratings were reversed. Ōkuma's rank had been attained through compromise and bargaining, while Tōyama had never known compromise. Ōkuma had over 200 Diet followers, Inukai 27, and Tōyama none. But Ōkuma would have no followers if he lost his wealth and power, whereas Tōyama's followers would gladly die for him. Ōkuma was pro-Western, and could not read Chinese classics. Inukai was less Western, but read the classics in translation. Tōyama was indifferent to all study; he knew human beings, and therefore he was far the wisest of the three. Ōkuma was vainglorious, boastful, and swaggering. Inukai was somewhat more reserved while Tōyama confined himself to cryptic remarks. Ōkuma had never been known to write, Inukai was a skillful calligrapher, while Tōyama's poetry was superb. In short, Dr. Miyake concluded, the ladies would rate them: Tōyama, Inukai, and, finally, Ōkuma.[11]

This tells us little about Tōyama, but a great deal about his standing, for Ōkuma was the most human and popular of the early leaders. Statesmen came regularly to consult Tōyama. Some probably came to escape the wrath of Tōyama's youthful assassins, but many came because they respected him. As military rule grew nearer in the 1930's, Tōyama's fame became even greater. Premier Hirota Kōki, a Fukuoka man and a *Genyōsha* product, said "[Tōyama's] personality has had an extraordinary influence on mine, and I have taken him as model for my life." Matsuoka Yōsuke, not to be outdone, said, "I do nothing before finding what Tōyama's opinion is."[12]

The bare facts of Tōyama's life do little to explain or justify such fame. He was born in Fukuoka to a penniless samurai family, and he was successively adopted by two samurai families. The second of these, the Tōyamas who brought him up, were an impoverished household, for their small income of 18 *koku* for five persons was further reduced with the coming of the Restoration changes. Nevertheless, Tōyama stayed with them, and at their home he received the rudiments of samurai education.[13]

Tōyama was involved in an early reactionary samurai revolt led by by Maebara Issei, and the three year prison sentence he received for this put him out of action for Saigō's rebellion.[14] After the death of Ōkubo at the hands of a disgruntled samurai in 1878, Tōyama went to Tosa to see Itagaki. He suggested that with Ōkubo gone there was nothing to prevent Itagaki from leading a successful revolt. Itagaki, however, refused to consider the plan.[15] Tōyama approved of the founding of the *Risshisha* and the *Aikokukōtō*, however, and, as has been mentioned, he represented the *Genyōsha* at the founding of a Kyushu liberal party.[16]

Like Hiraoka, Tōyama made money from mining enterprises. He acted as middleman in selling the rights to valuable tracts of land to operators for the peasant owners. Tōyama busied himself in getting the navy to set up a coaling station at Fukuoka. He also recruited labor for the unpleasant task of mining the coal, a job which had previously been reserved for the *Eta*. Tōyama was clearly a valuable contact for the mine owners, since he got them the mining rights, recruited labor gangs with his young rowdies, and helped them get markets with the navy. Tōyama's Pan-Asian goals promised to provide more opportunities for such industries, and it is not hard to see why some of the operators thought highly of him.[17] Yet the panegyrists would have us believe that Tōyama, like a true samurai, had no concern for money. We are told that when he sold a mine he gave away the money with complete disregard of self to his needy samurai comrades.[18]

The account of Sugiyama Shigemaru (1864–1935) gives one some idea of the charismatic effect Tōyama had on his followers. When he first met Tōyama in 1885, Sugiyama tells us, he had no purpose in life; he was using a false name to escape punishment for anti-government activities. After talking with Tōyama about the need of restoring rule to the Emperor, however, the old thoughts and the old name fell away; "heretofore I had thought only of myself, and henceforth I was to make a total change, thinking only of man and the world, and of projects to aid them." Sugiyama's personality and talents were better suited to official life than were Tōyama's. For a time he was a police official. During the Russo-Japanese War he went to America at Premier Katsura's request; he negotiated a loan from J. P. Morgan and Co., and arranged for the purchase of war materials.[19] Subsequently, Sugiyama played an important role in such imperialist enterprises as the South Manchurian Railroad and the Bank of Taiwan. He was an intimate friend and associate of outstanding Japanese military and political leaders.[20]

It is clear that Tōyama and his *Genyōsha* associates were destined to lose their early interest in the liberal movement. The government could hold out more attractive bait, for it could promise to employ them in pursuits that would further their interest in Asia. The *Genyōsha* rowdies were to be found in the employ of Home Minister Shinagawa in the 1892 elections, the first in which violence was deliberately used to discourage liberal candidates and voters.[21]

Tōyama retained his liberty to oppose "traitorous" policies on the part of the government, however, and he and his men registered prompt and emphatic opposition to the Inoue treaty revision plan by organizing mass meetings of protest and by threatening government leaders. Tōyama had to restrain his men from their plan to kill Inoue when he visited Fukuoka in 1886.[22]

When Ōkuma's treaty revision plans were revealed in 1888 it was a Fukuoka *Genyōsha* man, Kurushima, who threw the bomb which cost Ōkuma a leg. Kurushima's sensational act and prompt suicide revealed him as a man of great sincerity and valor, and Ōkuma sent a gift of money to help support the family. Nevertheless, the treaty revision plans were doomed. When Ōkuma formed his own cabinet with Itagaki in 1898 he is said to have offered Tōyama a cabinet post, an offer which was contemptuously refused.[23] Tōyama thus led a charmed life. Retribution for violence affected only his followers, so that he dared announce, after the Ōkuma bombing, "From of old, our principle is *sonnō, jōi.*"[24] A fitting conclusion to the episode came with ceremonies held November 18, 1921, to celebrate the thirty-third anniversary of the attempt on Ōkuma's life. Present were the giants of nationalism and imperialism; Tōyama, Sugiyama, and Uchida. Tōyama, after the ceremonies, visited Ōkuma and thanked him for providing for the Kurushima family.[25]

Tōyama and his allies, then, performed a valuable service for Japanese nationalism, politics, and imperialism by serving as intermediaries between the several levels and classes of government, business, and the lower fringes of society. As a whole these groups were militantly Eastern. Basing themselves on their fundamental tenets of Japanism, they could follow a shifting course between government and protest groups. They were an invaluable channel for government and business in providing unofficial aid and secret support to any purpose or group. With their keen interest in Asian expansion and their large constituency of adventurous youths intent on preserving the samurai tradition, the nationalist societies were perfectly situated to share in the hopes, plans, and activities of Asian revolutionaries.[26]

2. ŌI KENTARŌ AND KOREA

After the formation of the political parties in the years following 1881, many of the political leaders gave up the crude demands for war in Asia with which they had first fought the oligarchy. As long as their main aim was to embarrass the government, they could find adequate material for abuse in the program of total westernization and in the frequent exposures of political corruption. Political leaders were frequently dissuaded from such attacks by government positions and by business deals. Government repression discouraged the timid.

Nevertheless, an important group of liberals retained their early interest in China and Korea. Ōi Kentarō and his friends sought in those countries an opportunity to carry through reforms which had been blocked in Japan. Success in Korea would have political consequences in Japan, for if the Tokyo government failed to match progress elsewhere in Asia it would have lost its claim to leadership in Asia. Ōi Kentarō thus worked out the theories of aid and tutelage for Asia in the form in which Miyazaki Torazō and Sun Yat-sen heard them.

In many respects, the "radical liberals" like Ōi seem today to have been the most promising element in the Meiji political picture. Western political thought had made a profound impression upon them, and their humanitarian social programs set them off from their political opponents. Unfortunately, they were able to achieve very little. At times their political ideas had to be so changed to fit the Japanese context that little real liberalism remained. Unable to find solid bases of support in Japanese society, they became subject to adventurism which discredited them. Their tendencies toward adventurism led them closer to the chauvinist societies. Close association with nationalists like Tōyama inevitably conditioned the liberalism of an Ōi and a Miyazaki. Their failure was therefore indicative of the impossibility of a long-range coöperation between such forces and the Chinese revolutionaries.

With the radicals, as with the other political groups, personality loomed larger than ideology. In Ōi Kentarō (1833–1922), however, they had both. Ōi was a competent scholar who had interested himself successively in Chinese, Dutch, and French studies.[27] The French political philosophers had a great effect on him. He was a member of each of Itàgaki's early organizations and he persisted in their announced aims well after many of the other leaders had sold out to the opposition. In contrast to Itagaki, whose support derived mainly from the landowner class, Ōi and his men concerned themselves with the fate of the tenants, the poor, and the underprivileged. He was, in the words of Katayama Sen, "a figure that must not be forgotten in the history of the Japanese labor movement."[28] Ōi fought against the original limitations on the franchise, and argued for a larger constituency of share croppers, city artisans, and unemployed. He felt that a larger base would result in greater national unity.

Social goals of this order were rare in an age so class conscious that the first "liberal" organizations were restricted in membership to samurai. Ōi went so far as to consider disproportionate wealth and power disruptive of national unity, and as a remedy he advocated limits on wealth in order to aid the poverty-stricken peasantry. Equality was more important to him than individual rights and private property.

Despite his obvious familiarity with Western theories, Ōi was hardly pro-Western, for he feared Western imperialism as much as anyone.[29] Ōi sponsored the Japanese translation of Bellamy's *Looking Backward;* in his social thought he seems to have planned measures which would anticipate the West by avoiding the hardships resulting from uncontrolled capitalism.

When Ōi's nationalism is considered together with these theories, it is apparent that his position lacked stability. He was more concerned with the nation and its unity than with individuals and their freedom. For this reason, his activities resembled more those of the nationalist societies than they did those of the Parliamentarians. Ōi served in the Diet for a time, but he gave up politics in disgust. In his impatience with delay, his obsession with unity, and his indifference to individualism, Ōi showed his affinity to the ultra-nationalists.

The foreign policy that went with these theories was an extension of tactics. Japan, after having reformed, could aid Asia in bypassing the tortuous process of inequality and trial and error which the West had followed. Even if Japan should not reform, however, establishment of any part of this program in Asia would be of inestimable aid to the natives there as well as a goad to the conservatives in Tokyo. The liberals were nationalistic enough to believe that Japan, even in its present condition, was sufficiently ahead of the rest of Asia to be able to offer it all that was needed to equal the West. Japan had conquered feudalism, a condition which they thought still held the rest of Asia in subjection.[30]

In this manner, the liberals worked out their theories of Japanese guidance for Asia. Today their words seem contradictory and frequently deceptive, but the Korean, Filipino, and Chinese revolutionaries who heard these sentiments from their friends thought the arguments were quite sound. They had seen the modern army and navy, the new industry, and the efficient administrative system of Japan; they wanted the same things for their homelands.

Moreover, the Asiatics heard such phrases from known friends and proven allies. Ōi Kentarō, for instance, sincerely sought to rid the rest of Asia of "bureaucratic feudalism," for in so doing he was furthering greater Asian prosperity as well as fighting the Tokyo clan government. Ōi certainly sought to help, and not merely to use,

Korea and China. To quote the sympathetic view of a man who is also Ōi's biographer:

In any case, the propulsion outward of the principles of the Meiji Restoration, by which Japan set itself toward an East Asian administration in its mission to secure the peace of East Asia, did not merely proceed from a belief that it was necessary for Japanese self-interest or development, but from the desire to contribute to the cultural fame in the world of all the East Asian peoples by helping them to set up and preserve their independence and further their happiness.[31]

Unfortunately, there were others who held that the decadence and corruption of China and Korea were so far advanced that guidance alone would not avail. These could also be found in the *Jiyūtō,* and, calling themselves the *Kokkentō* (National Power Group), they advocated compulsory "guidance."[32] And since the end result of success by either group seemed to be so similar, once the radicals became convinced of Asian intransigence their acquiescence in power politics was assured. That conviction of depravity was first applied to Korea. In China, the charge was harder to sustain, and it was generally bolstered by theories that English, Russian, or Soviet advice and interference had prevented the success of the guidance experts.

Finally, the guidance line itself was weakened by its attractions for all groups. Superficially, at least, a "liberal" would have been in serious disagreement with the *Kokuryūkai* five point program only in his interpretation of the social and labor problems.

In other words, the ideological distinctions left much to be desired. Personal divisions seldom materialized, for even if all these groups opposed to the government's Asian policy had not had so much in common, the limited number of refugee revolutionaries would have forced some working agreement among them. One can learn more of the motives of these men by following their actions than by studying what they said.

a. The Korean Problem

Without coöperation from other groups, the liberals got nowhere. Their ambitious plans to reform Korea prospered only so long as the government authorized the extensive loans that were required.

After the government withdrew assistance, the liberals were reduced to spectacular but useless exploits like Ōi Kentarō's attempt to invade Korea.

The details of the confusion in Korea are of less interest here than the precedents that were set for Japanese relations with Sun Yat-sen. The Korean situation was complicated by a three-way competition for power among the conservative faction of the regent (the Tai Wen Kun), the progressive party of Kim Ok-kiun, and the family party of the Queen (Min), which was against whoever held the reins. The only constants were the consistent pro-Japanese orientation of the Kim party, which saw in Japan the model and ideal for modernization, and the overwhelming anti-Japanese feeling of all the other elements, who saw traces of the traditional Japanese enemy in the projected Western reforms. The political picture saw a succession of kaleidoscopic changes as the Japanese faction, after gaining influence, became the object of riots or palace revolutions. After the pro-Japanese group tried their own hand at a *coup d'état* in 1884, and thereby brought on Chinese intervention to quell the anti-Japanese disturbances that resulted, Kim and his friends fled to Japan, where the liberals and nationalists did their best to protect him and reform Korea.

Kim Ok-kiun's first visit to Japan came in 1881, when he managed to leave Korea as a student of Buddhism in order to learn more about Japan. The Kyoto Honganji priests gave him more than spiritual guidance, for they introduced him to Fukuzawa Yukichi.[33] Kim was on his way back to Korea six months later when the anti-Japanese outbreak of 1882 necessitated the sending of a Korean mission of apology to Japan; he returned to counsel the mission.[34] Kim was influential in the sending of ten Korean students to Japan. The first of many students from the mainland to seek the wellsprings of Japanese westernization, they studied the tax, post, police, and military systems.

The anti-Japanese violence of 1882 convinced the Japanese government that it would be wise to cultivate the Kim faction. At the same time, government repression of the liberals in Japan had become so effective that Gotō Shōjirō decided to shift his interest to Korea in order to build up a friendly force there. He found the Tokyo government willing to help, for after some prodding Foreign Minister Inoue allowed the Yokohama Specie Bank to make a secret loan of 170,000 yen to the Korean party.[35] The next year, Kim tried to get a loan of three million yen to reform the domestic situation in Korea. Those of his party were now in positions of prominence, and he saw hopes of success. The previous Japanese loan, and the presence and aid of numbers of advisers sent from Japan, had been of great help. Unfortunately, their work had been counteracted by Chinese agents who had money to bolster resistance to the reformers; some decisive steps were needed. The large sum of three million yen, however, posed a real problem. The nationalists claimed that although Mutsu Munemitsu, a Foreign Office official, backed the move, Inoue had decided to write Korea off to China, and so he blocked even a small loan of two hundred thousand.[36] Kim also tried to get funds from American representatives in Japan. He became discouraged, and returned to Korea in 1884.

The Liberals persevered in their attempts to help Kim. Gotō and Itagaki, after consulting with Fukuzawa, approached the French minister to Japan. Since the French were then at war with China, they tried to persuade the ambassador to supply one million yen and some warships to the Korean progressives in order to strike at China. The French were agreed, but asked the Japanese to guarantee the independence of Korea. Gotō was to go to Korea to insure responsible use of the money.[37]

When demands within Japan for a strong Korean policy seemed to be gaining ground, the government tried to buy Gotō off with a cabinet post. Gotō, flattered, foolishly revealed part of the plan to Itō; he offered to play Garibaldi to Itō's Cavour. When this came to the ears of Foreign Minister Inoue, he succeeded in stopping the operation. The Korean riots in 1884, in which the Kim faction first killed the pro-Chinese ministers, only to be counterattacked and forced to flee, ended all such plans.[38]

The liberals were still not prepared to abandon their interest in Korea. When Kim and his friends fled to Japan in 1884, the Korean government asked for their expulsion. After some hesitation, Inoue, realizing that Japanese public opinion was still favorable to Kim, allowed him to stay, and tried to protect him from Korean assassins.

Within Japan, Kim was helped by Gotō, Fukuzawa, and Tōyama.[39] Since Kim and his friends were penniless, the government quietly gave help to them through their Japanese friends. Meanwhile, the Koreans changed to Japanese names and awaited another chance.[40]

b. The Osaka Incident of 1885

At this point Ōi Kentarō tried to provide that opportunity by a scheme which has become known as the "Osaka Incident." The radical liberals were thoroughly dissatisfied with the Tientsin Convention which Itō Hirobumi had negotiated in 1885. They were also distressed by the domestic political situation; the major parties had been dissolved to await the Constitution which was to come, and the rank and file were restless and leaderless.

The plan called for Kobayashi Kuzuo, a liberal who had participated with Gotō in the conversations with the French, to assist Ōi in raising money and getting arms. Isoyama Seibu was to lead a party of some twenty *sōshi* (toughs) to Korea to force reforms there. Ōi and Kobayashi would then arouse public indignation with the government policy which ignored the safety of such valorous countrymen. This would force a change in Japan, probable war with Korea, and reforms in both countries.[41]

An Osaka Sinologist, Yamamoto Baigai, was enlisted to compose a proclamation in classical Chinese.[42] This was to be translated and distributed to foreign papers when the plot had matured. Kim Ok-kiun was consulted throughout, and he was in actual charge of many of the planning details.

The impulsive and irresponsible character of the *Jiyūtō's* constituency of rural youths was a source of both strength and weakness. For instance, when voluntary contributions of funds proved inadequate, the enthusiasts perpetrated a series of robberies to get the money they needed. The role of women in the project was also unusual. A Miss Kageyama Hideko of Okayama, who was a leader in women's rights, political reform, girls' education, and the emancipation of women, helped Ōi considerably with the planning.[43] But as the series of robberies continued and the day of action neared, the secret became harder to keep. By August, the plotters had accumulated several thousand yen, and substantial amounts of explosives were kept in the home of the unsuspected Sinologist, Yamamoto. In October, the advance guard under Isoyama left for Nagasaki. Many unoccupied *sōshi* got wind of impending action and converged on Osaka.[44] Isoyama's braves proved less amenable to discipline than to adventure, and before very long Isoyama, finding he could no longer control his group, gave up the cause for lost.

Isoyama's defection led to general confusion, and before long the police were able to crack the case, which can hardly have been a very difficult one. On November 23, 1885, one hundred and thirty adventurers and accomplices were arrested. The trials followed soon after. Ōi, Kobayashi, and Isoyama were sentenced to six years' imprisonment, while Miss Kageyama and Yamamoto received a year and a half.[45] The trials were strangely similar to those of the young army officers who took the path of direct action a half-century later. Ōi was allowed to express his ideas and ideals at great length, and he delivered an impassioned three-day oration in which he explained the difference between ordinary plans of conquest and the enlightened, brotherly goal of the *Jiyūtō*.[46]

After 1885, the Japanese government had no use for Kim Ok-kiun. Inoue even considered surrendering him to the Chinese.[47] Kim wanted to go to America, but he lacked funds.[48] The liberals continued in their friendship for him, and they persuaded the government to extend a small monthly allowance, but Kim was disappointed and embittered. In 1894, he was lured to Shanghai by Chinese agents who had convinced him that there was a possibility of help from Li Hung-chang. Instead, he was assassinated. The resulting indignation among his Japanese friends showed the affection in which they had held him.[49]

The liberals thus failed completely in Korea.[50] Instead of arousing gratitude among Koreans, their efforts had reaped only suspicion. It must be borne in mind, however, that there were many factors working against their program in Korea. The first was the behavior of Japanese to Koreans.[51] Next, they were blocked by Korean jealousies and incompetence. The Japanese government gave them little help. Finally, their case at home and abroad had been weakened by the familiar *Jiyūtō* propensity to direct action and violence.

When Sun Yat-sen came a decade later, all these factors were changed. Not all Japanese liked Chinese, but few despised them as they would an inferior race. The Chinese revolutionaries were far better organized than the Korean reformers, and they had secondary sources of help. The Japanese government had taken a definite stand against the Manchu dynasty of China. Finally, the group which concerned itself with China was for the most part the less volatile group of Parliamentarians allied with the business and educational world. Despite the *Jiyūtō* background of Miyazaki Torazō, his actions were usually subject to the approval of Inukai Ki.

3. MIYAZAKI TORAZŌ AND HIS PREDECESSORS IN CHINA

From the first, Japanese activities in China were far more restricted than they were in Korea. The Japanese government was content to follow a rather cautious policy. The liberals concentrated their activities on Korea, and as a result the spade work of research and exploration was left for adventurers allied with or sponsored by the patriotic societies.

The government's conciliatory policy was encouraged by foreign advisers, and attacked by the Japanese nationalists.[52] After 1890, that policy was gradually abandoned; the Japanese government was now stronger, and it was subject to new popular pressure through the new representative institutions. At that time, the earlier work of the pioneer adventurers proved invaluable.

Those adventurers who had penetrated inland China had done so at considerable risk, for the early Japanese treaties with China gave Japanese fewer rights of travel and residence than they gave Europeans.[53] The only chance for travel was thus in the disguise of native dress; Japanese had been growing queues in the hope of passing for Chinese well before Sun Yat-sen cut his hair in the hope of passing for a Japanese.

a. Commercial research

Arao Kiyoshi (1859–1896) inaugurated and directed the most important research activities. After some training as a foreign language student, Arao entered an army officers' school. Because of the excellence of his work, he was attached to the General Staff. There he was influential in the establishment of a special bureau to collect and coördinate information relating to China. In 1886, the General Staff sent Arao to Shanghai. He coördinated his activities there with the mercantile establishments of Kishida Ginkō, the proprietor of a highly successful patent-medicine shop on the Ginza who had extended its flashy name (*Rakuzendō,* Hall of Pleasurable Delights) and gaudy interior to a Shanghai branch in 1877.[54] Kishida needed young and adventurous workers and salesmen, and his business could conveniently be coördinated with intelligence activities. Arao opened a *Rakuzendō* branch in Hankow, and organized a small group of agents who made tours into the most remote parts of China to report on all aspects of the customs, political conditions, terrain, agriculture, industry, and commerce of the areas they visited. These agents of the *Rakuzendō* had to support themselves by selling medicines and books, and they suffered many privations. Arao convinced them that they were working for the eventual reform of China — the most important cause of the age.

In 1889, Arao turned his efforts to the promotion of Sino-Japanese commerce and trade to meet the growing perils of Western commercial domination of the Orient. He resigned his army commission, and, after consulting with prominent statesmen, he toured Japan for two years urging businessmen to enter the China trade. He started a new project, which he called the Institute for Sino-Japanese Commercial Research (*Nisshi Bōeki Kenkyūjo*), and sailed for Shanghai with two hundred students. He had counted on a subsidization by the Japanese Diet, but when this was not forthcoming contributions of businessmen kept the institute going. According to one source, the school's graduates did not live up to the commercial character of the institution; half entered the military, half became unattached *rōnin,* and only two entered the business world, as financiers.[55] To quote Norman's summary of the *Kokuryūkai* account, "At the end of their course the graduates of this school were divided into teams of about twenty to make trips into all parts of China, Manchuria, Siam, India, the Philippines, and the South Seas. Later, some would be employed as the local agents of the more enterprising Japanese trading firms; others would enter the Japanese consular service as specialists in Far Eastern trade;

many became scouts and official interpreters during the Sino-Japanese war, others again disappeared into the nebulous and ever growing army of Japanese adventurers. . ."[56] Arao was thus able to supply the army with interpreters and agents who were the more valuable because they functioned anonymously. Arao himself served in Korea, and he died in Formosa, where he had gone to develop new organizations to study the trade of South East Asia.[57]

Thanks to Arao and to others like him, Japan soon had available a good quantity of information about China. Almost anywhere in China, a Japanese consul might be as surprised as one at Yinkow was one day in 1897. Two haggard, dirty beggars appeared at the door. When they were contemptuously turned away, one exclaimed, "We're Japanese!" Now they were welcomed and feted. One, Yamada Yoshimasa, had been captured by the Russians in Manchuria; he had made good his escape, and had travelled through Shantung. His companion, Kogoshi Heiriku, had interrupted a career in the navy to check on the Russians. He had also seen much of the Yellow River area, and in a later publication he developed the theory that control of that river would save China, revive Asia; "it is the way to help the Yellow race make its way on the soil . . . it is essential to the Imperial Way."[58]

In short, many of these men probably came to have a knowledge of China greater than that of Sun Yat-sen, in whose cause Yamada was killed at Waichow, Kwangtung, in 1900. The deeds and travels of these adventurers, chronicled at length in the *Kokuryūkai* sources, show that such experiences formed highly satisfactory outlets for those discontented and dissatisfied with the humdrum course of peace and progress in Japan.[59]

b. The value of cultural bonds

Besides these commercial specialists, several groups organized to exploit the similarity of culture that existed between China and Japan. After the coming of the first Chinese Ambassador, Ho Ju-chang, in 1877, Ōkubo Toshimichi and others interested themselves in the interchange of students. A *Kōa Kai* (Rise Asia Society) was formed in 1880, and Ambassador Ho addressed its first session. The society set up a Chinese language school with Chinese teachers. It soon had over one hundred students, and it was later merged with the official government language schools (*Gaikokugo gakkō*). In 1890 came the *Tōhō Kyōkai* (Oriental Coöperation Society), which was set up by men of all shades of political opinion; its sponsors included the Russophobe peer Prince Konoe, Ōkuma, Gotō, Itō, Inukai, Ōi, Arao, and Tōyama. The manifesto of the group urged research in Asian studies in order to expand industry, commerce, and strength, and commended to the members the examples of adventurous Western pioneers.

The final product of this movement was the *Tōa Dōbun Kai* (East Asian Common Culture Society), which was founded in November 1898. This came during the height of Western imperialist activity in China, and the announced aims of the group were the preservation of China, reform and help for China and Korea, study and research in the affairs of China and Korea, and a revival of interest in the proper role of Japan in Asia. Again, the backers of the organization included leading figures of the political, business, nationalist, and educational circles. The *Dōbunkai,* through its numerous branches in China, performed a valuable intelligence service; its numerous expeditions throughout China and the publications describing their findings played a large role in providing Japan with excellent information about her neighbor.[60]

It was common for individuals really interested in China to avail themselves freely of the advantages offered by all the organizations listed above. Inoue Masaji illustrates this perfectly. Inoue was born in 1876; as a child he took Hideyoshi as his model, and he resolved to conquer China. He graduated from a naval school, but resigned his commission after the Sino-Japanese War. Inoue then met Arao Kiyoshi, who convinced him that he should study China and Asia first, and the West later. Arao taught him Chinese, the classics, and economics, and then got him a job with the General Staff in Formosa. In 1896, Inoue returned to Japan and entered Waseda, where he studied three years. He spent summer vacations with men like Uchida Ryōhei in hazardous trips through Siberia, China, and Korea. In 1898, Inoue joined the *Dōbunkai* group, and came to know Inukai, Miyazaki, and other China specialists, as well as the

Chinese reformers Liang Ch'i-ch'ao and K'ang Yu-wei, who were then exiles in Japan. Inoue then became secretary of the Shanghai *Dōbunkai* branch office, and he published a newspaper designed to counter Russian influence and propaganda. During the Boxer Rebellion, he travelled along the Yangtze, reporting regularly to Japan. In 1901 he went to Europe to study. After some time in Berlin and Vienna, he travelled from the Danube to Tashkent, to Teheran, the Black Sea, and then to Moscow, returning to Japan on the Trans-Siberian, in order to consider Russian policy in its setting. Inoue spent the next few years in Korea, placed as an adviser within the court. After 1912 his interest shifted to Southeast Asia, and he bought and operated a rubber plantation in Malaya. The second World War was to find him a wealthy Tokyo industrialist, author of some twenty books about his experiences, the China problem, and colonial history and policy.[61]

The conclusion reached by these pioneers of commercial and cultural promotion was that China was in a state of temporary degeneration. Her corruption was far less advanced than that of Korea; with Japanese help, China could still be saved from the West. This reasoning was, of course, very similar to the earlier *Jiyūtō* theories of Japanese guidance, but it received its classical setting from Ōkuma Shigenobu, whose party generally spoke for the commercial interests. The "Ōkuma Doctrine," as the Japanese called it, was set forth in 1898, at the time of maximum imperialist penetration in China. Its essential feature was a *noblesse oblige* whereby Japan, having managed to arrive first at the benefits of Western modernization, guaranteed to China freedom from Western aggression and aid in revamping her governmental system and reforming her social inertia. Ōkuma proclaimed that China would not long remain dormant; once a hero should arise, patriotism would well up, and China would resume her place among the powers. Japan, a grateful recipient of China's culture and spirit in the past, now promised to repay that debt by holding the West at bay and helping the Chinese hero in his development of a friendly, grateful, China.[62]

The search for such a hero, and the extension of aid to him in his mission, was the life work of Miyazaki Torazō.

c. Miyazaki Torazō

The autobiography of Miyazaki Torazō furnishes a striking instance of the way in which the intellectual currents, political struggles, and idealistic theories which have been described affected the relation of an individual Japanese to the cause of Sun Yat-sen. Yet Miyazaki is more than an isolated individual, for his background fits so perfectly into the broader pattern of influences and trends that he stands forth as an exemplification of theories and the personification of an ideal. Miyazaki was Sun's closest friend and collaborator in Japan, and his son stood with Tōyama and Inukai at the 1929 ceremonies to honor the memory of Sun Yat-sen. Miyazaki's account of his activities, *Sanjū sannen no yume* (The thirty-three years' dream) was written in 1902 to explain the failure of his mission.[63]

Miyazaki was born in Kumamoto Ken, Kyushu, in 1870. His was a samurai family, and they possessed enough land to make the transition to the new system fairly easily. In later years Miyazaki remembered wandering along the shore looking toward China, and dreaming of valiant deeds. At home, his mother taught him tales of heroes of the past. Almost as an object lesson, his oldest brother Hachirō entered the Satsuma Rebellion on Saigō's side, and was killed leading a small group of landless samurai against the government forces.[64] Life was not easy in rural Kyushu; of the eight sons and three daughters of the family, only four children reached maturity.

The boy Torazō was sent to one of the new government schools. Because of the family stories of his brother's feats and because of the unrest that pervaded the countryside, he wanted to study liberalism; he tells us that he stared long and hard at the characters *Jiyūminken* (liberty and people's rights), and sought to divine their content. In school, however, he found that his classmates desired only government jobs and official preference; they considered him odd for his anti-government sentiments and for his professed idealism.

Miyazaki's father died when the boy was ten years old, and his elder brother decided to send him to a boarding school run by Tokutomi Iichirō.[65] Tokutomi ran a "liberal" school. In Japan in the 1880's, "liberalism" came to mean almost as many things as "democracy" did after 1945. Private schools mushroomed all over southern Japan, and Tokutomi's was certainly one of the more remarkable of those. He established a democratic choice of studies and of rules, and he even trained the boys to give their own lectures. Instead of greeting Tokutomi with the usual *Sensei* (teacher), the boys proved their liberalism by using his first name. The stories of heroic revolutionaries were daily fare, and under the influence of Robespierre, Danton, Cromwell, and the others, Miyazaki came to associate liberalism, heroism, and rebellion together.[66]

Miyazaki next entered upon a period of intellectual and spiritual doubt; he felt a lack of direction in his life. No longer happy at school, he ran away to Tokyo, where he stayed with former friends who were now students there. He was shocked, however, by their foppish dress and sotted behavior. They wore silks, shoes, bowler hats, carried soap wherever they went, and washed their faces every few hours. Moreover, they were leading a wild, pleasure-crazed life which he despised.

At this time, Miyazaki was 15 or 16. One day he was passing a small missionary church. He heard the organ music, and entered the building. The service and scripture so impressed his restless spirit that he returned again; he was befriended by the missionary and his wife, and received lessons in the faith and in English from them. At this time he also attended Waseda for a time. During the (Baptist) missionary's summer vacation, Miyazaki decided to enter the Congregational church because he liked its republican government and liberal creed. To his amazement, the Baptist cut off his friendship with him, and so planted the first doubts in his mind. He persuaded his two elder brothers and his mother to become Christians, however, and seemed firmly rooted in his new beliefs.

It was around this time that his brother Yazō pointed out to him the danger that Western imperialism constituted for China and Asia as a whole. China, he pointed out, was degenerating, but if some way or person could be found to regenerate and unify its multitudes this would be a great blessing for the Yellow Race and for the world. This was Miyazaki's first contact with Asian problems, and it made a deep impression on him.

Financial troubles then forced Torazō and his brothers to stay home for a time. The expense of national industrialization was being borne by the peasantry, and the Miyazaki home became a center for discontented tenants as well as for philosophical and religious debates. The elder brother Tamizō, however, was furious because of the unjust burdens the tenants were forced to bear, and he swore redress. Tamizō did in fact devote his lifetime to the problem, and in future years his adaptation of Henry George's single-tax solution influenced both his brother and Sun Yat-sen. This period in Miyazaki's life was one of constant contact with hard, grinding poverty and distress. He went to a mission school in Nagasaki, only to be revolted by the false converts who sought free education. He extended his interests to include socialism. A period of religious doubt then set in, and ended with the rejection of Christianity by all three of the brothers. Their doubts began with the Trinity, and ended with total repudiation.[67]

Miyazaki once again lacked a purpose in life, and this time he seized upon Yazō's suggestion of work to save Asia. In several all-night sessions, the brothers discussed the feasibility and the means of saving China. Tamizō, a cooler head, discouraged these plans, but the two younger brothers were not to be discouraged. Their first step was to be the study of Chinese language and customs. An early scheme for Torazō to go to Hawaii to work among overseas Chinese there was soon abandoned, and instead it was agreed that he should try to go to Shanghai with a friend in 1891. The friend soon changed his mind, and Torazō, after foolishly lending him half his money on the promise that it would be sent to him, managed to get to Shanghai. He was now twenty-two, and the first sight of the land to which he had dedicated himself stirred him mightily: "My second native land!"[68] Just as he was about to embark on language study, Miyazaki learned that his money would not be forthcoming. Arao Kiyoshi and his Trade Research School tided him over, but the youthful idealist would not stay with people whose philosophy he did not share.

Miyazaki returned home for four years after this disastrous beginning. He married, but he never reconciled himself to an uneventful, domestic life. A letter from Yazō told him that he had met Kim Ok-kiun; as a result, he had changed his interest from

China to Korea. Torazō decided to do so too, and in 1894 he went back to Tokyo. Kim impressed him greatly by his honesty and ability. He agreed that China, too, must be saved, for it was the key to Asia. The two agreed to make detailed plans for their activities when Kim should return in three weeks from China. Shortly thereafter, Miyazaki read in the papers of Kim's murder in Shanghai; as a result, the brothers had to begin their plans all over again. Despite the heated objections of their family, they offered to serve as interpreters during the Sino-Japanese war. Nothing came of this and of several elaborate plans to study more Chinese, however, and Torazō's next plans centered on Siam.

Here his aims were threefold: to work into and through the Chinese community, to help the Siamese government reform and ward off imperialism, and to develop immigration of Japanese farmers. Yazō, meanwhile, had entered the circles of Arao Kiyoshi's Trade Research School. He had dropped all his acquaintances and friends in order to become a more effective Sinophile. Torazō's grandiose dreams soon faded, for he found himself in Siam with a small party of immigrants, only to realize that the Siam Immigration Company was no longer a functioning concern. Moreover, the coolies on the same ship had seriously worried him. These men were Chinese, and he should love them. Nevertheless, they were more like animals. Worse, they did not regard the Japanese as allies, but seemed to fear them. The same doubts obsessed the Siamese officials Miyazaki met. They admired Japan's rise, but they questioned her motives. Miyazaki finally decided that it would be necessary to reconstitute the immigration company, and to further this he returned to Japan, beset by conscience pangs for having left the immigrants employed in railroad construction in a malarial area.

When Miyazaki returned to Japan he found Yazō seriously ill. Yazō told him that he had met an important Chinese, and he urged him to hurry back again as soon as he could decently leave his Siamese affairs. Miyazaki returned to Siam with Hirayama and Suenaga, two men with whom he later worked in China. After a harrowing journey in which they were held up by plague, they stopped off in Singapore to see Ōi Kentarō, who was interesting himself in Sumatra. They arrived in Siam only to be beset by loneliness, despair, and cholera. The project soon collapsed for lack of food and money, and Miyazaki was sent back to arrange shipments. He never returned, and before long his comrades followed him home.

Miyazaki found that Yazō had died while he was gone. The loss of his favorite brother and main inspiration was a great blow to him. He made one more try to interest important people in the Siam project, and at the insistence of a friend he visited Inukai. Inukai was now in the government in the short-lived Ōkuma-Matsukata cabinet of 1896. From childhood, Miyazaki had been taught to distrust Ōkuma as a grafter and his party as opportunists; he made his visit very reluctantly. Inukai, however, won him over. He persuaded him that the immigration scheme was futile by pointing out that the government had even had difficulty in getting settlers for Hokkaido. The upshot of the whole matter was that Inukai was able to give Miyazaki and Hirayama secret Foreign Office orders and funds to investigate and contact the various groups able to promote reform and change in China. From this point on, Miyazaki's life work was set before him, and his friendship with Inukai never faltered. He was also on cordial terms with Tōyama and his group.

Miyazaki thus formed the perfect channel for Japanese aid to Sun Yat-sen. Like Sun, he had a considerable background in Western studies, English, and Christianity. The two shared fears of Western domination of the Orient. Miyazaki's family tradition of liberalism and social thought was strikingly similar in spirit to the positions later formulated by Sun. His contacts and affiliations with anti-government and liberal groups made him less dependent upon the whims of cabinet changes and government policy than would have been the case with anyone constantly in official life. Finally, the passionate intensity and genuine idealism of his hopes for Asia were doubted by none who knew him. One may question the presence of some of the Japanese at the ceremonies for Sun Yat-sen in 1929, but Miyazaki, had he lived, would have stood there with as much right as anyone in the procession.

SUN YAT-SEN

3

The Japanese search for a hero who could arouse patriotism and regenerate China for the cause of the Yellow Race led them to Sun Yat-sen. Sun, however, was in many ways an odd choice for that role. He spoke Cantonese, and so he could not converse with the Japanese China experts who had received their training in the Shanghai area. His education was almost entirely Western, and he could not hope to compete with the Japanese who claimed that their values and virtues were based on the traditional classics. Except for a single trip to the northern capital, Sun's knowledge of China was restricted to the Canton area. Therefore he knew less about the land and its problems than many of the Japanese who had spent dangerous years in trips of exploration and reconnaisance. Despite these shortcomings, Sun's character and ability as a revolutionary leader made such an impression on his Japanese friends that they seldom questioned their choice.

The Japanese government leaders were less certain of Sun's attributes. But since he was clearly one of the most important figures among overseas Chinese, the Tokyo leaders assigned contact men to meet and protect Sun. Their money and agents supported Sun in an early project to help Emilio Aguinaldo resist American imperialism in the Philippines. But Tokyo also kept track of the progress of the Chinese Reform Movement of 1898. When this movement failed, the Japanese welcomed reformers and revolutionaries alike to shelter in Japan, and tried to get them together on a united front movement which would deserve full sponsorship. To a Japan which was still not quite sure of its strength and status, and which was still smarting under slights from Western imperialist powers, a union of possible allies was of the greatest importance. Such a union would have solved the thorny problem of which group in China most merited Japanese aid. Moreover, it would also have lessened divisions within Japan.

1. Sun's Development as a Revolutionary Leader

Sun Yat-sen was born in the village of Choyhung, Hsiang-shan hsien, Kwangtung, in 1866. His father was a farmer, and until Sun reached the age of thirteen his life was probably not very different from those of the other village children. He received rudimentary schooling from an uncle who had served in the Taiping armies in the great rebellion that was crushed two years before Sun's birth. Sun later told his Japanese friends that he heard from this uncle the heroic tales of the Taiping leader Hung Hsiu-ch'üan. In games with other boys, Sun generally played the role of Hung.[1]

When he was thirteen, Sun was sent to Hawaii to join an elder brother who had emigrated some years earlier. In Honolulu, Sun entered an Anglican school. After three years, his brother sent him back home. Sun now had full opportunity to compare the progress and government of Manchu China with conditions in the Western world. Moreover, Sun returned a Christian, and he associated the old superstitions and religions with the general backwardness of his village.[2] When he scornfully broke some idols to show his contempt for them, the village head ordered Sun's father to send him away. As a result, Sun was sent to Hong Kong in 1883; there he was supported by monthly contributions from the brother in Hawaii. After a short period in the Hong Kong Anglican School, Sun entered Queen's College. Two years later, his brother called him back to Honolulu for a short time. When Sun returned to Hong Kong, he wanted to enter a Chinese military academy. Unfortunately, there was no army school, and the only naval academy had been destroyed by French gunfire in the disastrous Sino-French War of 1884–85. Sun apparently saw no alternative to studying medicine. He began his medical training in 1886, and completed it in 1892.[3]

During the formative years of his life, Sun had thus been subjected to a series of influences that resulted in an almost complete break with the values of traditional Chinese society. In comparing his homeland with Hawaii and Hong Kong, he found China deficient in government organization, scientific and educational progress, and material standards of living. Sun's Christianity further separated him from the traditionalists. Indeed, if Queen's College had not required complementary work in Chinese history and literature, it is uncertain that Sun would have had any contact with those fields at all. The war with France had demonstrated to him China's weakness in the face of Western aggression, and his observation of the life of Chinese in Hawaii must have confirmed reservations about the West's treatment of Asiatics. Sun became convinced that Manchu rule was the cause of all this; that rule was cowardly, unworthy, and outmoded.

While he studied medicine, Sun came into contact with representatives of organized opposition to the Manchus. Lu Hao-tung, a friend from his native village and a fellow Christian, had joined him in Hong Kong. Together they made the acquaintance of another student, Cheng Shih-liang, who was the son of a Shanghai merchant. In one of their discussions, Cheng disapproved of Sun's arguments for reform of the Chinese army and navy, and suggested that a revolution would do the same task more quickly. When Sun answered that revolt was impossible without an organization like that of the secret societies, Cheng revealed that he was an official of such a group, the *San Ho Hui*.[4] Sun and Cheng became close friends, and they worked together until the latter's death in 1901.

After Sun finished his schooling, he practiced medicine in Macao. Before long, however, he was forced out by the sudden enforcement of an old statute which required doctors to have Portuguese diplomas. Imperialism had now affected him personally.

Before this, in 1892, Sun had formed a secret society which he named the *Hsing Chung Hui* (Rise China Society). This was a protest movement, but it was not dedicated to a complete overthrow of the Manchus.[5] The final impetus for revolution seems to have come for Sun in 1894. In that year, he set out for Peking with Lu Hao-tung. At the capital they tried unsuccessfully to present to Li Hung-chang, who was then viceroy of Chihli, a memorial which urged the strengthening of the realm. The memorial was a lengthy and rather dogmatic explanation to the Viceroy of how the country could be made strong. Sun took as his goal the same "Rich country, strong defens " which had served as a slogan for Meiji Japan. He urged four steps. proper employment of human abilities, of the soil, of goods, and free circulation of currency. Under these headings

Sun denounced traditional learning as useless, urged new attention to production techniques and riparian works, and suggested the abolition of bothersome taxes on goods in transit (*likin*). Sun capped his argument by pointing out that Japan, which had followed these four steps, was now in a far better position than China, although it had met the West a good deal later.[6]

Li Hung-chang ignored this gratuitous advice, however, so the two youths spent several months traveling around the Peking and Yangtze areas before returning to the south. By now Sun was apparently convinced that a revolt would be required to upset the disastrous sequence of events upon which China had embarked. When the Sino-Japanese War broke out in August 1894, he decided to go to Hawaii in order to raise funds and arms. The Peace of Shimonoseki came in April 1895, before the plans for revolt had matured, but the war nevertheless gave Sun his first opportunity to capitalize on Manchu weakness. He was to wait until 1900, the year of the next great crisis for the Manchus, before launching his second attempt.

In Hawaii Sun formed a branch of his *Hsing Chung Hui*. He busied himself in plans to start newspapers and establish schools for Chinese, and he succeeded in arousing support from his brother and other overseas Chinese.[7] When Sun's friends in China wrote urging his immediate return in order to take full advantage of the unfortunate course of the war, he gave up his plans for a fundraising campaign in America and returned to Hong Kong.

When Sun returned in the spring of 1895, conditions for revolt seemed even more promising than they had during the war. Large numbers of demobilized soldiers roamed the countryside. They became more and more desperate, and terrorized the farmers. Sun and his friends opened an "Agricultural Association" in Canton, with three branches in Canton and one in Hong Kong. They planned to seize the provincial government headquarters in Canton in coordination with a group of disaffected troops from Swatow. At the last moment, a shipment of arms was discovered, the Swatow group was delayed, and the authorities were able to capture the headquarters and arrest a shipment of "soldiers" coming from Hong Kong. Lu Hao-tung was captured and executed. Sun escaped, however, and with Cheng Shih-liang and Ch'en Shao-pai made his way to Macao. After several days, he proceeded with his two friends to Kobe. The Manchu proclamation which announced their crimes, punishments, and rewards, rated the three appropriately. Sun's capture or death would bring one thousand taels, and Ch'en Shao-pai's but one hundred. Cheng Shih-liang, skilled secret society man that he was, failed to make the list of sixteen criminals implicated.[8] The Hong Kong government, disturbed by the use to which its territory had been put, added insult to injury by banning the rebels from its precincts for five years.[9]

From Kobe Sun proceeded to Yokohama, where he cut his queue and grew a mustache. This effected a startling facial transformation. With the Western clothes of Japanese cut which he adopted, he passed easily for a Japanese.

After the Japanese war, when the natives of Japan began to be treated with more respect, I had no trouble, when I let hair and mustache grow, in passing for a Japanese. I admit I owe a great deal to this circumstance, as otherwise I should not have escaped from many dangerous situations.[10]

Sun now left for Hawaii. Ch'en Shao-pai stayed on in Yokohama, and Cheng Shih-liang, who could safely do so, returned to China to organize and promote the revolutionary cause.

From Hawaii, Sun went on through America to England. All along his route he tried to interest the overseas Chinese in the cause of the revolution, but he found them discouragingly prosperous and contented. His harrowing experience in October of 1896, when he was captured by the Chinese legation in London and almost smuggled back to China for certain torture and death, marked a turning point in his determination as well as in his success. After his dramatic release, Sun wrote an account of his experiences.[11] He was now widely known as a revolutionary who would not be discouraged or stopped.

There followed close to two years of study and thought in Europe. Sun returned to the Orient with many new ideas and with a jumble of impressions gained from many authors. Many of his future revolutionary and political ideas had begun to form. His self assurance was adequate to his needs, and he now sought assistance in financial and military needs.

While Miyazaki's Christianity had early given way to a rather cynical fatalism, Sun's faith had emerged newly strengthened and bolstered from his experiences in London. Tōyama and his fellows had concentrated on Oriental values and learning in their attempt to revitalize and regenerate the native tradition. Sun, however, had almost no background in things classical, and sought to apply the fruits of Western speculation and experience directly to the Oriental situation.

It is not surprising, then, that most Japanese esteemed Sun more as a personality than as a theorist. Only the radical liberals had anything at all in common with Sun's theories of social and political democracy. Once Japanese hopes had been blasted, it was natural for the fascist theorist Kita Ikki to lay the blame for Japan's failure in China on the foolish hopes based on Sun Yat-sen. Sun's thought, claimed Kita, was mere Western froth poorly suited to the Orient, and Sun himself was little more than a bubble borne along on the revolutionary tide.[12]

2. SUN AND THE JAPANESE

Sun's first Japanese friend was Sugawara Den, a Christian minister whom he met in Hawaii in 1894. When Sun fled to Japan in 1895, he met Sugawara again, and introduced him to Ch'en Shao-pai. While Sun went to England, where he received unexpected notoriety through his experience in London, Ch'en stayed behind in Japan to further the work.[13] By this time there was a considerable population of overseas Chinese in Japan, and Ch'en concentrated his activities among them. Over one thousand were to be found in Yokohama alone.[14]

Among Ch'en Shao-pai's contacts was Miyazaki Yazō, the young member of the Sino-Japanese Trade Research Bureau who had dropped all other activities in the attempt to work into the Chinese community. Miyazaki Yazō realized that his health was failing. He was anxious to have his younger brother capitalize on his new contact, and he wrote Torazō urging him to return from Siam. Torazō did so. As has been seen, he arrived after his brother's death.

In 1897, Torazō was commissioned by Inukai to travel and do research in China with Hirayama Shū and Kaji Chōichi. Torazō became ill, however, and his colleagues left without him.

After he recovered, Miyazaki was about to follow his friends to South China when all his plans were changed as the result of a farewell call he made to Kobayashi Kuzuo, a lieutenant of Ōi Kentarō's in the Osaka Incident.[15] At Kobayashi's house he met Sone Toshitora, a former naval officer, China expert, and adventurer.[16] Sone had known Miyazaki Hachirō, the elder brother who had died in the Satsuma Rebellion. He welcomed Torazō warmly and urged him to come to his home to meet a Chinese friend. This friend was Ch'en Shao-pai.

Miyazaki, who still expected to sail for South China, headed for Ch'en's Yokohama address carrying his baggage. Ch'en had not heard of Yazō's death. At first he mistook Torazō for his brother, and greeted him warmly. From Ch'en Miyazaki first heard of the doings and organization of the *Hsing Chung Hui* and of its leader, Sun Yat-sen. Ch'en showed Miyazaki his copy of *Kidnapped in London* with Sun's picture in it. Miyazaki, anxious to learn more of the organization, asked Ch'en whom he should contact in Hong Kong. Ch'en gave him the name of one Ho Shu-ling.[17]

Miyazaki then proceeded to Hong Kong. He found that Kaji had grown discouraged and returned to Japan. Hirayama too was about to give up; he was thoroughly dispirited. He assured Miyazaki that the secret societies lived up to their name; they killed members who talked. Even Arao Kiyoshi had never made any headway with them.[18] Ch'en's note for Ho Shu-ling provided new hope, but no one would tell where Ho might be found. He was finally located after the Japanese had made a futile trip to Amoy. Even then, however, Ho was too cautious to tell them very much. The Japanese were surprised to find most people still resentful because of the Sino-Japanese War, and reluctant to share any confidences. Ho referred the Japanese to a man named Ku Feng-shih of Hong Kong. Miyazaki and Hirayama met with Ku's group in a church after the Sunday evening service, and found this new group far more friendly to the Japanese. When Miyazaki explained Japan's goals and ideals to them, they rejoiced in the prospect of Japanese aid. Ku Feng-shih decided to be completely free with the Japanese. He told them that Sun had left London for Japan. In fact, he was due to land at Yokohama the next day. That same night, Miyazaki and Hirayama left for Japan.

The morning after he arrived in Yokohama Miyazaki proceeded to Ch'en Shao-pai's house. He learned from the maid that Ch'en had left, and that another gentleman had recently arrived from abroad. While Miyazaki was trying to decide what to do, a tousled and sleepy head appeared at the door; Sun Yat-sen invited him to come in. Once inside, Miyazaki waited for Sun to dress. He wondered whether Sun was to be their man. Would this person be able to supply the strength and leadership needed for the many problems of China? Could he lead four hundred million people? Miyazaki was bothered by Sun's nonchalance; he had expected a different sort of person.

When Sun returned, Miyazaki lost no time in asking him about his political position and principles. Sun answered that he believed in the inherent right of self-government; for that reason, he advocated republican government for China. Sun warmed to his subject, and asserted that republicanism had actually been the ancient government of China; it furnished the only possible solution for the present difficulties. He insisted that there was a pressing need for a hero to appear, overthrow the Manchus, and save China. Sun readily admitted his own inadequacy to play such a role, but said that if it were heaven's will to favor his party he would give his all to help such a man when he should appear. The sense of destiny was strong with him. At the same time, he readily asked for aid. "The way to aid the four hundred million people of China, the way to heal the insults to the yellow race of East Asia, and the way to further the recovery of mankind," he said, "is to bring about our revolution." [19]

The conversation must have been rather halting, for the two lacked a common language. Miyazaki's English was scanty and his Chinese was poor. Sun's Japanese, at this early date, was almost nonexistent. The two communicated mainly by jotting down ideas in Chinese characters. Each supplemented this with snatches of language the other could understand. [20]

That Sun, despite these difficulties, and despite his original unfortunate impression, was able to win Miyazaki over as completely as he did, is a tribute to his personality and evident sincerity. For Miyazaki was won over, and tremendously impressed. He returned later with Hirayama to talk with Sun again. The two decided to take him to meet Inukai. Miyazaki went on ahead, and announced, "Instead of a report, I have brought you a living example." [21] Inukai was delighted. A high Foreign Office official, however, Komura Jutarō, was disturbed at the thought of bringing such a notorious enemy of the Chinese government into Tokyo. Sun was finally brought in as a language teacher for Miyazaki and Hirayama.

The first night the trio lodged at a Japanese inn. When Hirayama asked Sun what name he wanted to use, Sun answered that it made no difference to him. They had just passed the house of a Marquis Nakayama, so Hirayama scribbled that name down.[22]

Sun's meeting with Inukai apparently came during the closing days of the Matsukata-Ōkuma cabinet which was in office from July 1896, to January 1898.[23] Like Miyazaki, Inukai was highly impressed by Sun Yat-sen. He was also pleased to find him exceptionally well groomed and neat. Sun was in constant company of the Japanese, and he soon came to understand their language fairly well.[24]

Inukai now exerted himself in Sun's behalf. With help from Tōyama Mitsuru and Hiraoka Kōtarō, he was able to provide a house in Tokyo for Sun, who still posed as a language teacher. Official help was slow in coming. Foreign Minister Ōkuma, the "China expert," had cast his lot with the Reform Party in China. He rather distrusted the revolutionaries. Inukai was just making progress in his arguments with Ōkuma for aid to Sun, when the cabinet fell. He then had to start all over again with Ōkuma's successor in the Itō Cabinet.[25] During this period Sun Yat-sen met many important Japanese, and numerous channels of aid and friendship opened up for him. He met leading oligarchs like Soejima Taneomi, Parliamentarians like Ozaki Yukio, and he even met Ōkuma himself.[26] Perhaps more important, Sun gained favor with the nationalist wing led by Tōyama, Hiraoka, Suenaga Setsu, and Akiyama Teisuke.[27] Akiyama was particularly valuable in the days that followed. He had relayed money to a group of Japanese who had encouraged the revolt that served as prelude to the Sino-Japanese War in Korea in 1894, and he later served in a similar capacity in helping the Chinese revolutionaries get money.[28]

During this time, Miyazaki made one of his rare visits to his family. After a few months, he was called back to Tokyo by a telegram from Inukai. When he reported for duty, Inukai handed him several thousand yen in cash, and told him to travel in China again.[29] After Miyazaki gave Sun part of this money, Sun and Ch'en Shao-pai moved to Yokohama, where they established their headquarters on Yamashita-chō. Miyazaki proceeded to Hong Kong. Hirayama Shū, who had received similar orders from Inukai, proceeded to Peking.[30]

3. THE FIRST JOINT PROJECT: AID TO AGUINALDO

The first cause in which Sun Yat-sen and his Japanese friends collaborated was that of Philippine independence. This is of considerable interest, for it shows the degree to which Sun, notwithstanding his Western education and orientation, was motivated by a hatred of imperialism. As a result of the Philippine enterprise, the feeling of East Asian unity which the Japanese cultivated so carefully grew stronger. The details of the project illustrated the harmonious coöperation of the several strata of Japanese government and society in their common cause: Asian independence under Japanese guidance.[31]

Certainly the West never gave the feeling of Oriental solidarity as much help as it did at the close of the nineteenth century. In 1898 China was besieged on all sides for bases and territorial grants. Even the United States, who had entered the lists as protector and sponsor of self-determination and freedom, suddenly reversed itself to enter the imperialist scramble.

Japan had long been conscious of definite interests and ambitions in Southeast Asia. As has been mentioned, many of the Tokugawa *shishi* felt that the area should become a sphere for Japanese exploitation. The Triple Intervention of 1895 and the European grabs in North China in 1898 showed that nothing could be done to the north. Japan was still weak, and she could operate only by capitalizing on local discontent and national aspirations of dependent Asiatics. As a result, more and more of the expansionist theorists began to concern themselves with Southeast Asia. Uchida Ryōhei was one of those who encouraged all their official and military acquaintances to consider possibilities for action in the southern islands.[32] The government leaders were not unsympathetic. As early as 1896, Itō Hirobumi had considered the possibilities of Japanese naval bases in the Amoy area.[33]

In their turn, the Philippine nationalists realized from the first that they were most likely to get the help they needed from Japan. As early as 1895, the *Katipunan* leaders who were planning a revolt appointed a committee to negotiate with Japan for the purchase of arms. At that time a formal agreement was drawn up with a group of Japanese naval officers, but the Philippine leaders were apparently unable to raise the advance payment of three hundred thousand pesos. These early failures brought about a change in the Philippine leadership. Emilio Aguinaldo charged the incumbents with having deceived their followers with false promises of help from Japan.[34]

In 1897, Aguinaldo proclaimed a republic at Biak-na-bato, in the mountains of Luzon. His position was untenable, however, and in December of that year he accepted a Spanish proposition whereby he agreed to retire to Hong Kong in return for generous payments of Spanish money. Hong Kong remained the headquarters for the group until Aguinaldo was invited to return to Luzon by American forces who were fighting the Spanish in 1898. As Aguinaldo's relationships with the Americans grew more and more strained, the *Junta* which remained at Hong Kong, the Hongkong Revolutionary Committee, became more important. They soon developed plans to send representatives to countries whose governments might help them.[35] Miyazaki met this group when he returned to Hong Kong in 1898. They complained bitterly to him of their betrayal by the United States.[36] For the next few months, however, Miyazaki's interests centered on things Chinese.

The Hongkong Committee sent Mariano Ponce to Japan in June 1898. This was before America had decided to suppress the nationalist movement in the Philippines. Ponce found most Japanese very favorably inclined to his cause.[37] He did not press for official recognition. When it became evident that the United States was determined to put down Aguinaldo's forces, Ponce's position became more difficult. Early chances of official aid faded, and Ponce found his attempts at purchase and transport of arms blocked because of Japanese reluctance to antagonize America.

At this point, Ponce went to Sun Yat-sen. He described later, in a biography of Sun, how he found him in his humble Yokohama quarters from which he directed the enormous apparatus of political intrigue which "extended through all the planet, even to Africa." Ponce, like the Japanese, was immediately attracted to Sun. He found him a calm, reasoned speaker. "He does not produce violent emotions, he does not provoke passionate explosions, but he speaks without vehemence, in well-considered words."[38]

Sun was soon enthused over the prospects for action in the Philippines. Any victory against Western imperialism would be a victory for all Orientals, and a friendly Philippine republic would provide an ideal proving ground and staging area for work in China.[39] Sun suggested this to Miyazaki and Hirayama, who had returned to Japan again, and they referred the whole problem to Inukai. Inukai too was enthusiastic. He saw great possibilities in establishing a friendly and grateful Philippine state which would serve as a base for operations in China. Japan, of course, would benefit from the establishment of two friendly, grateful states.[40]

Ponce, too, met the important Japanese that Sun had come to know.

One cold winter night I was invited to Tokyo by one of the prominent politicians of Japan, member of the Diet, former samurai, former Minister of Education, and leader of the Progressive Party, Inukai Ki. The other people present, mostly politicians and Japanese men of letters, were presented to me. Among the invited was Sun Yat-sen.[41]

Nothing could be done through such official persons, however, and the project was handled quietly.

According to the Kokuryūkai account, the Japanese Army and most of the politicians were for all-out aid. The only arms available, however, had in the main been purchased from America. Foreign Minister Aoki felt they could hardly be used against Americans.[42]

Subterfuge was thus required. Inukai pointed out to Miyazaki and Hirayama that so delicate a matter could not be delegated to a merchant. A merchant would not be able to resist the temptation for gain. He suggested instead a friend and party stalwart, Nakamura Haizan, who was doomed to a short life because of diabetes. Inukai thought that Nakamura would be willing to engage in one last chivalrous, selfless enterprise. Nakamura proved more than willing to handle the arrangements.[43]

The Foreign Office had remained adamant in its opposition. Within the Army General Staff, however, General Kawakami, an extrovert expansionist who recurs constantly in the histories of the patriotic societies as a guardian angel, insisted that some help must be given. He doubted that the business would succeed, but felt that for the long-term interests of fifty or even one hundred years it was essential for Japan to have a friendly and grateful group of admirers in the Philippines.

It was finally arranged for army munitions to be sold quietly to the Ōkura Trading Company. Ōkura then sold the materials to a German, Weinberger, who, in turn, was a friend of Nakamura.[44] Sun Yat-sen was in control of most of the negotiations, probably because of Japanese fears of antagonizing the United States. The project seemed a Chinese one.[45] Finally all that was needed was a ship. An anonymous broker served as intermediary in the purchase of the *Nunobiki Maru,* one of the older Mitsui ships, for Nakamura and one Wan Chi.[46]

One final touch illustrated the close liaison of expansionist societies, army, and unattached adventurers. When the ship lacked coal, Uchida Ryōhei persuaded Hiraoka Kōtarō's younger brother to furnish three thousand yen worth of coal for the bunkers.[47]

On the night of July 19, 1899, the *Nunobiki Maru* sailed from Moji for Formosa loaded with six million rounds of ammunition, ten thousand rifles, one fixed cannon, ten field guns, seven field glasses, a pressing machine for gunpowder, and materials for the manufacture of ammunition.[48] It had been planned to take many Japanese military experts as passengers, but because of close police surveillance Hirayama Shū and a group of young officers went ahead without waiting for the ship to sail. With them, as a special gift,

Inukai sent a valuable Japanese sword to Aguinaldo. He enclosed with it a letter:

Inukai Ki, desirous of showing his sympathy and admiration for President Aguinaldo, herewith sends this Japanese sword. He hopes that the President will accept this sword. All those concerned for the security of East Asia will praise the strength with which the President pursues this war and the valor with which he plans its strategy. For this reason, I wish you every success.[49]

Hirayama's group ran out of funds, and they finally made the trip to Manila as deck passengers. The sword thus caused them a great deal of inconvenience, but it left little doubt as to the sincerity of Japanese sympathies.

Miyazaki's contact with the affair ended with the early arrangements. At Sun's request, he returned to Canton and Hong Kong to continue work on the Chinese situation. By mistake, he took a shore line ship instead of the express for Hong Kong. As a result he was en route eighteen days. When his ship put in at Fukien, Miyazaki heard that a ship had sunk off Shanghai. Its name meant nothing to him. In Hong Kong he discussed this with a Mitsui man, and learned that the vessel had been transferred to Nakamura Haizan. He then realized that the whole enterprise had come to naught.[50]

The superannuated, overloaded *Nunobiki Maru* had gone down in a storm, taking with her the lives of thirteen men. Three of them were adventurer-*shishi*. Meanwhile, the advance party of six Japanese had proceeded to Luzon. After many difficulties in eluding American guards they succeeded in reaching Aguinaldo. While there, they got the news of the ship's foundering, and realized that their mission had failed. Aside from occasional talks with Aguinaldo through an interpreter, they had a rather wretched and useless experience. They found Aguinaldo bitter and determined to fight to the end. He saw no difference between Spain and America, and he predicted that in the future the affairs of the East would be settled by China, Japan, and the Philippines. The word of white men could no longer be honored.[51]

At Hong Kong, Miyazaki reluctantly told the Philippine *Junta* of the fate of their arms. More arms remained in Japan, but it seemed doubtful that they could be shipped in time to save the situation. Miyazaki then waited for word of the fate of Hirayama and the other Japanese. Rumors circulated that the Americans had found out about them, and that they had been apprehended.[52] Hirayama, however, after great difficulties, succeeded in eluding the Americans by escaping in the guise of a Filipino fisherman. The story of his narrow escapes, and the clever devices whereby he was able to take with him more funds for use for weapons in Japan, make engrossing reading. But it is more than likely that the whole incident was embroidered in a natural attempt to forget the unpleasantness of the stay with Aguinaldo and the utter futility of all the Japanese activity.

The incident had two marked effects. One was the feeling of solidarity which this activity engendered in the Chinese, Japanese, and Filipinos involved. In August 1900, the Hongkong Philippine Committee issued a public statement of regret at the loss of the Japanese *shishi* in the cause of Philippine independence. At the same time, letters from Filipino generals to Japanese concerned expressed their appreciation for the Japanese bravery and help.[53] Ponce himself felt Sun's deep concern with the common problems of imperialism and nationalism.

For Sun Yat-sen the problems found in the various countries of the Far East presented themselves in such form that he could study them together. Many common points characterize these problems. For this reason Sun was one of the enthusiastic advocates of the group of young oriental students from Korea, China, Japan, India, Siam, and the Philippines.[54]

Within Japan, however, the net effect was disunion. After American soldiers captured one of the Japanese in Manila, the Japanese government saw to it that no further activity of this sort took place.

And when the *shishi* tried to use the rest of the arms in China, they came to the startling discovery that the diabetic Nakamura had embezzled most of the funds to ease his declining years with luxurious living. This was an unparalleled reflection on Japanese chivalry and samurai honesty. The fault naturally seemed Inukai's, since he had brought Nakamura into the case. Inukai was shocked; he tried to force Nakamura to make restitution. It was a delicate matter and it required discretion. But Uchida Ryōhei and the *shishi* knew nothing of discretion; they knew only that their sense of honor was outraged. Inukai thus found himself between two fires; the politicians felt he was making too much of a minor matter, and the *shishi* thought he was trying to hush the scandal. Inukai held a banquet, and tried to persuade the indignant adventurers to be quiet. They refused. When they redoubled their clamor, the papers got hold of the story. Inukai then had to expel Nakamura from the *Shimpotō*.[55] The final blow-up came at the end of 1900, when it was felt that Sun's failure at Waichow had been caused in part by Nakamura's dishonesty. In December 1900, the *Osaka Mainichi* reported that Nakamura had swindled Sun Yat-sen, and that general indignation was growing. Nakamura claimed he was a victim of political squabbles, but his protest was in vain. He remained a moral leper in the circles of Asian idealists. On December 17, the *Mainichi* remarked dourly that Mr. Nakamura had moved because the shades of fallen heroes sacrificed to his avarice were haunting him. He was assured that they would continue to haunt his new residence, however, since he still had their money.[56]

4. OTHER CHINESE CANDIDATES FOR AID

The Philippine enterprise was only a minor excursion for Sun and his Japanese hosts. It showed a warm sympathy in Japanese circles for Asian nationalists, and, on the part of Sun Yat-sen, a live appreciation of the strategic possibilities of Philippine independence. During the same period, however, the Chinese Reform Party was making its play for power in Peking. This posed an issue much closer to Japanese interests. By and large, the government circles in Japan much preferred the respectability and conservatism of the reformers to the more volatile republicanism of Sun Yat-sen. As long as the reformers had a chance of success, Sun got little real help in Japan. After the reformers fled to Japan, the Japanese concentrated on getting them together with Sun's group. Not until that attempt had failed did Sun dominate the picture in Japan.

China's disastrous defeat at the hands of Japan in 1895 stirred other emotions than the determination of Sun's party that the Manchu dynasty must be overthrown. A considerable group of literati and officials decided that what was needed was a reform of the government along the lines of the Japanese constitutional monarchy. The need for a speedy renovation of China was graphically brought home by the renewed pressure exerted by imperialist powers in the wake of the war. The reform movement, which culminated in the "Hundred Days" reform in the summer of 1898, was led by two Cantonese. K'ang Yu-wei and Liang Ch'i-ch'ao, his outstanding disciple, had been studying and teaching in Canton since 1891. The burden of their doctrine was that Confucius had been misinterpreted by the Neo-Confucian philosophers. Since all the significant essentials of Western progress were inherent in and justified by the classical canon, that canon, if properly read and understood, offered no psychological or doctrinal bar to the adaptation of modern schemes of government, education, and warfare. The reformers wanted to retain the institutions of monarchy, but they desired a speedy and guided renovation. Their thought was closer to that of most Japanese than Sun's republicanism was, and as a result they formed close friendships among the higher classes in Japan.

Shortly after the Sino-Japanese War, K'ang Yu-wei wrote an admiring study of the Meiji Restoration.[57] At that time, Liang Ch'i-ch'ao also regarded Japan as the ideal. Schools which used the slogan "Know the shame of not being like Japan" carried the reform message to many students.[58]

Since the reformers were scholars and writers, they found many kindred spirits among Japanese Sinologues who could establish no *rapport* with Sun Yat-sen. The cultural activities of the *Dōbunkai* organization meant more to the reformers than they did to the revolutionaries. The Osaka Sinologist Yamamoto Baigai, whose connection with the Osaka Incident of Ōi Kentarō had cost him several years in prison a few years earlier, traveled in China in 1896. He met many scholars, and translated several works into Chinese. He befriended many outstanding Chinese, among them Lo Chen-yu.[59]

Sentiments favorable to the reform party grew among the younger scholar-officials in China. They had the moral backing of the prominent viceroys Liu K'un-i and Chang Chih-tung. When the Kuang Hsü emperor tried to assert his independence from the Dowager Empress Tz'u Hsi in 1898, K'ang Yu-wei got his chance. Beginning on June 11, he master-minded a series of edicts which were to institute drastic reforms. K'ang was soon high in advisory councils, and Liang became director of the translation bureau. The reformers' Shanghai paper was changed into an official government organ, and agitation for a constitution grew. The reforms and reform decrees continued until September 21, when the Dowager Empress, aided by loyal military officers, reasserted her rule, imprisoned the hapless emperor, and moved to destroy the entire leadership of the reform party.

It will be remembered that in the summer of 1898 Miyazaki had gone to Hong Kong, where he first met the Filipino emigrees, while Hirayama had gone on to Peking. In the south Miyazaki soon became aware of the reform group, for it was attracting many young revolutionaries. Miyazaki tried to mediate between the two factions. Unfortunately, he was so obviously partial to the revolutionaries that his efforts had no results. Nevertheless, his mediation assumed a new urgency when word came from Hirayama in Peking that K'ang Yu-wei and his party were about to fall from power. Perhaps the new common anti-Manchu drive would make possible a new unity.[60]

At the time of the Empress Dowager's *coup d'état,* Itō Hirobumi was in China. He had gone to observe the degree of imperialist activity, and he remained to watch the political upheaval. Itō gave quiet instructions to the Japanese officials to protect the reformers.[61] K'ang was sheltered by the English. They helped him get to Shanghai, and from there an English mail boat took him to Hong Kong. Meanwhile, Liang Ch'i-ch'ao, who had fled to the Japanese consulate at Tientsin, proceeded to Japan with Hirayama on a Japanese gunboat.

Miyazaki met K'ang Yu-wei in Hong Kong. K'ang did not think very highly of Miyazaki, however, and he was not at all sure that he wanted to go to Japan. This was not surprising; Miyazaki had been arguing for weeks with K'ang's followers in the area, trying to get them to join the revolutionary party. Moreover, English aid and Japanese offers of help had flattered K'ang; he overestimated his own importance. When he finally decided to try Japan as an asylum, he had one of his students tell Miyazaki about it. There was never any of the easy comradeship that characterized Miyazaki's relationship with Sun. In fact, the final negotiations for K'ang's trip were handled by the Japanese consul at Hong Kong.

When K'ang did express a desire to speak to Miyazaki, his request illustrated his low opinion of that worthy. He told Miyazaki that the Empress Dowager was the only obstacle to reform in China, and expressed a desire to eliminate her by hiring some Japanese *sōshi*. Miyazaki regarded this as a reflection on the character of K'ang's followers. One determined patriot was all that was needed; was there not one such among the reformers? Evidently, K'ang took this to heart, for the next day a very nervous young man came to Miyazaki to take a tearful farewell. The tears were probably unnecessary, however, for that individual disappeared without a trace.[62]

K'ang's last doubts about Japan centered around the problem of his safety there. Although Miyazaki assured him of the excellence of Japanese police protection, K'ang desired Miyazaki's company on the trip. When this had been sanctioned by Inukai after an exchange of telegrams, the final plans were made.[63]

In Tokyo, Foreign Minister Ōkuma saw to it that the proper preparations were made.[64] A small ship was sent out from Hong Kong with only English and Japanese passengers besides K'ang and his party. They were quietly transferred to the *Kawauchi Maru*, which headed for Japan.[65] Five days later the party of eleven arrived at Kobe, where Hirayama met them as they debarked in the early morning darkness.

K'ang Yu-wei arrived early in November of 1898, just after the *Kenseitō* cabinet had fallen. Ōkuma was now no longer able to provide official assistance, but he continued his help on a personal basis. For a time, K'ang lived with him. Afterward they wrote each other frequently, and their friendship continued on past the World War.[66]

The new Yamagata cabinet was less cordial to the reformers.[67] The situation was complicated by the distrust with which European powers were beginning to view the presence of such prominent troublemakers in Japan. The reformers, however, needed official protection more than the revolutionary group, for they did not have the enthusiastic backing of the action societies which Sun enjoyed. The Chinese government, of course, added its complaints at the presence of K'ang Yu-wei in Japan. Its fears were not entirely unjustified; one group of enthusiasts wanted to spirit the Kuang Hsü Emperor to Kyushu to form a government-in-exile there which would have advanced K'ang's purposes and strengthened ultimate Sino-Japanese friendship.[68] K'ang himself had counted on Japanese help to drive the conservative party out of Peking, and when this aid was not forthcoming he became embittered.[69] The Tokyo government finally decided that it would be wisest to have K'ang leave Japan. Yamamoto Baigai, who served as intermediary, was given secret Foreign Office funds with which he was to help K'ang and Liang. He also agreed to help in the publication of their materials in Japan and in China.[70]

Liang Ch'i-ch'ao remained in Japan, as did many other adherents of the reform group. In the months that followed, the Japanese concentrated their efforts on a proposed union of the two groups of Chinese. At the very least, they wanted close coöperation between Sun Yat-sen and K'ang Yu-wei. This was an obvious attempt for them to make. Indeed, the Chinese had been trying to bring about such an alliance themselves. As early as 1896, a group of Chinese in Hong Kong led by Hsieh Tsan-t'ai had done their best to unite the two factions.[71]

Three basic disagreements prevented such attempts from bearing fruit. The two factions were divided in their ideas of government. They both sought to control the same sources of revenue. Worst of all, the personalities of their leaders, as well as those of the rank and file of the membership, were basically antithetical to each other.

In the early period, the groups were divided by the issue of the monarchy. Had this been the only stumbling block to union, it is possible that the mutual concern with overthrowing the rule of the Empress Dowager might have sufficed to make an alliance possible. Tz'u Hsi herself helped this along by classing K'ang, Liang, and Sun together as the three greatest criminals of China.[72]

Competition for revenue was a greater problem. The overseas Chinese were at all times the main source of money for the revolutionaries and reformers alike, and their allegiance was essential if the exiles hoped to keep free of foreign domination. The Chinese in Hawaii had financed Sun's first revolt. After he fled to Japan, the Yokohama Chinese colony sponsored the early travels of his agents.[73] As the Chinese community in Japan grew in numbers, its members realized the necessity of establishing Chinese schools. Inukai served as godfather to the project, and thanks to his mediating influence both groups of Chinese supported the schools. Kashiwara Buntarō, an assistant of Inukai's, was named executive secretary of the schools, which were named *Da t'ung,* or Great Harmony. The first head master was a protege of Liang Ch'i-ch'ao named Hsü Ch'in.

Despite the early coöperation in this project, differences were not slow to arise. Sun and his friends traveled more, and they furnished the schools with fewer students. The schools gradually came to take on a definitely conservative character. Before long Miyazaki was investigating complaints by Sun that his group was being ignored. The answers by Hsü Ch'in assured Miyazaki of great respect for Sun and a deep desire to work with him, but they also revealed that the schools' teaching was conservative. Hsü's letters left no doubt as to Miyazaki's importance. He portrayed China as a boat in a storm, and confessed that it would be helpless without Japanese assistance.[74] Nevertheless, protests and denials could not change the trend of the schools. Many of the students had studied previously at Liang's schools in China, and the type of political philosophy which they had studied naturally made them partial to the reformers. No one was more earnest than Inukai in his efforts to promote agreement and avert a wider split, but his sincerity was rewarded by little more than gratitude from both parties.[75] At one time, Liang Ch'i-ch'ao seemed close to agreement with Sun. K'ang, who opposed this, ordered Liang to Honolulu on a fund raising tour, and thereby disrupted any possible harmony. For the next years, overseas Chinese all over the world were subjected to double appeals for help by organizations whose branches covered the globe in parallel lines.

In the final analysis, however, personality problems counted for fully as much as ideological or financial differences in the widening split between the two groups. The day after K'ang landed in Japan in 1898, Sun Yat-sen called to greet him, but K'ang refused to see his rival.[76] From K'ang's standpoint as a loyalist, Sun was a rebel without dignity or virtue. From K'ang's intellectual perspective, Sun's represented a barbarous accommodation to the Western materialist philosophies of gain and utility. Sun, for his part, rejected the elaborate synthesis upon which K'ang had lavished care, and dismissed its premises as irrelevant and unimportant. Sun neither knew nor valued the classics. As a result, the two groups were not likely to get along. According to Kashiwara, the school secretary,

Although Inukai urged Sun and K'ang to work together, such harmony was difficult to achieve. For example, many of Sun's followers at that time were a rascally set of near-scoundrels. Since K'ang's group were scholars and gentry, the two didn't get along at all. K'ang would say of Sun, "Sun himself isn't a bad character, but he is too unlettered; he doesn't understand when you talk to him." Sun, meanwhile, said of K'ang, "That rotten Confucianist is worthless." I won't say which was in the right.[77]

Although Ōkuma and Inukai continued to be interested in K'ang Yu-wei, the Japanese activists deserted him for Sun Yat-sen. In the action-filled years that lay ahead, personality evidently counted for more than ideology. So it was that the Japanese nationalists, exponents of the Imperial Way and Oriental values, allied themselves with a representative of republicanism and Western values. For the less conservative Miyazaki, of course, that choice had never been in doubt.

K'ang Yu-wei, in turn, became so distrustful of his erstwhile saviors that the last attempt at reconciliation between K'ang and Sun Yat-sen that Miyazaki made in 1900 resulted in a real altercation and permanent hatred.

The early period of experiment and friendship had thus ended with a firm alliance established between Japanese adventurers and Sun Yat-sen. The Chinese reformers, despite Tokyo preferences, had been abandoned when their personnel and personalities proved antithetical to the Japanese and Chinese adventurers through whom

Tokyo could best furnish help. The first joint enterprise had demonstrated how well suited the Japanese adventurers were in temperament and aptitude for collaboration with their Chinese guests. The Philippine trial balloon had also provided useful precedents for coöperation with business and army circles. What was needed next was another opportunity to capitalize on Chinese weakness and disunity. The Boxer Rebellion of 1900 furnished that opportunity.

1900: WAICHOW AND AMOY

4

The turn of the century marked a decisive point in the collaboration of the Japanese with the Chinese revolutionaries. By 1900, Japan had rid herself of the worst features of the unequal treaties, and her citizens and leaders took a more active and vocal interest in the fate of neighboring Asiatics than ever before. In that year China was suddenly engulfed by a startling wave of anti-foreign frenzy that promised to give foreign aggressors and dissident Chinese unparalleled opportunities for action. The revolutionaries and reformers were not slow to profit by this state of affairs. After K'ang Yu-wei's men tried to stage a rebellion in Hankow, Sun Yat-sen and his allies began a more ambitious revolt in South China.

Japan's participation in the events of that summer was of the greatest importance. In North China, where she had so recently been deprived of her war-time gains, Japan's moderation won her Western friendship and admiration that was a prelude to full equality and alliance with England. Her conscientious participation in the allied expedition to Peking reflected a realization that little could be gained in North China by power politics. If Russia was to be prevented from initiating the partition of China, it would require the concerted and coöperative policy in which Japan played such a prominent role.

But if, despite this caution, the partition of China seemed likely to proceed unchecked, Japanese public opinion would force the Tokyo leaders to see that Japan shared in the loot. It was never easier to do. Disorder, rebellion, and outrages directed against foreigners were so widespread in China that excuses for action could be found or forced at will. Japan advanced to the brink of open aggression in South China, and held back only when it seemed possible that Russia might forego her opportunities for expansion in Manchuria. The discovery that Russia was not so inclined, and the bitter recriminations that followed after the opportunity in South China had been lost, then caused the fall of the cabinet in Tokyo.

While all this was going on, the architect of the abortive invasion in South China, the governor general of Formosa, offered Sun Yat-sen the use of his territory as a base for a new revolt. Until he was stopped by Tokyo, General Kodama's plans for help to Sun included Japanese equipment and Japanese officers as advisers. Sun was never again so close to getting full-scale Japanese help. Here, then, Japanese imperialism fused so completely with the work of the expansionist societies and their Chinese wards that little chance remained for the liberals with their theories of guidance.

The confusion was not limited to Tokyo, Peking, and Formosa. For a time there was talk of a separatist movement in which Li Hung-chang, one of the most faithful servants of the Manchu dynasty, was to coöperate with Sun Yat-sen. And after this failed, Sun Yat-sen showed himself almost as uncritical of Chinese allies as he did of Japanese. His rebellion was waged by a loose league of secret societies, and led by men who had little agreement on concrete plans in the event of success. If his plans had been successful, Sun would have found himself at the head of an imperfect union which owed its existence to Japanese military help.

Small wonder, then, that in such chaos the vague idealism of the Japanese radicals was submerged in the more purposeful plans of the military and their lackeys in the patriotic societies. They alone came prepared. When their plans too were discarded, the way was open for a realignment and re-evaluation of Chinese revolutionary programs and groups, and a re-thinking of Japanese policy goals in Tokyo. This produced, in 1905, a shift to the left in revolutionary thinking that coincided with a shift to the right in Japanese policy thinking.

1. THE BACKGROUND

Since the fall of the Ōkuma-Itagaki *Kenseitō* cabinet in November 1898, the Japanese government had been headed by Yamagata Aritomo, the spokesman of the military. Itō Hirobumi, who had left for China shortly after the formation of the coalition cabinet, was unable to prevent its fall or to anticipate Yamagata's moves to form a new cabinet. For most observers, Itō's attempts to regain control of the political situation after his return from China dominated Tokyo politics for several years. Yamagata's government, however, seemed quite strong. By means of working agreements with Itagaki's branch of the old *Kenseitō,* the Premier was able to get the tax increases he needed from the Diet. Nevertheless, the administration gradually aroused determined opposition among the political leaders. Itō utilized this dissatisfaction to form a new party, the *Seiyūkai,* in September 1900. By then, Yamagata had been subjected to fairly constant pressure in the Diet. As usual, the opposition used the China policy as material for debate. Ōishi Masami, a "liberal" chauvinist who had served as ambassador to Korea shortly before the Sino-Japanese War, led this assault in the Diet with persistent questions about the government's plans for stopping foreign gains in China.[1]

As political differences widened in Tokyo, China was beset by the Boxer Rebellion. Anti-foreignism had grown steadily in the wake of foreign encroachment and missionary advances. Rural superstitions and rumors were aggravated by economic ills attendant upon new technology and transportation. Before long, the Manchu court saw in the movement a means of satisfying its desire to strike the foreigners. The Boxers entered Peking in June, and the expedition of the Powers to rescue their nationals and punish the Chinese did not reach the city until mid-August. Japan took a leading part in the Allied Expedition; she supplied the bulk of the troops.[2] Russia took advantage of the occasion to occupy Manchuria, while Japan seemed likely to realize nothing for her efforts. In Japan, professional patriots were understandably annoyed by such bungling. Their concern for China's territorial integrity was heightened by their inability to share in its probable violation.

Meanwhile the Chinese revolutionaries were completing plans which had been under way for several years. It had long been evident that a union with the secret societies of South China would be necessary. In the preliminary arrangements for such a union, the Japanese played an important part as emissaries of Sun Yat-sen. Hirayama Shū had made contact with many secret society leaders in the Yangtze area on his way to Peking in 1898. The busy days of the abortive reform movement had temporarily eclipsed these activities, but by 1899, while Hirayama was in the Philippines, Miyazaki was to be found in Hong Kong. There he worked with Ch'en Shao-pai. About this time, the revolutionaries made an important convert in the person of Pi Yung-nien, whose earlier allegiance had been with the reform party. The reformers had many friends along the Yangtze cities, and they were planning a revolt of their own. Sun Yat-sen thus faced competition for the help of the secret societies.[3]

When the representatives of several secret societies met in Hong Kong to confer with Miyazaki and Ch'en Shao-pai on the problem of unity, they chose Sun Yat-sen as their leader. Sun had much to recommend him. He was better known than any other person, and he had worked with the societies before. The society heads were anxious to be able to utilize the monetary resources of the overseas Chinese as well as whatever foreign aid might be available. Sun, in view of the efforts of his Japanese colleagues, seemed a logical choice.

The representatives of the *San-ho-hui* and the *Ko-lao-hui* thus threw in their lot with Sun's *Hsing Chung-hui,* and the result was a new organization which was called the *Hsing Han-hui* (Rise Han Society) which carried on the revolt of 1900.[4]

After these arrangements were completed, Miyazaki returned to Japan. Hirayama, who had just returned from the Philippines, replaced him in Hong Kong. In Shanghai, Miyazaki enlisted another *shishi* for the cause. Kiyofuji Koshichirō resigned his *Dō-bunkai* post, and accompanied Miyazaki to Tokyo.[5] In Tokyo, Miyazaki continued his recruiting. Thanks to his efforts, several businessmen and mine operators contributed generous sums.[6]

Sun Yat-sen was now ready to proceed. He was not aware that there were no weapons left from those purchased with the sums entrusted to Nakamura for the Philippine incident, and he now had money to buy more. Several of the comrades were sent off to raise more money. All those involved in the operation received a tremendous psychological boost when Uchida Ryōhei offered to lead a group of *sōshi* as shock troops.[7]

By summer of 1900, then, the planning of several years had borne fruit in the form of a new union of anti-dynastic societies. The union had considerable support from the Japanese. With the Chinese government and the Western powers which supported it preoccupied by the Boxer outbreaks in North China, it is not surprising that Sun Yat-sen was confident of success.

2. NEGOTIATIONS WITH LI HUNG-CHANG AND K'ANG YU-WEI

Sun Yat-sen and his entourage of Japanese spent most of June on shipboard. Travel was necessary to secure financial backing from the overseas Chinese. The fund-raising activities were also supplemented by a last attempt to unite the faction of K'ang Yu-wei with that of Sun Yat-sen. Tied in with this was a possibility of coöperation with the venerable Viceroy Li Hung-chang. In retrospect, the hopes for coöperation with K'ang and Li seem foolish, but they fitted easily into the sanguine mood that was Sun's in June 1900.

The southern provinces of Kwangtung and Kwangsi were farthest removed from the court at Peking. They had the longest history of contact with the West, and also of anti-foreign sentiment. They produced most of the early agitators and revolutionaries. It was, then, not surprising that among the societies formed by Cantonese in the Tokyo area in the early revolutionary period one took the name of "Society for the Independence of Kwangtung."[8] Still, it was something else again for a viceroy to entertain thoughts of secession.

In 1900, the viceroy of these provinces was Li Hung-chang. Li was in the last year of his long service to the Manchu court, and, although he was temporarily out of favor with the Empress Dowager's coterie, he could still be expected to act the part of the good and faithful Manchu servant. It was, therefore, a highly astonished Sun Yat-sen who received, early in June, a letter from one Liu Hsüeh-hsun of Canton, telling him that Li Hung-chang wished to confer with him in regard to a plan for declaring the two Kwang provinces independent of the faltering Peking court.[9]

Sun consulted with his friends. They confirmed his doubts as to the motives of the wily old viceroy. They felt it was a new and clever scheme to capture Sun Yat-sen.[10] It was finally decided to use the Japanese allies as emissaries, since they were not likely to be molested by the viceroy. Hirayama was sent on ahead to confer with the secret societies in Hong Kong, and the main body followed shortly after. Early in June, the *Nippon Maru* sailed for Hong Kong with Sun, Cheng Shih-liang, Ch'en Shao-pai, Kiyofuji, Uchida, and Miyazaki among her passengers. They worked out their plans on shipboard.[11]

When the *Nippon Maru* reached Hong Kong, a small Chinese naval vessel put out under cover of darkness to meet her. Liu Hsüeh-hsun had sent this out for Sun Yat-sen. Instead, Miyazaki, Uchida, and Kiyofuji transferred to it. They sailed up the West River, and were taken to Liu's splendid home in Canton. The talks proceeded slowly because of linguistic difficulties. Liu and Miyazaki spoke a little English, and they clarified obscure points by scribbling notes in Chinese. No sure account of the conversation is available from any of the participants, for Miyazaki professed himself unable to tell the interesting details, while the other two probably understood very little of what went on.[12] According to the research of the eminent scholars Yoshino Sakuzō and Katō Shigeshi, however, the conferees agreed that it would be a good plan to try once more to line up K'ang Yu-wei in a united front in which he, Li, and Sun could coöperate to secure at least part of China from imperialism and internal unrest. Liu said that the Canton gentry were particularly eager to bring this about, and that they had contributed several thousand *taels* for the project. He suggested that the Japanese should take along a generous sum in token of aid to K'ang Yu-wei, and he assured them that more would be forwarded to them in Singapore.[13]

After reporting all this to Sun Yat-sen, Miyazaki, Kiyofuji, and Uchida proceeded to Singapore. Sun stayed in Hong Kong to check on the progress of plans for the revolt. The stage was now set for the final attempt at uniting the reform party with the revolutionaries.

When Miyazaki arrived in Singapore, he wrote to K'ang asking for an interview. K'ang sent polite regrets. He explained that his English hosts guarded him so sedulously that he could not possibly receive visitors. One of K'ang's followers had a better explanation; he told Miyazaki that K'ang had received warnings from Yokohama that Sun and his Japanese friends were determined to kill him. Miyazaki then wrote K'ang again, assuring him of his pacific intentions. Several days passed. Uchida Ryōhei, impatient at Sun's delay in coming from Hong Kong, lost interest and returned to Japan. Miyazaki persisted in his attempts to see K'ang, but he had no success. K'ang was evidently still convinced of Japanese superiority in rough-neck tactics. He became more and more nervous. Finally, he could stand it no longer; he told his troubles to the Singapore police.[14]

So it was that one warm evening while Kiyofuji was playing *go* to the accompaniment of Miyazaki, who was strumming on his *biwa,* the Colony Constabulary entered and took them both off to prison. It is not difficult to see why the subsequent interrogations produced a reasonable doubt in the minds of the officials. The search of the prisoners' baggage produced two Japanese swords, thirty thousand *taels,* and no explanation other than assurances that the Japanese were just calling on old friends. Miyazaki explained that to the *shishi* a sword was as essential as a cross to the Christian, and he assured the astonished British that the sizeable sum of money was not at all unusual for *shishi* who lived and traveled on a common, share-alike basis. The Japanese spent six days in prison while the officials tried to decide what to do with them. Despite the readiness of the Japanese consul and a Buddhist missionary from Japan to support all of Miyazaki's statements, the British could not be persuaded. They hardly were reassured when Miyazaki explained that it was his long-range purpose to save China.[15]

Six days after the arrests, Sun Yat-sen arrived from Hong Kong. He assured the police that the Japanese were old friends of his, and that the money was actually his. This offered a basis on which the prisoners could be released. The Japanese of whom K'ang had complained — Miyazaki, Kiyofuji, Uchida, and Hirayama (who was in Hong Kong) — were then banned for five years as troublemakers, together with Sun Yat-sen. The British escorted them to the *Sado Maru,* bound for points north.[16]

This ended any possibility of coöperation with K'ang Yu-wei. From now on, the Japanese adventurers despised him as an ingrate and a coward, and they ended their efforts to mitigate the acute dislike in which Sun Yat-sen held him.

The *Sado Maru* put in at Hong Kong several days later. Miya-zaki and Kiyofuji went ashore immediately to ask Hirayama about the preparations for revolt, but when the Japanese consulate warned them that the English intended to extend the Singapore ban to Hong Kong, they returned to the ship in order to avoid arrest. When the order to stay on board was brought out by the police, Miyazaki was discouraged at finding himself barred from the place he had used as a second headquarters since 1896.[17] This was not calculated to lessen his dislike for K'ang Yu-wei.

The incongruous idea of an alliance with Li Hung-chang, how-ever, had not yet been renounced. This time Peking intervened. The Empress Dowager, anxious to profit from Li's prestige in reaching a settlement with the West, called Li to Peking. Li was rather re-luctant to go, and the Canton gentry, who felt that his departure would bring chaos, did their best to get him to stay.[18] At the same time, friends within the Hong Kong government asked Sun to stay until it became clear whether or not Li would heed the call from Peking. Li finally decided to go, and he left Canton on July 17, 1900.[19] This ended any possibility of coöperation between the two extremes in the Chinese political world.

Several possible interpretations suggest themselves for Li Hung-chang's original bid to Sun Yat-sen. One theory holds that he was merely trying to divide the anti-Manchu forces by arousing K'ang's suspicions of Sun Yat-sen. It can also be held that he felt a revolt was inevitable, and that he planned to temporize and delay the revolutionaries by giving them hope of a bloodless victory. Yoshino Sakuzō's conclusion, however, is more likely. From a consideration of the role of the Hong Kong government in holding Sun available on shipboard, it can be argued that the scheme was not Li's, not Sun's, and certainly not K'ang's, but rather that of the English authorities on the spot. Fearful of riots and revolts, and desirous of preserving order in South China, they may well have offered encouragement and vague promises of protection to a regime which would unite the strongest elements in the area. Li may have played along with this until he was sure of regaining the upper hand at court, at which point he walked out on the whole plan.[20] Most likely of all is a modification of this theory. In all probability the Canton gentry and merchants, with the knowledge of some of their Western counterparts, were willing to pay and pay heavily in order to avoid disorder and rebellion.[21]

One other project which occupied Sun Yat-sen in mid-summer showed that he realized fully the importance of the Hong Kong government in planning a revolt in South China. In June 1900, Sun applied to the Hong Kong government for help or, at the least, for neutrality in case of a revolt. While the Japanese were busying themselves with Li Hung-chang's representative, Sun and his Chinese assistants prepared a statement for British consumption.

The document they drew up was, in the main, a bitter excoriation of the corruption and inefficiency of the Manchu court and its gentry-official supporters. It pointed out the crucial nature of the situation in China, and warned that the hardships that resulted would be borne by the ordinary people. The officials, far from helping those people, sought only their own gain and profit. England, in the past, had shown integrity and sincerity, and England prized commerce. England was especially victimized by these officials, for they were parasites on trade. Sun promised to build a new China, with no divisions, and with friendly treatment for all countries. All merchants would be welcome, and no special privileges would be reserved for Chinese. The document ended with a six-point declaration of purpose. The revolutionary government would remove the capital to a central location, it would set up a federal government, establish civil rights for Chinese and equal opportunities for all foreigners, it would institute increased salaries for officials in order to end corruption, it would adopt an Anglo-Saxon code of law, and it would create special schools for the study of law, science, and the arts.[22]

This interesting document shows that the revolutionaries had little faith in the gentry-sponsored plan proposed by Li Hung-chang. The play for British help showed that Sun was not averse to varying Japanese aid with other assistance. Finally, the detailed outline for the new government was the fullest statement Sun had made up to that point. It showed that Sun Yat-sen would not rest content with

Kwangtung and Kwangsi, but that his goals were national in scope.

Unfortunately, Sun's appeals, and his travels, brought no results. The British ignored his overtures. By banishing his Japanese allies from their territory and by denying admittance to Sun himself, they threw him further on the grace of the Japanese allies. Such personal setbacks from Western imperialism unquestionably affected Sun's later denunciations of that system more than any reasoned analysis of its effects.

After mid-July, all efforts were devoted to the rebellion that was to follow.

3. The Second Attempt: Waichow

In considering the Waichow revolt, it would be fitting to follow the preparations of those who led the rebels and incurred the danger and the disappointment. The activities of Cheng Shih-liang and his men deserve more attention than they have received. Cheng, however, was responsible to Sun Yat-sen for his plans and actions. And since Sun in turn was dependent upon other forces for help and advice, it will be necessary to continue to follow that ubiquitous group on board the *Sado Maru* off Hong Kong. Their course led them, by a circuitous route, to Formosa, but a proper study of their activities ends in Tokyo.

a. A provisional government

On the way south from Japan in June, Miyazaki questioned Sun about the role he envisaged for the Japanese in the revolution. After some discussion, they agreed that Kiyofuji should be in over-all charge of the Japanese share in the operation, and that Uchida Ryōhei was best fitted to lead the *sōshi* in the actual fighting.[23] The plotters further agreed that the general goal of the revolt would be the city of Waichow (Postal Atlas: Waiyeung), about one hundred miles east of Canton. It was felt that it would be wisest to gather momentum at a safe distance from Canton. Sun was confident that once an early success had been achieved, defections from Manchu troops to the revolutionary side would become general.[24]

These early tactical plans were ruled out by the British refusal to allow the revolutionaries to land at Hong Kong. Another council was held on shipboard to meet the new situation, and it produced the first serious split between Sun and the Japanese.[25] Sun's plan was cautious. He wanted Fukumoto Nichinan, a new member of the group and one who was not on the list of those barred, to go ashore to raise money.[26] Pi Yung-nien was to go along the Yangtze to contact the secret society leaders, while Sun, Miyazaki, and Kiyofuji would return to Japan. They could then go back by way of Formosa and Amoy after the revolution had begun.[27]

These plans were much too circumspect to suit the Japanese. Fukumoto argued that the Japanese government was watching them too carefully to make any activity in Japan possible. He suggested landing secretly and starting a revolt immediately. Sun opposed such rashness as suicidal. Miyazaki, possibly conscious of how ridiculous his earlier ruminations on a splendid death would seem if he now returned sedately to Japan, threatened to quit the whole enterprise. Soon a violent argument was in progress. Miyazaki countered Sun's charges of idiocy with suggestions of cowardice. After the other contestants slipped quietly out one by one, Sun broke into tears and retreated to his cabin.

This nadir of Sino-Japanese brotherhood was soon forgotten, for shortly afterward Miyazaki and Fukumoto spotted Chinese and English police on deck. The realization that they were being watched canceled out the possibility of an immediate *putsch* and removed the hard feelings. The next day, long-range planning was resumed. This time, Japanese aid was more essential than ever. At Hirayama's suggestion, Sun drew up a provisional cabinet so that action could be taken in his absence. As before, Cheng Shih-liang was in charge of the military effort. Assisting him were Hara Jo[28] and Yang Fei-chang. Fukumoto was named head of the Civil Administration, and Hirayama was to be his assistant. Miyazaki reports that there was some disagreement with these posts, but that Sun's word prevailed.[29]

Sino-Japanese coöperation had suddenly recovered from a low of disunity to reach its apogee of trust and confidence. After this conference Sun, Miyazaki, and Kiyofuji returned to Japan, while Fukumoto stayed in Hong Kong to raise money for the cause. Cheng Shih-liang went ashore to begin recruiting his troops.

b. Over-eager allies

In Japan, Sun and his friends found that the *sōshi* who were to form the shock troops were becoming discouraged and restless. When Sun went on to Shanghai, he arrived just in time to keep the Japanese from taking steps to utilize those restless spirits.

The discouragement could be traced to the fate of T'ang Ts'ai-chang, a member of the reform group who had tried to launch a revolt at Hankow. T'ang was a close friend of Pi Yung-nien. Unlike Pi, he had decided that it would be better to lead a revolt for K'ang Yu-wei than to shift to the party of Sun. T'ang decided to take advantage of the Boxer unrest and to coöperate with the secret societies. Rumors of this movement had been discounted by Miyazaki when he met with secret society men in Hong Kong earlier.[30] The Yangtze branch of the *Ko-lao-hui* had responded enthusiastically to plans for simultaneous risings at Hankow, Tatung (Anhwei), Anking (Anhwei), Changteh (Hunan), and Hsinti (Hupeh). Since T'ang's group lacked funds, they had to extend their deadline for action several times. A declaration of purpose was drawn up which differed conspicuously in tone from Sun's letter to the Hong Kong government. It proposed only restoration of the Kuang Hsü Emperor, a modern government, and full coöperation with foreigners. Viceroy Chang Chih-tung's men found out about the plot late in July, and they arrested the conspirators early in August. T'ang and nineteen associates were executed.[31]

Tidings like these discouraged Uchida Ryōhei's *sōshi*.[32] Their interest was likely to evaporate if they did not have something to do. Unfortunately, chances for another revolt on the Yangtze were more remote than ever. All through the area, officials were more watchful than they had been, and retribution was likely to be swift and sure. The officials knew that Sun also was planning a descent upon the coast.

An answer to this problem was worked out by Uchida Ryōhei, who was in Shanghai with a group of *Genyōsha* members. They were joined by Yamada Yoshimasa, who had just left his position as Nanking *Dōbunkai* representative. Uchida and Yamada decided that only three viceroys — Chang Chih-tung, Liu K'un-i, and Li Hung-chang — stood between order and anarchy in the provinces free of Boxer outbreaks.[33] The assassination of any two of these, they thought, would end the repression of revolutionary activities that seemed to be delaying Sun's revolt. Uchida and his men proposed to take care of Li Hung-chang, while Yamada would see to Liu K'un-i. Once this was done, the way would be open for the volunteers to come from Japan. Sun Yat-sen found out about this just in time to stop it. He felt that the attempt was sure to fail, and he realized that his entire movement would be discredited.

The Japanese were unable to convince Sun, and they finally sent telegrams to Japan to keep the assassination squads from coming.[34] Uchida was disgruntled. He shifted his attention to Korea, and several other Japanese returned to Japan from Shanghai. Sun seemed likely to lose the enthusiastic support of the Japanese firebrands who had been expected to serve as his assault force.

c. Formosan sanctuary

Unlike Uchida Ryōhei, Yamada Yoshimasa was not prepared to abandon his hopes for a revolution. After he went to Formosa armed with messages from expansionists in Japan, Governor General Kodama Gentarō instructed Civil Governor Gotō Shimpei to extend help to Sun Yat-sen.[35] As soon as Sun got word of this, he hurried to Formosa. Now his plans included the use of Japanese officers in the revolutionary army.[36] Sun sent Kiyofuji back to Japan to ask Hiraoka and other donors for more funds. Miyazaki, who was apparently less close to all this, was still in Tokyo.

While all this was taking place, Cheng Shih-liang had been rounding up members of the *San-ho-hui* in Kwangtung.[37] By August, he had assembled about six hundred men. Their headquarters was at Sanchoutien, a mountainous coastal area which could be supplied by pirates.[38] The men had only three hundred rifles and hardly any ammunition. Through contacts within the Canton military garrison, plans had been made to secure large amounts of ammunition, but the combination of Hong Kong and Canton police surveillance made this impossible. Cheng's men stayed up in the hills, and before long they were short of food. Many left for their homes, and for a time the force dwindled to eighty men. When rumors spread through the countryside that a group of men were holding a mountain redoubt, the Manchu military officials decided to move some of their Waichow garrison to clear up the situation. The local troops furnished no problem for the rebels. Cheng won all the initial skirmishes, and he was able to send word to Formosa asking for ammunition. Sun's answer assured Cheng that help was sure to come soon. He advised avoiding contact with the enemy troops and heading for Amoy, where help from Japan could be expected.

It was now October. Sun had been sending frantic messages to Miyazaki, telling him to hurry the shipments of ammunition left from the Philippine project. When Miyazaki sent back word of the Nakamura swindle, Sun went to Japan himself. He took Miyazaki severely to task, and returned to Formosa. Evidently he still expected the Japanese to make up for Nakamura's dishonesty. After a time, Sun received a long letter from Miyazaki which detailed the entire course of the Nakamura case and investigation. It was a dreary recital of the indifference of Ōkura officials, political considerations, and mutual recriminations. Miyazaki begged for understanding and patience, but it was clear that no ammunition was on the way. Sun had failed again.[39]

But Cheng Shih-liang and his men had not been idle. Their initial victories gave them more and more arms, ammunition, and men. Both defeated government troops and the peasants of the area joined them. In Waichow, the inhabitants routed the Manchu garrison and welcomed the rebels. The rebels followed Cheng's orders which forbade theft from villagers, and their popularity and numbers grew apace.

As the rebels proceeded in the direction of Amoy through rugged country, they had relatively few engagements with the enemy. But they were also cutting themselves off from possible sources of supply from Hong Kong. The Manchu troops concentrated on blocking any links with the outside sources of help, and then closed in on the rebels with superior and better equipped troops. Food supplies also became a problem. With twenty thousand men now under his command, Cheng needed help and supplies more than ever.

Seventeen days after the fighting had begun, word arrived from Sun Yat-sen. He reported that there was no longer any prospect of

Japanese aid or ammunition, and he sorrowfully advised disbanding the army. This dismayed the revolutionaries. Some wanted to turn back to try to win over the Canton garrison, while others counseled a dramatic last-ditch stand. Cheng realized the futility of such measures, and he reluctantly ordered the men to disband. The great majority of them had been swept along as the force passed through their villages, and they were able to melt back into the countryside with little difficulty.[40] The rebellion had lasted from October 8 to October 25, 1900.[41]

The leaders were less fortunate. Yang Fei-chang managed to make his way to Hong Kong. There he set himself up as an English teacher, but it was not long before a gunman killed him to collect the reward posted by the Manchus. Pi Yung-nien was particularly disconsolate at the failure of the revolt. He entered the Buddhist priesthood, and died soon afterward. Cheng Shih-liang fled to Southeast Asia, where he fell ill and died the following year.[42]

There was another noteworthy casualty. Yamada Yoshimasa carried Sun's final message to Cheng Shih-liang. On his way back to the coast he fell into the hands of the imperial troops, who executed him. He thus became, in Sun's words, "the first foreigner who laid down his life for the Chinese Republic." [43]

4. THE AMOY INCIDENT

The Waichow revolt had failed. Its leaders had scattered, and many of them were to disappear permanently very soon. But the background of Governor General Kodama's promise of help to Sun Yat-sen and the subsequent failure to make good that promise have never been made clear. Failure to get help from abroad was certainly a major cause for the collapse of the revolt. The popular response to the rebel campaign had been so enthusiastic that Sun continued to regard the whole affair as distinctly encouraging. Then why did the revolt have to stop just as it was gaining momentum, and why did the officials in Formosa fail to live up to their promises of help?

Miyazaki's failure to get arms in Japan was a contributary factor in Sun's decision to stop the revolution, but it was not the most important factor. One night, a week after Sun and Hirayama had been established at Taihoku, a messenger came from Governor General Kodama for Hirayama. The man told Hirayama that Civil Governor Gotō Shimpei had received an order from Tokyo to expel Sun from Formosa, to expel Hirayama for his work with the Chinese revolutionaries, and to have no more to do with such movements. This ended Sun's hopes of advisory, military, and financial aid from the Formosan officials.[44]

Sun later explained this change in policy by relating it to a change of governments in Tokyo. On September 26, 1900, Yamagata Aritomo resigned, to be succeeded by Itō Hirobumi with the first *Seiyūkai* cabinet.[45] Sun was content with the theory that Kodama favored the revolution, and Itō did not. Subsequent historians, Japanese and Western have followed Sun in this conclusion.[46]

This theory is not without truth, but stated in this way it creates more problems than it solves. There is the discrepancy of dates. Sun's instructions to Cheng to disband his troops came almost a full month after the cabinet change in Tokyo. Kodama's position in the new regime was stronger than it had been in the old, for he served concurrently as minister of war. One might explain the timing by crediting the delay to reluctance on Kodama's part to carry out Itō's orders. But even then, why should Gotō and Kodama, representatives of the military and the right, have replaced Inukai and Miyazaki as Sun's guardian angels? What made Sun so confident that the revolutionary army would find Japanese help at Amoy? Some writers dismiss these questions by inferring that there were certain stipulations attached to Kodama's help.[47] If so, why did the new cabinet not continue help to Sun? Or indeed, why should Yamagata have resigned at such an unfortunate time?

Most of the answers to these questions are to be found in an examination of the political scene in Japan during the Boxer Rebellion.

a. Pressure on the Government

The pages of the *Osaka Mainichi,* one of the great metropolitan dailies, show that in September of 1900 the situation in China was of overriding importance for Japanese readers. The newspaper reflected the intoxication which accompanied Japan's consciousness of her new status as ally and valued friend of the West. Headlines and stories told of little else but China. Special features described tours through the Forbidden City, and maps and pictures gave relatives good opportunities for following their soldiers' activities in Peking. Sensational headlines told of rumored meetings of Li Hung-chang with the Russians, and readers were well aware that the crafty old viceroy might be able to deprive Japan of the honors and privileges due her for her part in the advance on Peking. The speed of Japan's transformation from feudal to modern times was graphically illustrated by parallel serials of Tokugawa tales and accounts of the foppish westernization crazes of a mere dozen years before. Already both seemed equally distant. Editorials on law reform, on anti-prostitution campaigns, and on foreign relations served as notice of the continued drive for further gains and the expectations of international recognition of past achievements.

With all this concern over North China, however, the affairs of Sun Yat-sen in the South came in for far less coverage. Moreover, the news was very late and very sketchy. In October, readers learned that Sun was in Formosa conferring with "six Chinese and two Japanese" and that something seemed to be brewing.[48] Reports of the rising did not come in for another fortnight. Stories told of disturbances near Canton, the taking of Waichow, and the siege of the rebels there by a huge government army. The confusion with which the revolt was obscured implied a chaotic situation. It was successively a movement led by Sun Yat-sen, then obviously dominated by the *San-ho-hui,* and finally "without doubt" led by K'ang Yu-wei.[49] In short, the public stood to learn little about actual events. The revolt never ended, but dribbled out to a conclusion with the news (in November) that the Formosan authorities had imposed temporary landing restrictions.[50]

The reader had reason to be confused about events in South China, but he was left in no doubt about the broader issue of Japan's interests in China. It was clear that most political groups agreed that the government lacked a policy and that it was allowing Russia to take advantage of its aimless drift. Remnants of the *Kenseitō* and the *Jiyūtō* met separately to form associations for investigation of the China problem.[51] Pressure mounted steadily, and a league which united all political groups was formed. The *Kokumin Dō-meikai* (Peoples' League) aimed its charges directly at the government's failure to safeguard North China from Russia.[52] The concern the league showed was not limited to Manchuria or to North China, but it extended to the entire field of Japanese interests in China. These were no ordinary anti-government machinations. The *Seiyūkai,* which had not yet assumed power, joined the government in opposing such groups.[53]

The charges of these groups were demonstrably false, for the Tokyo government had a far better eye for long range gain in China than most of its critics.

b. Expansion to the South

Ever since the acquisition of Formosa, Japanese governors general had been suggesting practical implementation for the general plans of expansion in South China and Southeast Asia that dated from Tokugawa days. The second governor general, Katsura Tarō, was minister of war in the Yamagata cabinet in 1900. During his service on Formosa, Katsura had submitted an elaborate plan for expansion southward. He advised concentrating on Amoy as a beginning, and developing that port as a focal point for trade and gain in South China and the South Seas.[54]

The fourth governor general of Formosa was Sun's benefactor, Kodama Gentarō. Like Katsura, Kodama was from Choshu, and their careers had been quite similar. Kodama's report did little more than elaborate on Katsura's ideas.

Kodama too stressed the importance of commercial ties with Amoy. He held that Amoy and Formosa were interdependent, and that they should be under the same control. He suggested several methods for accomplishing this end. A branch bank at Amoy would help, as would Japanese commercial, mining, and language schools in Amoy. Amoy, in turn, was only a foothold for the province of Fukien, whose government was in a state of deterioration and collapse.[55]

These ideas were highly congenial to Gotō Shimpei, who was civil governor of Formosa in 1900. Gotō's favorite project was the Amoy branch of the Bank of Taiwan. In April 1900, he went to

Fukien to inspect this with a party of Japanese experts. He gave many talks to groups of overseas Japanese, Chinese gentry, and Chinese officials. In these meetings he emphasized the Buddhist and Confucian bases of Japanese culture, and he pointed out that Japan had a ready-made synthesis of East and West for China to use.[56]

In other words, Tokyo critics were decidedly unjust in charging a government made up of such officials with laxity toward Japan's rightful place in China. Indeed, the mere presence of Saigō Tsugumichi as minister of interior should have sufficed to show that the government would not be slow to take advantage of any opportunities that might develop in China.[57]

c. Proconsular Difficulties

When the Boxer Rebellion broke out, Governor General Kodama was in Japan. He hurried back to Formosa, and sent the Tokyo government word that Japan's great opportunity had come. The Powers were busy in the North, and it was Japan's job to take care of Fukien. In that province, rumors that the Japanese were contemplating action had caused considerable unrest. Gotō wrote Chinese officials to assure them of Japan's pacific intentions, but the rumors would not down.[58]

Kodama had strong support from Navy Minister Yamamoto Gombei. Admiral Yamamoto argued that it was futile to oppose anti-foreignism in the North while ignoring it in the South, and he called for a consistent foreign policy. Yamamoto finally persuaded his colleagues to take a more active course in South China.[59]

On August 10, 1900, secret instructions were sent to Taihoku. The telegram explained to Kodama that since Russia had taken Newchwang and the English had landed at Shanghai, Japan would have to take steps to protect her nationals in South China. Kodama was to make all preparations for an occupation of Amoy.[60]

Kodama was perfectly willing, but he felt that the operation would require more preparation. He felt he did not have enough troops or transports. On August 15, he received further instructions from Katsura. At a given signal from Tokyo, Kodama was to be ready to bombard the Amoy batteries and move into the city. Kodama was to cite the safety of Japanese nationals as justification for this move, and he was cautioned to avoid conflict with foreigners.[61] Kodama was still uneasy about the operation, but he sent several agents and engineers to Amoy to make the necessary preparations.

On August 23, Katsura telegraphed again to check on preparations. Gotō Shimpei went on ahead to Amoy with a Navy captain to make plans for holding the city after its capture. As Gotō's biographer modestly states, the fate of Asia now hung in the balance.[62]

The next day came the provocation that was needed to justify Japanese action. Shortly after midnight on August 24, the Honganji temple in Amoy was attacked and burned. The abbot, a former samurai who had turned to Buddhist missionary work as an alternate way of advancing Japanese aims, reported that a Chinese mob had perpetrated the outrage.[63] A. Burlingame Johnson, United States Consul in Amoy, gave a slightly different account in his report to the State Department. The Japanese "temple," he found, was an old house which some Japanese priests had rented. Three days before the fire, they had a dispute with their landlord over the amount of rent due. On the day of the fire, the priests moved all their valuables out. That night, the "abbot" was the only Japanese who slept in the house. At one o'clock in the morning, he rushed to the Japanese consulate with the news that a Chinese mob had burned his temple. No one else had seen the mob, however, and everyone had seen Chinese soldiers and civilians who helped to put out the fire.[64] Hirayama Shū, who was in Amoy at the time, reports that some people thought the Japanese might have set the fire themselves.[65]

A small force of Japanese marines was landed immediately to guard the consulate. They were soon the cause of anti-Japanese demonstrations and riots. "It will be a wonder," reported Mr. Johnson, "if an outbreak does not occur as a result."[66] On August 27, Katsura ordered Kodama to proceed as planned.

All mail ships were seized at Formosa. Transports were loaded, and the island was in a state of war. The schedule called for gun emplacements to be stormed on the twenty-ninth. The same day, foreign consulates were to be informed of the intended occupation, which was to take place on the last day of August.

An ultimatum was drawn up, complete except for the deadline. All was in readiness. Ships were on their way. On Formosa, two groups of volunteer *sōshi* awaited transportation.[67]

Then came a telegram from Tokyo which wrecked the whole enterprise. On August 28, Katsura advised Kodama that the cabinet had decided to delay the invasion. He told Kodama to anchor the warships in Amoy harbor, and to keep the transports out of the harbor.[68]

Kodama was beside himself with anger. Both he and Gotō sent frantic wires to Tokyo to say that the time was growing short. Action could still be taken; to delay would be fatal. To no avail. The cabinet persisted in delay, and all hope was abandoned when, within a week, British marines and warships made a quiet, inconspicuous act of aggression no longer possible.[69]

Kodama had now had enough. He asked a change in assignment. This denied, he sent an angry wire asking to be allowed to resign. This, too, was turned down. Kodama then sent Gotō to Tokyo to see what was going on.

In Tokyo, Gotō had long conferences with Saigō Tsugumichi. Saigō was anxious for Kodama to remain on Formosa, and he explained to Gotō what had happened. The unanimity of the cabinet had been broken by the opposition of Itō Hirobumi. Itō was not a member of the cabinet, but as head of the Privy Council he retained a voice in matters of policy. Itō was worried about the European reaction to Japanese seizure of Amoy. He warned Foreign Minister Aoki of this, and finally persuaded the latter to oppose the invasion. Yamagata, in trying to counter these arguments, had relied more and more upon the Russian moves in Manchuria as full justification for any steps Japan might take. Then, on August 26, a report had come in that Russia was considering withdrawal from Manchuria. By using this, Itō had been able to delay the invasion in order to check on the report. By the time it proved unfounded, the arrival of foreign warships in Amoy harbor had made the invasion impossible.[70]

By this time, the *Mainichi* readers were becoming aware that all was not well in the government. In September, the papers carried word of the Amoy temple fire for the first time. Further dispatches told of bands of ruffians who were endangering Japanese lives and property in Amoy.[71] The "abbot" was also on his way back to Japan to give his account.[72]

On September 19, the paper revealed that Kodama, who was described as furious over his treatment (which was not described) had asked to be replaced. The emperor had appointed Chamberlain Komeda to accompany Gotō back to Formosa in the hope of getting Kodama to reconsider. Before long the emperor was gratified to hear that Kodama had respected his wishes, and that he was on his way to Tokyo to express his appreciation for the imperial solicitude.[73]

The Yamagata cabinet fell before Kodama reached Tokyo. Its collapse had been precipitated by Kodama's request for retirement. Had Kodama been allowed to resign, the responsibility for the incident's failure would have seemed his. On September 11, therefore, Yamagata informed Kodama that he and his cabinet would accept the blame and submit their resignations.[74] It is true that there were other factors involved. Yamagata had apparently been ready to step down for some time, and the formation of Itō's *Sei-yūkai* furnished a convenient excuse — one which Japanese historians have perpetuated. But the correspondence of the government leaders leaves little doubt that Kodama's dissatisfaction was an important reason.[75]

Itō was a consistent opponent of military adventurism, but he accepted Kodama as his minister of war. Probably, the premier was willing to compromise on minor issues once he had won his main point. A week after the cabinet change, the Waichow Rebellion broke out, and two weeks later Kodama deprived Sun Yat-sen of his Formosa headquarters. Yet there is no reason to suppose that Kodama, a military man and a realist, was particularly reluctant to oust Sun when the time came. The greater chance, at Amoy, had been irrevocably lost. The rebels were beginning to have difficulty in the field, their supply routes were cut, and their outside sources of help had run dry. Kodama would not be one to take undue risks. He limited himself, said Sun, to "promising that *if there were a serious outbreak* he would support us."[76] Within a week of its beginning, the Waichow Rebellion was no longer serious enough to affect Japanese policy.

When Japan's greater chance was dissipated through indecision in Tokyo, the secondary interests of Cheng Shih-liang's fate were expendable. Katsura, Kodama, and Saigō had been forced to moderate their enthusiasm because cooler heads feared the opposition of Russia to the North. The next step was to find all factions together on the Russian problem which had blocked each such enterprise since early Meiji.

For Sun Yat-sen, Waichow had demonstrated that, given favorable auspices, a rebellion would snowball into a revolution. He returned to his task of soliciting, recruiting, and organizing for the revolution. But when it came to Japanese help, Sun was often living proof of his slogan, "To act is easy, to know is difficult." [77]

5

The confusion of factions and motives that marked the events of 1900 was not duplicated in the years that followed. During the decade before the Revolution of 1911, both Chinese and Japanese concentrated on thinking, planning, and organizing. At the end of the decade, the relationship between the Japanese and the Chinese was very different from that of 1900. By 1911, one can approach Japan with many of the preconceptions of the 1930's. Japan was firmly in the imperialist camp. Nationalism, crowned with success in war, had produced a conviction of the sanctity of Japanese institutions. Any idea of "guidance" for a neighboring state was conceivable only within the framework of authorized constitutionalism that had been set up in Japan. The likelihood of substantial Japanese support for liberal and republican forces in Asia was very slight.

The change in attitudes could be derived first of all from the transformations in Japanese political and national life. The decade after 1900 was dominated by power politics on the grand scale. The Anglo-Japanese Alliance of 1902, the Russo-Japanese War of 1904–1905, the network of treaties which the Foreign Office was able to weave about China thereafter, and, finally, the absorption of Korea in 1910 — all this resulted in a new situation for the former "poor boy" of Asia. And the Japanese were well pleased with their success and the power it had brought them. Their consciousness of power, and their pleasure in it, hardened national self-esteem. This was particularly noticeable in terms of policy. There were advantages in respectability. A great power could gain concessions from the tottering Manchu dynasty simply by demanding them. It could feel itself above negotiating with men like Sun Yat-sen.

And when the Manchus saw the need of change, as they did, Japan stood to gain most by coöperating with them. The Manchus represented known factors of accommodation to the imperialist presence. Who could be sure that the revolutionaries would be as coöperative? Even if they were, would not a constitutional monarchy be a more fitting neighbor for Japan than a republic? Power thus brought Japan the luxury of selection among the factions in China. And the choice of the oligarchs would not long be in doubt. Their own institutions, once the object of their experimentation and design, were now sacrosanct and immutable. They must be kept from contamination. The Meiji leaders, like their emperor, were getting older, more respectable, less imaginative, and more conservative. They preferred to deal with their social equals across the waters. And as their neighboring officials hired Japanese legal experts and military advisers, and sent thousands of young men to Japan as students, the Tokyo leaders saw that they had chosen well. Japan now had a large and a growing stake in the preservation of the old order in China.

It is true that the top leaders had never in the past had much use for Sun Yat-sen. But now that their policies were demonstrably successful, the expansionists who formerly dogged their steps followed but to serve. Manchuria and Korea provided ample opportunities for their talents in lines approved by the government. Official projects brought more reward than did escapades in China. Such a shift in interest, of course, weakened the theories of "guidance" which the expansionists had shared with the liberals. In Korea, the adventurers showed a cynical disregard of the national consciousness of their neighbors. For a time, the opinions and feelings of the Chinese guests became less important. Especially was this the case when the Chinese moved closer to the forces of radicalism and socialism which were beginning to emerge in Japan. The *shishi* were self-appointed guardians of the national conscience, and their opposition to radicalism at home inevitably made them reflect on its effect in China.

Sun Yat-sen's real friends — Inukai, Miyazaki, and the like — did not change their minds. But their position in the political picture was decidedly less advantageous than it had been. They had lost contact with power. As the Japanese government became more conservative, and as its money was less available, men like Miyazaki, no longer channels of government help, tended to become little more than messengers for Sun Yat-sen.

Finally, the Chinese revolutionaries both reacted against and benefited from the changes in Japan. The inspiration that Japan's victory over Russia provided was a tremendous boon. Sure now of the inevitability of his victory, Sun Yat-sen concentrated on organizing and preparing a new movement. Then, as the conservative viceroys poured students into Japan, the revolutionaries profited by their presence to organize anew. And, as the students reacted against Japanese discrimination and Japanese nationalism, the movement swung more to Chinese goals and Chinese nationalism. At the same time it swung to the left. New theories, Sun's study in Europe, and friendships with Japanese leftists contributed to this shift. No longer was there any serious likelihood of a facile acceptance of Japanese constitutionalism. The revolutionary movement insisted that one of its aims was a permanent alliance with Japan, but it was much less pro-Japanese than before.

The revolutionaries thus became an ever less likely group for Japanese support. As Japanese leadership grew older and more conservative, the revolutionaries, thanks to the student influx, became younger, more radical, and more nationalistic. The coöperation between the two groups was less general and more discriminating than it had been. At the dawn of the revolution Miyazaki, once a secret agent of his government, was the object of surveillance by his successors.

1. A JAPANESE LEAGUE

The changes that came over Japanese political life and Chinese revolutionary activity were symbolized by two leagues which were set up. The Japanese *Dōmeikai* of 1900 is written with the same Chinese characters as Sun's *T'ung-meng-hui* of 1905. Sun Yat-sen's league lasted until the Revolution of 1911. Although its Japanese equivalent had a much shorter life span, the nationalist-military leadership which it showed remained in firm control of Japanese policy for over a decade.

The *Dōmeikai* was an expression of a national determination to end the Russian threat in Northern Asia. The vigorous and purposeful course which marked Japanese policy in foreign affairs, however, was not matched by as colorful conduct in domestic politics.

Between the Boxer Rebellion and the Chinese Revolution, the Japanese government was under the experienced leadership of elder statesmen and bureaucrats. The old political parties fell on evil days, and political affiliations became increasingly confused and misleading. Katsura Tarō had been selected by Yamagata as his successor for premier. Katsura's cabinets alternated with those controlled by the *Seiyūkai,* which Itō had turned over to Saionji. Such a cabinet, dominated by bureaucrats, succeeded Katsura whenever parliamentary difficulties made it too difficult for the latter. The party men oscillated between the Katsura and Saionji camps, and they were guided chiefly by political opportunism and economic gain. Several of the early leaders, among them Itagaki, left politics in disgust. Ōkuma carried on for a time to preside over the wreckage of the old coalition group of 1898. When he too left, Inukai took over for him until he led in the formation of the *Kokumintō* (Nationalist) party in 1910. Although treaty autonomy and international equality were accomplished facts, the government continually pressed for further military budgets. The Diet seemed dominated by petty squabbles in which the politicians alternately sought to deprive the government of the budgets and pressed for policies which would have required far greater expenditures.

In foreign affairs, however, the issues were simple and direct. Russia had offended Japan by her role in the Triple Intervention and her subsequent seizure of Dairen and Port Arthur. To this she now added a direct challenge and threat in the occupation of Manchuria. Besides this, the completion of the Trans-Siberian Railroad and Russian intrigues in Korea showed that Japan's position there might not long be "special."

Most of the adventurers who had worked with Sun Yat-sen now shifted their attention to the Russian problem. Uchida Ryōhei, it will be remembered, had made the shift even before the Waichow revolt. The machinery of the pressure groups was at hand to warn the people that Europe must not be allowed to benefit from China's weakness. When the Amoy adventure caused the fall of the Yamagata cabinet, it was rumored that all was not well in South China.

But Manchuria remained the focus of attention for the country as a whole. Concern for the situation there had led Yamagata and Katsura to repudiate Kodama and Sun at Amoy in 1900.

During the summer of 1900, secret reports from the numerous adventurers like Uchida who had ventured into Manchuria confirmed rumors of a new and secret Russo-Chinese treaty which was to give Russia sweeping control over the railroads of all Manchuria. The *shishi* lost no time in warning the proper authorities of the dangers of such agreements. One of their leaders, Nezu Hajime, had been one of Arao Kiyoshi's first followers in China. Subsequently, he held important *Dōbunkai* posts. He now resigned these to enter the employ of the General Staff. At first, he advised against aggression, since he felt Japan should not provide Russia with an excuse for action. Before long, however, he became convinced that the time had passed for hesitation, and he advocated immediate war with Russia.[1]

The professional patriots had new cause for misgivings in 1900 when Russia, in a conciliatory move, suggested a deal whereby Japan would rest content with an undisputed mastery of Korea up to the line of the Tadong River. To the dismay of all, Itō, who was prime minister, was inclined to regard this proposal with favor. This was the immediate cause for the organization of the *Kokumin Dōmeikai* on September 25, 1900.[2] This powerful group was sponsored by men of all factions and parties, and it worked for a united expression of public opinion to force expulsion of the Russians from Manchuria for the protection of China.[3]

The League was predominantly a *Dōbunkai*-sponsored organization, and its varied constituency was headed by Prince Konoe, head of the House of Peers. Itō, who feared lest Konoe's name should embarrass the government-sponsored *Dōbunkai,* used his influence at Court to prevent Konoe's election as President of the league. But Konoe was not restrained from lecturing, and he was the undisputed leader of the drive to block Russia.[4]

The patriots were never more convinced that they spoke for the nation. Tōyama called on Itō, and warned him sharply that his life would be in great danger if he agreed to the Russian plan for Korea.[5] Itō agreed to decline the Russian offer, but he persisted in his opposition to a plan to move Japanese troops from Peking to the Korean border. The combined pressure in Diet and press resulted in sharp Japanese protests to Russia.

The proposed Russo-Japanese treaty was dropped. In April 1902, the Russians announced their decision to evacuate Manchuria. The next month the *Dōmeikai* was dissolved.[6] Its leaders, of course, retained their official positions and influence.

a. The Role of the Expansionists

It soon became evident that Russia was not going to honor her agreement to evacuate Manchuria. The adventurers had decided much earlier that war would be necessary, however, and they had formed several organizations to hasten its coming. The most important of these, the *Kokuryūkai,* which was formed in 1901, has already been described. It was essentially an improvement on the earlier *Genyōsha,* and it concentrated on the elimination of Russia from the sphere south of the Amur. Its early activities included establishment of "Amur" (Russian) language schools, publication of maps and pamphlets, and the financing of secret agents who reported on Russian activities. Uchida Ryōhei, *Kokuryūkai* head, was also prominent in another group that deserves mention, the *Nichi-Ro Kyōkai* (Japan-Russia Society). In 1902, Uchida explained its purposes to Itō, who was still undecided about war with Russia. Uchida told him that, although war was inevitable, it was proper for statesmen to seek peace, soldiers to prepare for war, and *shishi* to awaken popular opinion to the necessity for war. "We are all working for the same end," he stated, "but until we reach it we take different paths, and it is hard for us to work together." [7]

As planning for the war progressed, the role of the adventurers became greater. In 1903, Hiraoka arranged for Uchida to meet Kodama Gentarō, who was now army chief of staff. Uchida reported at length on his extensive travels and reports from Siberia, and he stressed the necessity for special measures to counter Russia's new logistic capabilities in the Trans-Siberian Railroad. Kodama showed keen interest in Uchida's offer to organize and use the many bandits in the area to break Russian communications near Irkutsk and Baikal.[8]

These plans were in fact adopted, and although the effectiveness of the strategy is open to question, there can be no doubt but that the adventurers became more closely allied with the army as a result. In turn, there is little question but that the army helped finance their activities.[9] As the nationalist military faction grew in power in Japan, its liaison with the patriots grew ever closer. Their slogans and chauvinistic professions "only anticipated by ten years the watchwords which later became the official principles of the government itself." [10]

In this setting, the aid the *Kokuryūkai* gave to Sun Yat-sen leaves few doubts as to motivation. To quote the society's official history:

It should be explained with what motivation our *shishi* plotted such uprisings. First, they naturally considered Sun Yat-sen's principles, designed to save a great China about to decay after countless years of oppression, as an essential step toward aiding the general situation in East Asia. Accordingly, it was a pleasure for them to participate in the Chinese revolution and pour out the blood of chivalry as neighboring *shishi*.

Another very important element in the plan was the fact that Sun Yat-sen's revolutionary thought was revealed in the slogan, "Down Manchus, Up China!" Once the Chinese revolution should be carried out by the Chinese nation, the Manchu race would be eliminated, and their former home in Manchuria would be left to an uncertain fate. Russia would move in to settle this, but in that case Japan, allied with a China whose revolution she had made possible, would oppose Russia's southward expansion. She would put Manchuria and eastern Siberia under Japanese control, and Japanese power would expand into the continent. Thus love of country and chivalry went hand in hand in the Japanese help of the South China revolutions.[11]

After Japan's startling victory over Russia in 1905, it was no longer necessary to encourage Sun Yat-sen in order to speed a war with Russia, but the ultimate aim of furthering Japan's continental position remained valid. Post-war Japan was ready and eager to strengthen its position in Manchuria and China. In ideology, as in politics, the war ended an epoch. Japanese became increasingly proud of their heritage and tradition, and any question of accepting Western ideology was far more remote than it had been. Scholars returned to their own culture, and fostering of Oriental studies and consciousness became a deliberate national and governmental policy.[12]

In this picture, the role of the liberals who had sought a spontaneous regeneration for China and who desired guidance rather than mastery for Japan tended to diminish in importance.

Miyazaki was sick and dispirited after the collapse of the Waichow revolt. He felt that all his efforts had failed completely. For a time, he drank heavily. Then, to the astonishment of his friends and family, he decided to enter a school of ballad recitation. Thereafter he wandered around Japan, trying, in a half-hearted way, to raise funds for Sun Yat-sen. He took up the writing of poetry, and he wrote his autobiography, which was published serially in Akiyama Teisuke's newspaper. Miyazaki's wife and friends tried to dissuade him from his new vocation, but he remained firm in his resolve. He felt that his life had been a failure; it had passed as a thirty-three years' dream.[13]

2. CHINESE STUDENTS IN JAPAN

During the years in which Japan became more self-confident and nationalistic, Tokyo became the training ground for thousands of impressionable young Chinese. The Dowager Empress had foresworn the ways of obscurantism after the Boxer fiasco, and in a series of sweeping reforms she now tried to effect the renovations that had long been needed. One of the first steps taken was the decision to send students abroad. From every consideration of language, cost, ease, and speed, Japan was the logical center for the students. Before long the number of students in Japan was increasing in geometric proportions. Japan's victory over Russia furnished the final impetus for the student movement. The number of students, which had grown from five hundred in 1902 to fifteen hundred in 1904, now swelled to eight thousand in 1905, and to over thirteen thousand in 1906.[14] Unfortunately for the Manchus, however, their belated reforms served only to exacerbate the opposition and stimulate further demands. The student movement played a central role in undermining the dynasty.

The student movement had an equally important effect on Japan's hopes for domination of the ideology of China's new intelligentsia.

Many students did form lasting friendships in Japan, friendships which stood the Japanese in good stead when they needed collaborators thirty years later. But the greater percentage of the students restricted their admiration to Japanese nationalism. As they became more conscious of their own country's political disadvantages, they became very nearly as nationalistic as their Japanese hosts. Under such circumstances, guidance of a grateful nation was a goal the Japanese could not attain.

Nevertheless, the students offered an unprecedented opportunity for Japan to influence the future leaders of China.[15] And for the revolutionaries, the opportunity was even greater. Before the Boxer Rebellion, the Chinese students were carefully selected, and they were assured of government jobs on their return. Most of them sought only institutional training in Japan to supplement their Chinese education.[16] As the number of students grew, however, their average age diminished. The newer groups were without roots in their own culture. For a time their only ideology was a shallow worship of the Meiji institutions, and they restricted their studies to law, politics, and military studies. The smaller number of students that went to Europe tended to become even more radical. Their findings were harder to apply to China on their return, however, and the students from Japan were a larger and more important group.[17]

Chinese students in Japan found themselves in an entirely different environment. In the face of Japanese power, self-confidence, and condescension, their animus against their own government naturally increased. But this did not mean that they became pro-Japanese. In fact, the reverse was often the case. The students' contacts in life and in education were with Japanese nationalism. Most of them absorbed its spirit while rejecting its direction. Just as European nationalism had aroused Japanese patriotism, Japanese thought now turned many of the Chinese against Japan. Many of the students became conscious of past Japanese acts which justified a new anti-Japanese attitude. "The weak and the strong," as one Japanese author sorrowfully concluded, "are seldom friends." [18]

As the students increased in numbers, the educational facilities became more inadequate. In China, special examinations for government posts were given to returned students. In proportion to their numbers, those from Japan fared worse than their counterparts from Europe and America. The Japanese press, speculating on this, wondered whether the more expensive western trips were reserved for the most able students, or whether their own educational institutions were inadequate. The vast majority of the students in Tokyo, however, were not even enrolled in regular schools. Their stays became shorter, and their restlessness and dissatisfaction were transmitted directly to their families and friends in China.[19]

In this setting the revolution found good ground. A Szechwan youth of seventeen, Chou Yung, wrote a little book entitled *The Revolutionary Army* which was soon widely known among students everywhere.[20] Chang Ping-lin organized a meeting to mourn the passing of China. At the request of the Chinese government, it was banned by the Japanese authorities.[21] Other students organized military groups to express their indignation over the Russian failure to evacuate Manchuria. Efforts to stage revolts within China by men like Huang Hsing and Sung Chiao-jen resulted in new flights to Japan, and new heroes for the floating student population.

Instead of theorizing further about the cumulative effect of the new environment on the Chinese students, it may be of value to cite a few of the impressions gained by one of their number. A citizen of Honan began his diary in Shanghai on December 15, 1905, and he ended it with his return to China on June 12 of the following year.[22] He thus hit the flood of the student movement, a period in which youths in their teens often came together with their parents, each determined to learn the secrets of Japan's strength. At that time, the Kanda section of Tokyo was so full of Chinese students that even the maids knew a few phrases of Chinese.

The diary tells a great deal about the indirection and confusion that was in its author's mind. From his initial surprise at the neatness and compactness of the ship, the months in Japan form a continuous series of new impressions for the student. Soon after his arrival, fellow students give him a list of mores he should observe; regulations for speaking softly, warnings about spitting and otherwise infringing Japanese concepts of neatness, suggestions for giving up his seat to elders and women on trolleys, and warnings to be careful about his watch and loose change. The diarist never attends any one school, but he goes to many lectures and meetings held by professors of law and government. Each of these seems to feel that his field and its findings were vital to the success of the Restoration in 1868. The student is displeased by the political activity of some students, particularly the rowdies who gang up on conservatives, cut their queues, and then disappear. Students, he feels, should study. Japanese is difficult for him, and he works at it diligently. He has almost no contacts with Japanese students. He hears several lectures by Ōkuma Shigenobu and others about Japan's proffered guidance for China, and he hears about Inukai. What impresses him most, however, is Japanese patriotism. The stories of General Nogi's sacrifice of his sons at Port Arthur win his admiration. He finds that even Japanese girls are so patriotic that few marry Chinese students.

Japanese nationalism thus made its impress upon even profoundly unpolitically minded students. Upon the great majority of the students, its impact was even greater, and the urge to build for themselves as strong a country and as united a populace as the one they had seen dominated their every thought.[23]

3. THE REVOLUTIONARY MOVEMENT

During the early years of the student movement Sun Yat-sen lived quietly in Yokohama. To a Western journalist who interviewed him there, he seemed far from despondent about the future of his revolution. He felt that the Waichow failure had been due only to the lack of ammunition, a lack that had been caused by the Japanese contractor's dishonesty.[24] Sun was little in the news, but his house was a center for Chinese. Inukai reported that he spent money as soon as it came in, and that he lived happily in borrowed clothes when out of money.[25]

Sun's interest at this time centered in military tactics. The Boer War fascinated him, and he thought that its guerilla tactics might be of use in China. In 1903, he visited the Hanoi Exposition at the invitation of the governor of Annam, M. Doumer. Sun found the French interested in his activities, and the overseas Chinese seemed more disposed to furnish funds than they had been previously.[26]

When he returned to Yokohama, Sun found that the Manchus

had wisely taken steps to restrict the numbers of Chinese students attending Japanese military schools. To overcome this, he consulted his friends among the Japanese military. A Major Hino, who had invented a magazine-loading gun and who was in high favor with the Japanese high command, set up a secret military academy for Sun at Aoyama. Hino and a Japanese army captain gave the instruction. An eight-month term was set up, with courses on general military science as well as the manufacture of cannon and other arms. The first class of fourteen were sworn to obey the laws of the school and the leader of the revolution. Internal dissension prevented effective work, however, and the school closed soon after Sun left for Europe and America in the fall of 1903.[27]

Sun remained away from Japan for two years. In Hawaii, America, and Europe he sought funds, workers, and ideas for the future government of China. To some who had known him earlier, he seemed less optimistic.[28] Nevertheless, he continued unshaken in his sense of destiny. The readiness of the considerable numbers of Chinese students in Europe to accept his proposals gave his mission new strength.

Within Japan, other groups continued their efforts. The small but enthusiastic group of Japanese socialists were keenly aware of the revolutionary tide in China, and many of the Chinese worked closely with them. The *Heimin Shimbun* (Commoners' Paper), short-lived organ of the Japanese socialist party, reflected the common concerns of Oriental socialists. Unfortunately, the pacifist stand of the Japanese socialists cost them their position within Japan for a time, and thereafter they could contribute little of the material aid which Sun needed.[29] As the Japanese government became more hostile to the Chinese revolutionary movement, however, friendships with the socialists and other leftists became more important.[30]

Huang Hsing, after his abortive Ch'angsha revolt of 1904, joined the refugees in Tokyo.[31] He lived quietly under the name of Momowara, and for a time the Japanese police did not realize that he was a revolutionary leader. Sung Chiao-jen lived with him, and their house became known for the numbers of Chinese who frequented it; loud conversations took place late at night. The police thus became suspicious, and once Huang's identity was known the Japanese *shishi* lost little time in meeting the two revolutionaries.[32] Huang still thought in terms of nationalism alone, but Miyazaki convinced him that the revolution should benefit Japan and the rest of Asia as well as China. The two became good friends, and Huang was soon popular with the other Japanese adventurers.[33] With student enthusiasm running high, student numbers constantly increasing, and a pervasive feeling of confidence and strength everywhere, the stage was set for the return of Sun Yat-sen to act as a catalyst in the formation of a new and greater revolutionary league.

a. Organizing

Sun returned to Japan late in July of 1905 with his revolutionary principles and theories better worked out than they had ever been before. The three principles of nationalism, democracy, and livelihood, and the five-power constitution which was to safeguard them, had been tried out on meetings of students in Brussels and Paris. As he returned to the Far East by way of Singapore, Sun felt the surge of confidence that accompanied Japan's victory over Russia. Twenty years later the memory was still fresh in his mind.

On my way home, in going through the Suez Canal, I met an Arab. Looking at my face, he said, "Are you a Japanese?" I told him, no, I was a Chinese. He told me he had observed vast armies of Russian soldiers being shipped back to Russia from the Far East, a fact which seemed an undeniable sign of Russia's admission of defeat. The joy of this Arab, as a member of the great Asiatic race, seemed to know no bounds.[34]

Several hundred Chinese students were waiting to welcome Sun at the dock in Yokohama. Soon Miyazaki introduced Sun to Huang Hsing, and the heads of the two revolutionary groups became fast friends. They had a long talk and agreed on the necessity of a new organization.[35]

Among the Japanese, Kayano Chōchi, who had previously served as messenger and counselor, now became increasingly important as a friend and follower of Sun Yat-sen. He was present at many of the important meetings that followed.[36]

On August 13 a student meeting was held in Tokyo at the Fujimiken restaurant in Kōjimachi to welcome Sun. Over a thousand attended, and the streets were thronged with those unable to gain admittance. Suenaga, Miyazaki, and others delivered welcoming speeches for the Japanese. Sung Chiao-jen translated these for the students. Sun Yat-sen then gave an inspiring presentation of his revolutionary ideals.[37]

The Chinese embassy, understandably alarmed by this, pressed the Japanese authorities to regulate student activities more carefully. As a result, greater caution was exercised for the next meetings. The next gathering took place in the home of Uchida Ryōhei, who had just moved to spacious quarters in the Akasaka district of Tokyo. The fifty or sixty guests, representing many groups and opinions among the students, once again overflowed the confines of the building and filled the garden.[38] Sun spoke again about his three principles, and found Huang Hsing in substantial agreement with him. Uchida's house, in turn, became too small, and the meetings shifted to the home of Sakamoto Kinya. By this time the plans for the League were well worked out, and the charter members were required to take an oath of loyalty to the new organization.[39]

The formal inaugural meeting was held at Sakamoto's house. Several hundred members, representing each province of China that had students in Japan, were sworn in. Sun Yat-sen was president, and Huang Hsing vice-president. Although the formal rules of membership made no allowance for non-Chinese, Miyazaki, Hirayama, and Kayano Chōchi were members of the *T'ung-meng-hui*. Miyazaki, in 1907, was given full authority to negotiate for arms and supplies as Japanese representative of the League.[40]

The League adopted a broad and comprehensive program that included essentially all of Sun's later ideas, including that of nationalization of land. On this point, Sun's convictions were unquestionably bolstered by those of his Japanese friends. Miyazaki's older brother, Tamizō, had concentrated his efforts on working out a solution to agrarian inequalities ever since the hardships the family had suffered in early Meiji days. His final solution was along the lines of Henry George's single tax plan. In 1906, he published an influential little book on that theory. Miyazaki Tamizō had many contacts among the Japanese socialists as well as among the Chinese students. It would probably be wrong to believe that he was influential in persuading Sun Yat-sen to adopt the same program, but

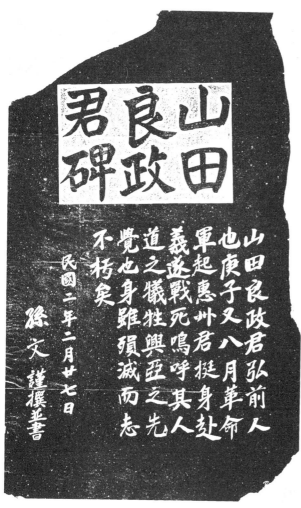

Rubbing of inscription composed by Sun Yat-sen in Tokyo in 1913 to honor Yamada Yoshimasa, who died in the 1900 revolution. During World War II the Japanese made use of this and similar writings in their attempts to lend legitimacy to the puppet regime of Wang Ching-wei in Nanking.

MEMORIAL TO MR. YAMADA YOSHIMASA

Yamada Yoshimasa was a man from Hirosaki. When the revolutionary army rose at Waichow in the intercalary eighth month of 1900, he came forward and went to his death in battle for the cause of righteousness. Truly, he sacrificed himself for humanity and became a pioneer of the new Asia. Although he is no more, his spirit will endure forever.

February 27, 1913.

Written in homage by Sun Wen.

委任狀

中國革命　　理孫文逸仙

委任宮崎寅藏君在日本全權辦理

籌資購械援濟革命軍所有與貿

主交涉條件悉便宜行事此委

宮崎寅藏君

天運歲次丁未年九月十三日

POWER OF ATTORNEY

Sun Wen Yat-sen, Leader of the Chinese Revolutionary Alliance *(T'ung Meng Hui)* appoints

Mr. Miyazaki Torazō as attorney with full authority in Japan to raise funds, purchase equipment, and obtain supplies for the revolutionary army. All terms negotiated with capitalists shall be arranged at his discretion. This commissions

Mr. Miyazaki Torazō.

October 19, 1907.

(Seal: *T'ung Meng Hui*, China Federal Association)

Power of attorney given by Sun Yat-sen to Miyazaki Torazō in 1907 when the Japanese government asked Sun to leave Japan. Original copy in the possession of Mr. Miyazaki Ryūsuke, Tokyo.

there is no reason to question a sympathetic strengthening of Sun's convictions.[41]

The membership of the *T'ung-meng-hui,* however, was far from united on all points of Sun Yat-sen's program. There was complete unanimity only on the issue of doing away with the Manchus. Future events were to show that, once that issue had been disposed of, the League would no longer be an effective organization.[42]

Despite this drawback, Sun Yat-sen and his friends had never been so well prepared. They worked out manifestoes and detailed regulations for martial law, for a provisional government, and for the treatment of foreigners.[43]

b. Publishing

On the propaganda front, the revolutionary paper *Min Pao* (People's News) occupied first place. *Min Pao* began publication in February 1906. Its editorial board was headed by Chang Ping-lin and included Hu Han-min, Wang Ching-wei, and others.[44] These three were able to work closely with the various Japanese whose support was essential to publication of a subversive journal.[45] The editors, by their skillful play upon the dissatisfaction of the students and the intelligentsia, gave Sun a counterweight for the several journals of Liang Ch'i-ch'ao's reform party.

The split between the two groups had become deep and permanent, and the violence of the editorial conflict reflected and stimulated the greater personal animosity that divided the students. Liang Ch'i-ch'ao's paper, at one point, reported somewhat hopefully the death of Sun Yat-sen.[46] In the Tokyo propaganda struggle, Sun's group had more concrete plans and more tangible focuses of resentment than Liang could offer. The restless and the enthusiastic flocked to join the *T'ung-meng-hui.* They did not hesitate to use strong-arm methods. In October 1907, Liang's group met in Tokyo. Inukai was among those on the stage. Suddenly about 1500 students of the other political persuasion invaded the meeting. The hall was soon in turmoil, and opposition harangues were substituted for the talk scheduled by Liang Ch'i-ch'ao. The Japanese police intervened on this occasion, but such events were not calculated to increase Liang's student following.[47]

But the pages of *Min Pao* were not given over entirely to invective. The journal adopted a basic program of six points. These included overthrow of the Manchus, republican government, world peace, nationalization of land, coöperation with Japan, and world support for the revolutionary cause.

The point of Sino-Japanese friendship was naturally closest to the Japanese interests.[48] It could be expected to cause grave reservations among Chinese, however, and in the articles from *Min Pao* that are available we can see the editors trying to explain and justify this point.

Wang Ching-wei contented himself with explanations that Japan, with England and America, had shown her pacific intentions when she did not try to take advantage of China at the time of the Boxer Rebellion. He also cited the example of Japan as an inspiration. Both China and Japan had been beset by Russian aggression, but Japan had done something about it, thereby delivering China from the Russian paw.[49] These were arguments which Sun, who once termed Japan "the watchman of Asia," would also have used.[50] Unfortunately neither argument held true. Japanese aggression in 1900 had been restrained only through fear of Russia, and in 1907 Japan was to enter into cordial treaty-relations with Russia.

Hu Han-min, in an editorial explaining the six-point program, devoted least space to the fifth point. There are, he explains, two schools of thought about China in Japan. One advocates conquest by force, but it is a small and unimportant group. The other favors close guidance and ultimate assimilation for China, since China lacks self-consciousness. This, Hu agrees, is true at present, but it will not be so in the future. The two peoples must plan to work together, and Japan must give up her ambitions. Japan owes her culture to China, and she must not try to take advantage of her now.[51] Hu thus distinguished the Japanese anti-Manchu policy from what he hoped would be a pro-Republic policy. At times Hu carried this distinction to its ultimate conclusion by implying that Manchuria and the Manchus had little relation to China at all.[52]

The Japanese explanations and rationale were thus accepted, at least in part, by the *Min Pao* editors. Hu Han-min, in fact, cited Ōkuma by name as authority for the opinion that a weak China was a danger to world peace, and that a change was essential.[53]

Min Pao had a wide circulation, and it performed a valuable service for the cause of Sino-Japanese relations. Its services were needed, for there was much to arouse suspicion and dislike among the Chinese students in Japan. A month after it had begun publication, the Japanese Ministry of Education put out rules regulating activities of Chinese students. This infuriated the students, and they split into groups between those who advocated a move to the Shanghai International Settlement and those who wanted to stay on. The split extended to the editorial board of *Min Pao*. Wang Ching-wei and Hu Han-min, however, wanted to stay. The paper resumed publication after a brief interruption.[54] Had *Min Pao* and its leaders been removed from the Japanese setting so soon, it is not difficult to imagine how thoroughly anti-Japanese the revolutionary movement might have become.

c. Soliciting

The editors had reason to feel a debt of gratitude to Japan. The League had been formed with Japanese help. But the numerous unofficial and zealous helpers and contributors were more important for the coffers and morale of the organization. One of the most important fund raisers was Akiyama Teisuke, a man who had supported Japanese adventurers' activities in Korea prior to the Sino-Japanese War. Akiyama's account of his work with Sun tells us much of the personal effort and enthusiasm that went into the work.[55] With Akiyama, the charismatic charm of Sun Yat-sen apparently counted for as much as idealistic theories. "A man like Sun," he said enthusiastically, "will not be seen tomorrow, or in fifty, or in a hundred years. Even in dreams you cannot imagine such a man. I had not dreamt of such a person until he appeared. Sun is the world's great revolutionary."[56] Mingled with this admiration, however, was an unmistakable annoyance at being dunned so regularly and so mercilessly. Almost daily, Sun would come in, smile cheerily, and announce, "Akiyama-san, it's a monetary question again today!" Occasionally Akiyama would rail at Sun and accuse him of ingratitude and insouciance, but Sun always countered by pointing out the pleasures of participating in such great and noble enterprises. Sun was constantly busy with new and expensive projects, such as printing presses for a new *Min Pao* plant in Shanghai. In fact, Sun's powers of persuasion seem to have exceeded Akiyama's resources, for the latter went so deeply into debt that he had a six month nervous breakdown.[57] At that time, the solicitous Sun merely shifted his appeal to the several other people who were supporting him. When Sun's needs outran private sources, his friends were able to interest Mitsui officials in his work.[58] Fund raising was a basic assignment for all the Japanese friends as well, and a man like Kayano, who converted a Kobe shipping magnate to the revolutionary cause, would find his status and popularity considerably greater among the Chinese plotters.[59]

4. DIFFICULTIES OF THE T'UNG-MENG-HUI

The steady increase of enthusiasm among the students after the return of Sun Yat-sen was cause for concern to both the Manchus and the conservatives within the Japanese government. In Japan, the nationalist group, secure in its war-time prestige and power, felt no particular need to support Chinese intrigue and revolt as long as Japan could utilize her newly won status as a great power to achieve her ends. Moreover, conservative and military factions were beginning to fear that Chinese republicanism might infect the Japanese spirit. Even Tōyama Mitsuru shared these doubts.[60]

a. Sun's expulsion from Japan

The Chinese government's misgivings were confirmed by a speech which Sun made in Tokyo in January 1907. According to the *Kokuryūkai* sources, Sun intimated that since the revolution was aimed at the Manchus and the revival of China, he would have no complaint if Japan felt she deserved territory north of Changchun for her help. When this reached the ears of the Peking government, they used it as an excuse to demand Japanese expulsion of Sun Yat-sen.[61] Whether this was the case, or whether, as the Chinese accounts claim, Sun's speech was devoted to a particularly aggressive presentation of the three principles,[62] there is no question but that the meeting attracted enough students and enough Japanese interest to justify a Chinese request for Sun's expulsion.

On February 13, 1907, Uchida Ryōhei was called to Tokyo by

Prince Itō, who showed him the Chinese demand. Uchida explained to Itō that it was important to keep on good terms with the revolutionaries, and he suggested that Sun should be allowed to leave voluntarily. Itō referred future discussions to Yamaza Enjirō of the Foreign Office, who agreed completely with Uchida. It was decided that Sun should be allowed to return in three or four years.[63] Yamaza gave Uchida seventy thousand yen for Sun. Sun received sixty thousand of this sum, and the rest was used for an elaborate farewell banquet. Most of the Chinese and Japanese active in the movement were present; the total number of guests exceeded sixty. Miyazaki and his group were aggrieved and indignant at their government's blindness. A Tokyo broker felt so strongly about his government's action that he gave Sun ten thousand yen of his own.[64]

The loss of Sun weakened the headquarters of the *T'ung-meng-hui* severely. A latent distrust of the Japanese, allayed in large measure by Sun's personality and presence, now revived. Relatively few of those who remained in Tokyo were members of the old group which had known Miyazaki and the others for a decade. After Huang Hsing and Sung Chiao-jen also left to raise money in Southeast Asia and America, the basic differences in aims and ideology within the League came to light again. At the same time, increased Japanese surveillance and control contributed to the irritability among the revolutionaries.

b. The Tokyo remnant

Even before Sun's expulsion from Japan, several developments suggested that the previous cordiality of his adventurer-military backing would not long continue. Shortly after Miyazaki and the others helped to start *Min Pao,* they themselves put out a magazine that was frankly international and socialist in nature. From the alacrity with which the Japanese police swooped down upon it, there can be no doubt that this publication represented a definite break between Miyazaki and his former sponsors.

After the February Revolution of 1905 in Russia, several refugees and revolutionaries had made their way to Nagasaki. There they formed a revolutionary party with Dr. Nicolai Russel at its head. They tried to publish a paper, but they were so short of funds that they resorted to measures like robbery and the sale of maps of the Russian shoreline. In 1906 Sun Yat-sen traveled to Annam with Kayano Chōchi. On his way, he met Russel. The two discussed general problems, and agreed that their revolutions had complementary aims. The Doctor's scientific training made research in bomb assembly possible, and before long materials were being smuggled to him inside rubber dolls. We are told that the explosives Wang Ching-wei intended for the Prince Regent in 1909 were made from photographic supplies by the Russians in Nagasaki.[65]

Miyazaki, Kayano, and several others met these Russians in 1906. Together with several socialists, they published a magazine called *Kakumei hyōron* (Revolutionary review) which was to speed both revolutions. The Japanese police, however, closed it down after a few issues.[66]

It is understandable that enterprises of this sort caused considerable concern among Japanese conservatives. Their distrust of the Chinese revolutionaries was heightened after Sun's exit from Tokyo, for the publicists that remained were on the whole a more radical group than their predecessors. Chang Ping-lin, Chang Chi, and Liu Kuang-han continued the close relations with the Japanese socialists that had begun earlier. In 1907, an anti-imperialist organization was founded under the name *Ashūwashin kai* (Asian Peace and Friendship Society). Its publications were issued in Chinese and in English, the latter entitled "Asiatic Humaniturian [sic] Brotherhood." Meetings were held to discuss socialism, and at one lecture by the Japanese socialist leader Kōtoku Shūsui ninety people were present. The group was international in its appeal: Annamese, Filipinos, Indians, and Chinese were present. Meetings were held in the Tokyo India House and in a Unitarian church. Such developments did not constitute the kind of Greater Asian movements that the Tokyo government favored, and the various publications were banned by the police. In 1908, Chang Chi went to France, where he turned his thought more and more to anarchist doctrines.[67]

In the absence of Sun Yat-sen, the early unity of the *T'ung-meng-hui* gave way to division and discontent. Rivalry and jealousy threatened to wreck the league. In 1907, Sun Yat-sen wrote to Miyazaki urging him to accept a power of attorney for the revolutionary organization. Sun suggested that it would be best to keep this arrangement secret, unknown to Hirayama and the Japanese; it should even be kept from the Chinese group in Tokyo.[68]

c. French support in Indo-China

Internal squabbles among the Tokyo comrades hindered several attempts Sun Yat-sen made between 1907 and 1911. In 1907 two revolts were based on Annam. There, French officials and officers were generous with advice and help. On the whole, their aims were probably not dissimilar to those of General Kodama.[69] The revolutionary troops in Annam were under the command of Huang Hsing, and they were aided by several well-timed peasant riots along the Chinese frontier. The Manchus dispatched two generals with good sized armies. Sun's men and money were everywhere, however, and for a time it seemed likely that the generals themselves would switch sides and lead the combined armies against the Chinese government. The rebels lacked only arms and ammunition. Kayano Chōchi, who was now a full-time ally of Sun with considerable experience in getting ammunition, returned to Tokyo to arrange for the shipments.[70] A combination of internal disunity among the revolutionaries and government surveillance proved too much for Kayano, however, and Sun Yat-sen was once again doomed to disappointment. Although Huang's troops fought well and showed considerable courage, the Manchu generals, noting that all was not well in the rebel camp, decided to carry out orders and crush the revolt.[71]

In November 1907, Sun made another attempt to capitalize on French good will and rural discontent in South China. He proposed to turn the attention of the semi-savage mountaineers and bandits along the Tongking Kwangsi border from aimless marauding to fighting the Manchus. The bandit leaders were amenable to this, and Sun and Huang Hsing were both present for the campaign which followed. Once again, lack of ammunition stopped the revolt after a few isolated successes. Of the Japanese, Ike Kyōkichi was present throughout, and at Sun's request he wrote a history of the revolt.[72]

After this Sun was banned from Indo-China. By now few Asian countries would give asylum to so prominent a revolutionary. He therefore went to Europe, hoping to interest M. Doumer, the former Governor of Annam, in further use of that colony as a base in a joint effort to establish French democracy in China. Although Sun got no official support, he was able to raise a moderate amount of money. In November 1909, he went to America, where he stayed some eight months. He returned to Yokohama in June of 1910. The Japanese government was still not willing to let him stay, however, and so he continued on to Penang. His family moved there, and for a time that island became the revolutionary headquarters. In November 1910, Sun divided his lieutenants and assigned them fund-raising areas throughout Southeast Asia. At the end of that year he left again for Europe, and early in 1911 he was in America. Sun kept in touch with Miyazaki and Kayano. His letters told of meeting important leaders in America, and he seemed confident of success. His letters always included questions about the possibilities of permission to re-enter Japan, and they usually ended with best wishes for Inukai and Tōyama.[73] The answers from Tokyo never contained the news Sun wanted. Until the outbreak of the revolution in October, he was in North America, traveling quietly between America and Canada.

d. The overseas Chinese

Time was on the side of the revolutionaries, but in the years before 1911 their prospects seemed far from bright. Internal dissension had weakened the once united League. Repeated failures, loss of Japanese and French support, and the constant threat of hired assassins discouraged the revolutionaries. Discouragement bred violence, and a series of acts of terrorism lent the revolutionary cause less honor than it did publicity. It was therefore fortunate that in the last years of Manchu rule the overseas Chinese gradually came to support the revolution.

In Southeast Asia, a preference for Sun as against K'ang Yu-wei among the overseas Chinese was only slowly and laboriously established. It is true that the Chinese there had grudges against the Manchus. They received no legal or diplomatic protection worth mentioning. Then too, the revolutionaries were from South China, and hence frequently kin to the overseas Chinese. But prosperity bred caution and conservatism, and in the struggle for allegiance Sun's agents were finally forced to offer more attractive rewards than their competitors. As a result, it gradually came to be a good investment to support Sun's revolutionary cause. One hundred *yuan* brought citizenship in the New China, one thousand earned promises of mining concessions and other business preferences, ten thousand earned one a term as representative in the new government, one hundred thousand would find a bronze statue in the home town of the lucky donor, and he who parted with a million for the cause would be honored by statues in parks named after him in his town and in the capital.[74]

The financial efforts of the years immediately preceding the establishment of the republic were thus largely concentrated on the overseas Chinese in Southeast Asia, and their support was unquestionably the most important source of help and money for Sun. With an elaborate network of propaganda papers and agents scattered throughout the area, and with Sun himself established at Penang, Southeast Asia clearly displaced Japan as the seedbed of the revolution.[75]

The Chinese in America were also a valuable source of funds for Sun Yat-sen.[76] America also contributed a remarkable adventurer in the person of Homer Lea, a man who helped by training Chinese cadets, raising money, and donating the proceeds of the Japanese edition of his *Valor of Ignorance* to Sun's cause.[77] Lea was strongly anti-Japanese. The overseas Chinese too had no particular reason to be favorably inclined toward Japan.

5. SUN YAT-SEN AND THE JAPANESE ON THE EVE OF THE REVOLUTION

The influence and importance of Sun's Japanese friends was thus very much reduced in the years immediately before the revolution. Sun was less in Japan, there were fewer Japanese with him, and the Japanese government was definitely against him. Anti-Japanese sentiment grew among all classes in China, and it was worsened by high-handed Japanese policy. In 1908, for instance, Japan adopted such an uncompromising tone after the Chinese had stopped a Japanese freighter loaded with arms in Amoy that a general boycott of Japanese goods spread all through South China. Thanks to the combined efforts of the Japanese Ambassador Hayashi Gonsuke and Sun Yat-sen, the Chinese government and Chinese students respectively were mollified. The boycott, however, was an ominous indication of what was happening to Japan's hopes of guidance.[78]

If Sun Yat-sen still had any faith in the expansionist leaders, that trust should have been seriously weakened by the role they played in the annexation of Korea. Their preoccupation with Korea was central to Sun's loss of support, for while men like Miyazaki had the good will, Uchida had the organization.

When Itō Hirobumi went to Korea after the Russo-Japanese War, he took Uchida Ryōhei with him at the request of Sugiyama Shige-maru. Uchida devoted his energies to the control of a protest group, the Il-jin-höe (Advance Society). This was headed by two puppets, I Il-sik and Song Pyong-jun. After forming a close friendship with these men, Uchida was able to control the group by funds which were sent from Japan by Sugiyama. Uchida thus became a direct agent of army imperialism, and his policy was approved and strengthened by occasional visits to Japan in which he was interviewed by men like Katsura and Yamagata.

The Advance Society furthered Japan's interests by furnishing workers for Japanese railroad projects which were opposed by Korean nationalists, and they helped Japanese propaganda with special publications of their own. When the Korean king was forced to abdicate in favor of his son in 1907, the crowd outside the palace which demanded the step was made up of members who had been paid for their service. In other words, it was a well-informed Korean crowd which gathered outside the Japanese legation after the abdication, shouting "Kill I!" Kill Uchida!" [79]

Such techniques and such reactions were far from what the early liberals had envisaged. By the eve of the Wuhan Revolution in 1911, the dream of a friendly, imitative China seemed very distant indeed. Within one year, the liberals saw Sun expelled from Japan, Min Pao closed down for a time, and the negotiation of a friendly treaty with Russia. Just as the once-hated symbol of Western imperialism, Russia, had become a friend, Sun Yat-sen, the epitome of republican and democratic opposition to Manchu despotism, had now become a subversive influence to be feared.

Since the end of World War II, the secret files of the Japanese Foreign Office have become available. They show as nothing else could how hostile the government attitude was toward Sun Yat-sen and his Japanese friends. It was known from Miyazaki's writings that he felt he had fallen on evil days. His house had become suspect, and after one police search for arms and explosives Miyazaki received a letter from Sun asking his patience, and praising again his unselfish help for a foreign cause. In 1910, when Sun returned to Japan for a few days, he brought his elder brother with him. They stayed with Miyazaki, sharing his poverty. It was not long before the Japanese police told Sun to keep moving.[80]

In the Foreign Office files we find Miyazaki and Kayano watched as though they were foreign subversives. Secret agents, identified by number, detailed their every movement, their mail, and, second-hand, their opinions. The Foreign Office was well informed. Weeks before Sun's "secret" visit to Japan in 1910, their agents reported that Sun had written Huang Hsing, who was back in Tokyo for a time, asking him what he thought the Japanese government's attitude would be if they should discover his presence. His progress was reported by Japanese consuls all along the line, and once he was closeted with Miyazaki and Kayano the agents strained to catch the conversation.[81] Such surveillance was probably the more troublesome in that it was noticeable. Kayano, in fact, reports that it was a nuisance to realize there was a police agent just outside the door so constantly.[82]

The agents reported from Hong Kong and Shanghai as well. There was very little chance of eluding their scrutiny; when Miyazaki, returning from China in May 1910, neared Kobe, his imminent arrival was announced to the Foreign Office and the Home Ministry, which then alerted the Prefectural Governors of Nagasaki, Yamaguchi, Osaka, Tokyo, Gifu, Aichi, Shizuoka, Kanagawa, and Shiga.[83]

Other agents, all along the line, reported the speeches and activities of Sun Yat-sen. Sun's stops in Hawaii and in Southeast Asia got particularly full coverage in 1910 and 1911. His speeches radiated confidence, chiefly on the issue of Manchu army reforms. As the army was enlarged and modernized, he told his hearers, it would not remain loyal. There is little doubt that the Tokyo Foreign Office agreed all too well with the British treaty-port papers that reported these speeches. In Singapore, an approving consul included with his report a clipping from the *Straits Echo* which, after noting that the speech was "of a kind to do the Chinese no good," ended with the lofty comment that "the *Echo* ridicules the whole speech especially his appeal to local Chinese for financial support." [84]

Unlike the British, the Japanese officials had constant indications that their citizenry remained partial to the movement led by Sun Yat-sen. The consuls and the secret agents reported Sun's numerous contacts with Tokyo financial and business circles. They recounted the activities of the ubiquitous messengers and adventurers. Not all the expansionists had shifted to Korea; although the name of Uchida Ryōhei did not appear in the agents' reports, others of his persuasion were represented.[85] Almost all the reports, however, dealt with Sun or with his closest friends, Miyazaki and Kayano. Their status was indicated by the heading of each report: "The man that needs watching."

In a Japan fearful lest the old virtues and ideals should be discarded, the aging *Genrō,* alarmed by increasing signs of radicalism, warned against revolutions and advised the Manchus to make reforms in order to ward off the inevitable. A friendly China was desirable, but a strong China unthinkable. Thus reforms that might have produced a really strong army were discouraged, and China was prevented from forming alliances with potential friends by a prior series of Japanese treaties. The last of these, the Root-Takahira notes of 1908, completed China's encirclement. Yuan Shih-k'ai, a strong man and a confirmed enemy of Japan, was now discredited.[86] Japanese advisers were dispatched to help China draw up a sane, conservative, constitutional monarchy that should be modeled on that of Japan. The revolutionists naturally came to think less kindly of Japan and Japanese institutions.[87] For the Tokyo government, the diplomacy of force seemed more promising than that of guidance. Shortly before Yuan's fall, Katsura's demands for further territorial and commercial rights in Manchuria bore fruit in treaties signed in September 1909.[88]

Japan's relationship with Peking thus held out little hope for help for Miyazaki, Kayano, and their Chinese friends. When Sun Yat-sen's revolution broke out in 1911, most observers expected Japan to intervene in support of the Manchus.

THE 1911 REVOLUTION

6

Despite all their research, and despite their cautious support of the several groups likely to lead China, the Japanese awoke, in October 1911, to the fact that China was very much out of control. The sudden overturn of the Manchu dynasty caught them off guard and completely unprepared, and the vacillation of their bewildered policy makers soon gave the impression of deliberate guile and duplicity. Japan's attempts to work out a policy for China deserve close attention, for they show unmistakable evidence of wide disagreement and considerable bewilderment within Japan. The complete failure of Japan's hopes and plans for China can then be ascribed less to overambitious and cynical opportunism than to governmental indecision, fumbling, and weakness. The very groups that worked hardest for a policy of double dealing were, in fact, the most critical of their government because it failed to follow their ideas. In many ways, the picture of the reluctant Tokyo government, restrained by its allies from striking out alone, and beset on every hand by pressure groups demanding a positive policy in China, strikes one with a startling relevance. Japan's hesitant course reflected a disunity at home in which vocal oppositionists prevented their government from acting on its conservative and reactionary inclinations.

There were three broad courses open to Japan in treating with the revolution in China. Support for a truly national revolution which expressed the determination of the Chinese for an independent government and nation would have been destructive of any hopes Japan might have held for domination of China. A democratic China would have increased the demand in Japan for the benefits of liberalism which later comers to modernization were enjoying. Partisans of change would then have pointed out that those innovations had not weakened China, but had actually strengthened her.

A China whose successful revolution owed much to Japanese support, however, might have been expected to be a friendly state and a probable ally. Early liberals like Ōi Kentarō had counted upon such results when they schemed for reform in Korea. Miyazaki Torazō and Kayano Chōchi, who worked with Sun Yat-sen in good times and bad, undoubtedly favored such a policy of support for the Chinese revolution. It would have suited their goals within Japan, and it would have gratified their emotional bonds with their Chinese friends. It would also have pleased Japanese public opinion. The adventurers and their colorful foreign allies were far more popular than the conservatives in Tokyo; but a policy of help to the revolution was manifestly unacceptable to the Tokyo government leaders.

Japan could also have supported the Manchus. A narrowly averted revolution in China would have made for the continuation of the previous system of gradual encroachment by all imperialist powers upon the prerogatives of the dynasty. Japan had been doing very well in the pre-war years with increased activities in Manchuria and a role in the railroad development consortiums that dominated Chinese diplomacy. Such a policy would not have appealed to chauvinists, for it could not be designated as independent or forceful. Nevertheless, conservative politicians and business circles had watched with favor the steady integration of Japan's China policy with those of England and Russia.[1] Japanese public opinion, however, was strongly for the revolutionaries. This, combined with English hesitation to interfere in China, prevented such a course.

The last possibility was one with which most writers have credited Japan. This involved running with the hare and hunting with the hounds. Official participation in the Powers' non-interference, along with quiet help to the Manchus and surreptitious aid to the revolutionaries, would have indebted all factions to Japan, without enabling any one to establish a stable and effective government. Internal disorder would probably have resulted in provincial autonomy. This might have led to great advantages for Japan, for in a divided country the army and business-sponsored *shishi* and *rōnin* and their carpetbagger colleagues could have sought personal gain. Nevertheless, such a policy would have required considerable astuteness in Tokyo. Moreover, the political uncertainty that would have resulted in China would not make for the business conditions Japanese exporters sought. Then, too, similar opportunities of parceling China would have awaited other countries. If exclusive spheres had been set up, England was fairly certain to obtain the Yangtze region, thereby restricting Japan to Fukien and Manchuria — areas she already controlled to a large extent.

The puzzled Japanese tried each of these policies in turn. Some aided the revolution. Others, who tried to set up autonomous puppet states, were stopped by their government. No one could be quite sure which group would win out, and as a result the government hesitated to clamp down on the activities of the adventurers. The government itself tried half-heartedly to support the faltering dynasty before it reluctantly joined the other powers in sponsoring with a loan the new government of Yuan Shih-k'ai. Tokyo thus managed to make itself unpopular with each group in China, and with foreign governments as well. As reward it received only the sharpest of criticism on the home front. Such capital bungling is a far cry from the picture most writers have given us of the crafty leaders of Japan. Explanations for it lay in unpreparedness, uncertainty, and political strife at home.

1. THE *Mainichi* READER AND THE REVOLUTION

For an understanding of the confusion and debate with which the revolution was obscured for the average citizen in Japan, it will be of value to follow its events briefly through the pages of the *Osaka Mainichi*. The *Mainichi* reader could be expected to have the interests of the business class in mind, for the paper openly catered to them.[2] The reader was also well informed on the virtues of the revolutionary cause, for on the whole reporters were conspicuously pro-revolution in China. They often formed special groups to advocate policies that would further the revolution, and, thereby, Japanese aims.

On October 10, the paper made no mention of disturbances in China. The next day it noted disturbances in Szechwan, and reported that some people had been killed. On the twelfth, however, the number of casualties was given. This time some information was added about discoveries in the Russian consulate in Hankow. These implied that trouble was brewing again in China. The reader, however, was used to revolts and rumors of revolts in China, and there was certainly little to prepare him for the next day's issue.

On October 13, monster headlines announced a real revolution. Subsequent issues contained little else. The revolution dominated the news columns, and even after other items reclaimed part of the front page it continued to fill the rest of the paper. Before long, news features were supplemented by special articles such as the history of the movement by Miyazaki which has been cited above.

The *Mainichi* then brought its readers up to date. At Hankow, Viceroy Jui Cheng had discovered a revolutionary plot. His discovery forced the hands of the revolutionaries, and their rising resulted in the defection of the entire garrison. The viceroy was soon in flight up the Yangtze in a Chinese gunboat, and punitive forces were dispatched from Peking on October 15. As more government troops joined the rebels, the Hanyang arsenal fell. Within little more than a month, the rebels had sacked Nanking. As the imperial troops counterattacked, however, the issue remained in doubt for some time. Revolutionary successes were not achieved without some hard fighting.

While this was going on, the *Mainichi* was trying to decide what the Japanese policy should be. On October 14, an editorial observed that the Manchus were apparently unable to put the revolution down. It suggested that the government had better start thinking about its policy. Either intervention against the revolution or friendship for the rebels should be adopted.

But the government was in a rather poor position to do either. Saionji had replaced Katsura as premier for the last time in August 1911. He was distinctly not a militarist, and that made him less likely to heed army suggestions for intervention. At first the communications minister, Hayashi, held the Foreign Office post in addition to his own, pending the arrival of Ambassador Uchida Yasuya from Washington. Until the latter's arrival in October, no action was possible. And even then Uchida, long out of touch with the Chinese situation, relied more and more upon Ijuin Hikokichi, the Japanese representative at Peking. Ijuin, meanwhile, was a friend of Yuan Shih-k'ai. The latter had received an Imperial Mandate to put down the revolution on October 27.[3] Thus a pro-revolutionary policy was also unlikely. For a time, Japan had neither a foreign minister nor a China policy.

On October 15, the *Mainichi* pointed out the dangers of continued unrest to trade and commerce. It held that the disturbance in China was already doing more damage to Japanese trade than the Sino-Japanese and Russo-Japanese wars had done, and it hinted that the Foreign Office had better start thinking about putting the revolution down. Fortunately, Foreign Minister Uchida would know what to do. The same day's issue had an interview with Ōkuma. Ōkuma agreed that the situation was serious, and he advised co-operative action with England to restore order quickly so that Japan could resume her task of leading Chinese modernization. *Mainichi* reporters had also found K'ang Yu-wei and Liang Ch'i-ch'ao vacationing at Hakone and Suma, but the reformers had refused to comment on the Chinese situation.

On October 18, the paper reported that Uchida Ryōhei had called on Mr. Kurachi, head of the Political Section of the Foreign Office, to ask about the China policy. Uchida told reporters that he had pointed out that the rebels were not likely to lose. Even if the Japanese government felt obliged to support the Manchus, it would be foolish to alienate South China. Economically, that area was more important to Japan than North China. Mr. Uchida had been told that the government was weighing all such matters, but that it had not yet arrived at a decision. To help it make up its mind, the adventurers staged meetings in Tokyo. The *Rōninkai,* an organization that had been formed by Tōyama and his *Genyōsha* associates in 1908,[4] staged a mass meeting in Hibiya Park. Some two hundred people gathered to hear speeches which stressed the importance of events in China. They were told that there was a real danger to the yellow race, to world peace, and to trade in a policy which followed European leads. Japan should follow an independent, sincere foreign policy. Miyazaki, present as a China expert, gave a short talk.

The *Mainichi* editors continued to be confused. They weighed the pros and cons of intervention with other powers, only to be shaken by reports that the rebels had captured so many arms at Hanyang that they might be able to win. The Reformers also complicated things. On November 10, Liang Ch'i-ch'ao departed for Peking. The next day he was reported in Mukden, where he told correspondents that foreign troops might have to protect the court in Peking. That same day, the *Mainichi* suggested policing Manchuria together with Russia in order to guarantee foreign lives and business interests. By now, the editors had shown themselves very uncertain about policy. They were growing fidgety and impatient with inaction.

Many news items showed that influential quarters favored the rebels. On November 12, a *Shishi konshinkai* (Gathering of *Shishi*) met under the direction of Tōyama Mitsuru and his friends. It adopted resolutions which held the Chinese Revolution to be indigenous and just. On December 20, Inukai's *Kokumintō* warned that intervention could lose Japan the friendship of China. The government was urged to strive for peace without wounding Chinese sensibilities.

On the other hand, former Premier Katsura predicted on December 20 that lack of provisions and munitions would soon stall both sides, and that the result would be general lawlessness. Katsura felt that Japan and England should force their good offices upon China to bring about the establishment of constitutional monarchy.

The *Mainichi* editors finally cast their vote for safety and conservatism. On November 23, an editorial warned of the rise of anti-foreignism in China. It urged the government to take strong steps to protect Japanese lives and interests. It complained about the apparent indifference of the Saionji cabinet to such problems.[5] By December 2, the editors were frankly annoyed. In an editorial entitled, "What is our China Policy?", they blasted the do-nothing Saionji cabinet. Every other country, they complained, was exercising more influence than Japan in China. It was necessary to *do* something to protect Japanese business and to keep Japan's rightful place in China.

At that time, the Imperial troops had just retaken Hanyang and Hankow and intervention seemed likely to succeed. Germany was reported to be supplying the Manchus with arms. It would certainly never do to have the victorious side owe nothing to Japanese help.

But there were numerous indications that the Chinese people themselves were unreservedly for the revolution, and the government in Tokyo was wise not to follow the demands of the *Mainichi* editors. On December 2, a three days' armistice was signed between the rebel and Peking forces. This was extended to fifteen days, and by then arrangements had been made for a general cease-fire until December 31, at which time a peace conference convened in Shanghai.[6] Despite the petulance of the government's critics, the government could do very little once these developments had taken place.

Meanwhile those who sympathized with the revolutionaries were equally displeased with their government. They organized numerous meetings to protest the pro-Manchu stand, and they did not hesitate to do what they could to act as midwives in the birth of what they hoped would be a friendly China. Their work seldom reached the columns of the *Mainichi*, but it had an important bearing on Western and Chinese opinions of Japanese motives and policies.

2. The First Manchukuo

Of these active groups, we may select one led by Kawashima Naniwa as most closely allied with the predatory aspects of Japanese militarism and imperialism. The Machiavellian schemes attributed to all Japanese unquestionably dominated Kawashima's thinking, and yet he was able to get little coöperation in Tokyo. According to the expansionists' apologia, however, even Kawashima's motives were of the highest kind. We are told that he, like the other adventurers, considered no help too great for Sun Yat-sen. This was because Sun had renounced Manchuria, and because he seemed to promise a friendly, well-run China. The advent of Yuan Shih-k'ai made Sun's promises worthless, however, and a new plan had to be worked out. As a result, the *shishi* were split into groups that were for and against the revolution. Of the former, a further distinction existed between those who wanted to have a unified China under the revolution and those who desired to have most of China

under Sun Yat-sen with Manchuria and part of North China reserved for Japan under nominal Manchu rule. Kawashima exemplified this last group.[7]

Kawashima fits squarely into the main stream of adventurer
activity. He came of samurai stock. After the Restoration, his family
had moved to Tokyo. Surrounded with the evidence of westernization, Kawashima himself experienced a conversion to Christianity,
and then left the faith for a new belief in the necessity of ridding
the world of white aggression. In 1886, he made his first trip to
China, where he was depressed equally by the poverty of the natives
and the opulence of the Westerners. Before long, he became a China
specialist with a command of the language and many friendships
among Japanese army and navy circles. During the Sino-Japanese
War, he served as interpreter for the army, and after the Boxer
Rebellion as head of the police in the Japanese zone of Peking.
Afterward he organized a school to instruct Chinese police in
Japanese methods. When Peking reverted to Chinese control,
Kawashima continued as head of the school. Kawashima installed
Japanese at all important posts. They served as Chinese officials, and
revamped the entire system on the Japanese model. When other
countries protested this favoritism, Kawashima's post was changed
to that of instructor. Later the school was shifted to Japan.
Kawashima remained in charge, able to place his graduates and
control promotions. The five thousand-odd graduates of the institution were scattered all over China, and it was hoped that they
would exert great influence.[8]

While he was in Peking, Kawashima met Prince Su, who came
to head the Police Bureau. Kawashima succeeded in convincing
him of the benefits of an East Asia for the Asiatics. Prince Su
was forced out of office for a time by the Tzu Hsi cabal, but when
he came into favor again in 1907, he became an important ally.
Ultimately, he became the first candidate for investiture as a Japanese puppet.

In 1911, Kawashima returned from China with the prediction
that a revolution was about to break out. When it did, he returned to China. On his way, he saw General Terauchi in Korea,
and secured his agreement to a plan which called for helping the

rebels to take all of China south of the Yellow River and helping the Manchus to the north. This would satisfy the rebels, and it would ensure Manchu subservience. Terauchi discussed with him the possibility of using reserve troops the Japanese had stationed in Korea.

When Kawashima went on to Peking, he found Minister Ijuin interested in the plan; but when Yuan Shih-k'ai was recalled to head the government, Ijuin favored complete support for the Manchus. Kawashima was attached to the Japanese legation. Before long he and Ijuin were completely at odds; Ijuin had his men watch Kawashima, while the latter sent home reports that were uncomplimentary and disparaging.

Kawashima now worked alone. He persuaded his friend Wu Lu-chen, a general who had had a prolonged period of study and residence in Japan, to bar Yuan's return to Peking.[9] Yuan got word of this, however, and he had Wu assassinated before the plan was carried out. Next Kawashima plotted with Japanese officers to bomb Yuan's train. This plan was foiled by Ijuin. A last attempt to bomb Yuan's residence failed when he moved his headquarters.

Kawashima then decided to set up Prince Su in Manchuria. He helped him to slip out of Peking with the help of some young Japanese officers.[10] The Prince, who had opposed any surrender to the revolutionaries, was eager to re-establish even a part of Manchu rule.

An elaborate plan was worked out; it included two Mongol princes, who were to set up a regime in Inner Mongolia.[11] The Tokyo army headquarters gave its tacit assent, and sent out several officers with vague orders to "help Kawashima." The latter worked out his scheme carefully. He signed a treaty with one of the Mongol princes which ensured Japanese primacy in Inner Mongolia in return for arms, material, and economic assistance. All advisers were to be under Kawashima's direction, and the Mongols were to check with Japan before making any agreements with Russia. Japan was guaranteed sweeping commercial privileges. The boy emperor, thought to be in Jehol, was to be informed about these plans, for his eventual participation was desired.

Weapons were sent over the mountains of Jehol rather than

through Shanhaikuan in order to escape detection by Chinese and Japanese officials. Several skirmishes with bandits who wanted the arms and with several forces of Chinese troops took the lives of thirteen Japanese, nine Mongols, and about thirty Chinese.

In answer to a wire from the Assistant Chief of the General Staff, Kawashima returned to Tokyo expecting to receive official aid. Instead, he was told that the cabinet had discovered the plot and that it wanted it stopped at once. An interview with Foreign Minister Uchida revealed that Japan was entering the international loan consortium, thereby underwriting Yuan's new government.

This ended the first attempt to set up a puppet state in Manchuria. Although it ended in complete failure, and was kept quite secret,[12] by 1934 the scheme seemed so prophetic of the future that the victims were honored at a memorial service in Tokyo. In 1911, however, Kawashima bitterly complained about the lack of direction and lack of planning in Japan's China policy. Far from judging this policy deceptive, he would have condemned it as naive and idealistic.[13]

3. THE JAPANESE AND THE PROVISIONAL NANKING GOVERNMENT

Kawashima and his men found out that the Tokyo government was not willing to take the risks of a policy of deliberate double-dealing in which both sides would receive support. What of those who wanted to help the revolution? How did they regard their government's actions and policy?

The real friends of the revolution were to be found among the small group that helped Sun Yat-sen in many of his hopeless and dangerous *putsches*. Working with them were many whose motives were less than idealistic. Even a man like Kawashima, after all, favored giving help to the revolutionaries in South China. The *rōnin* themselves, in their conflicts of opinion, were representative of the confusion in all strata of Japanese thinking about China. A *Kokuryūkai* history, for instance, laments the fact that the people and government did not agree. Within the government, Foreign Office and Army were at odds, Army and Navy disagreed, and even Army and War Office were not always together.[14] It was thus only natural that there were disagreements among the China adventurers, since at one time or another some of them were to be found working for each of the above groups. Nevertheless, in the case of workers like Miyazaki Torazō, Kayano Chōchi, and Ike Kyōkichi, we are well justified in believing that the sentiments so many expressed were sincerely held. Others, like Kita Ikki, might favor the revolution in China simply because the Tokyo government seemed to oppose it.[15] Men like Miyazaki and Kayano, however, served Sun so faithfully that Kita scorned them as lackeys.

a. A late start

The Japanese were of little direct help in the early stages of the revolution. They were as unprepared for its outbreak as was Sun Yat-sen. To make up for their late beginning, the society histories stress their contributions in men and money that preceded the revolt. The *Genyōsha* history, for instance, claims that the Japanese contributed over 250,000 yen to Sun's movement before 1911.[16] But all admit that the adventurers had little part in the actual events of the revolution. Kita Ikki, who was in Shanghai just before the revolt, says that the *rōnin* were able to do little because the police and army surveillance in Shanghai made it impossible to stock-pile arms. Kita says that the bombs which were said to be imported from Japan were actually procured from corrupt Chinese officials and officers, and points out that the Japanese had very few men, and no arms, on hand in October.[17]

During the early weeks of the revolution, the Japanese were further handicapped by the absence of Sun Yat-sen. Their activity had focused so exclusively upon helping him personally that until his return late in December they could do little more than keep in touch with individuals of less importance. By the time Sun returned, the developing jealousies and distrust among the Chinese leaders demanded his full attention, and the Japanese advisers played a secondary role. The close coöperation of the early days was never revived.

As if to make up for their minor role, the Japanese engaged in a great amount of bustling activity. Sung Chiao-jen had promised Kiyofuji and Kita that he would call upon them when help was needed. When he wired them after the Wuhan outbreak, they hurried to Shanghai. Kayano was also summoned. He could not leave immediately, for he was devoting all his energies to the first election campaign of Kojima Kazuo in Tokyo.[18] As soon as it was possible, he headed for China, disguised as a Honganji priest to avoid attention. Many others went to China, where they performed varied tasks for the revolution. Some hired barbers to cut queues and so prepare citizens for the new Chinese Republic.[19] Others entered the fighting with great enthusiasm; they even led charges, and three were killed at Wuhan.

Within Japan, the enthusiasts extended themselves to mobilize public opinion for the Revolution by such manoeuvers as staging parades of Chinese students on their way to fight for the Revolution, by forming political action societies, sponsoring meetings, and prodding government and business firms as to their attitude toward the Revolution.[20] A new organization, the *Yūrinkai* (Neighborly Society) was formed to send medicines, doctors, and nurses to China. It was to found the Nanking Army Hospital. Still other groups tried to smuggle arms to China. Inukai had secured agreement of the Nippon Yūsen Kaisha to carry such materials free of charge, but the shipments were discovered and stopped by customs agents.[21]

In China, the Japanese did their best to keep close to the leading revolutionaries. Whatever planning had gone into the Wuhan revolt had been done by Huang Hsing on the basis of the Yangtze *T'ung-meng-hui* organization built up by Sung Chiao-jen, and so Sung and Huang naturally came in for special attention. Kayano was with Huang Hsing through the November battles for Hanyang, and thereafter he stayed with Sung Chiao-jen.

There was a Japanese near each important individual or center of activity. Besides Kayano's presence with Huang and Sung, Hirayama was in Peking, while Ozaki Yukimasa was in Hankow.

Kayano reported that Huang Hsing instilled in his men the valor and *bushidō* of the Japanese warrior. When the rebel forces were forced to retreat after an imperialist cross-fire, one soldier with two wounds hailed Kayano and asked him to note that a Hunan soldier, like his Japanese counterpart, was not afraid to die.[22]

b. The arrival of Sun Yat-sen

Any real chance of close coöperation between the revolutionaries and the Japanese depended upon the presence and influence of Sun Yat-sen. The revolution had caught him on a fund-raising tour in America. Instead of rushing back to China, he determined to proceed to Europe to try to ensure the coöperation of England in blocking the newly arranged consortium loan to the Manchus. In this he was successful. Britain also rescinded his banishment from her colonial areas, and agreed to consider a loan to his government when it should be established. Sun then went to France for an interview with Clemenceau before he returned to China. This he did by way of Penang and Hong Kong. He arrived at Shanghai on December 24, 1911.[23]

It is important to note that Sun no longer had the optimistic view of Japanese policy that had been his previously. In England, he asked help in preventing the rumored intervention against the revolution by Japan.[24] On his way back to China, he was accompanied by his newly acquired military adviser, the California theorist Homer Lea. Lea's chief claim to fame lay in his vigorous anti-Japanese writings; *The Valor of Ignorance* had furnished the world with a sensational warning of the potentialities of Japanese might and aggression. There is even a letter from Sun to Lea in which he offered to try to get Japan's secret mobilization plans for the United States.[25]

Lea was interviewed at Penang as Sun's ship neared China. He stated that, in order to preserve the balance of power in the Far East, it would be necessary for Japan to be weakened or China to be strengthened. The British press expressed considerable pleasure with the views of Sun's new adviser.[26] In Hong Kong, American Consul General Anderson cabled the State Department that it was evident that Lea, Sun's Chief of Staff, had great influence over him. The new government was apparently going to be set up on the American model, and Lea's influence would extend to foreign relations.[27]

Sun's entourage grew as he neared China. Among the newcomers that joined the party in Hong Kong were Miyazaki and Ike.[28] The old friendships had not died, but the Japanese were now outnumbered by others who strove to please and influence Sun Yat-sen.

By the time Sun Yat-sen arrived in Shanghai, numerous rifts had opened in the rebel camp. The *T'ung-meng-hui* had united on a program of doing away with the Manchus. Now that this aim was all but achieved, the secondary fears and jealousies came to the fore. The nationalists that dominated the scene in Nanking were disconcerted to find Sun putting so much trust in his peculiar, self-styled American general.[29] The Japanese reminded them of his past alliances with Japanese imperialists. Sun's position was far from impregnable. To quote a Western critic, "the Revolution had been started without his knowledge, directed without his presence or advice, and would have ended without his active participation, or any suggestion that he was the 'Father' of the movement, had he not arrived at a moment when it suited the real leaders to have a figurehead as a foil to Yuan Shih-k'ai." [30] This is a tremendous overstatement, but the elements of truth in it suggested to men like Kita Ikki the advisability of urging the other leaders not to put all their faith in Sun, who was more Western than Oriental.[31]

But Kita's advice had no effect. The revolutionaries needed a figure behind which they could rally. Moreover, Japanese were now extremely suspect as advisers among most of the revolutionaries. This was due in large part to the vacillating policy of the Tokyo government. Suspicion of that policy was heightened by the clear evidence of rascality on the part of many Japanese who had gone to China. Under fraudulent promises of getting arms, Japanese carpetbaggers were everywhere trying to get what they could in the confusion. A Professor Terao who left his university post to go to advise the republicans on their new constitution reported that Japanese merchants had taken advantage of the Chinese in almost every instance. They charged huge prices for guns that would not fire. According to Terao, if Yuan had attacked Wuchang at one point not a shot would have been fired in its defence, for the guns were all defective.[32]

c. *Tōyama and Inukai go to China*

These rogues became so great a problem that their control was finally undertaken by Tōyama Mitsuru himself. Tōyama, with eight followers, sailed for Shanghai on December 23, 1911, and he stayed until April 13, 1912.[33] The effect of his coming upon the Japanese profiteers was magical. If we are to believe the panegyrists, the scoundrels disappeared at a single wave of the master's Shinto wand. Upon those who were working for the Chinese, the moral effect of his arrival was, to use the same conservative sources, the equivalent of an army of a million.

Inukai also went to Shanghai. Together with Kashiwara and other friends, he arrived on December 19. Except for several trips to Nanking to see Sun Yat-sen and Huang Hsing, and one short trip to Japan in January, he remained in Shanghai. Both Tōyama and Inukai stayed in houses on Szechwan Road in Shanghai, and they saw Sun together on at least one occasion. We are told that Sun was so delighted to see them when he returned to China that he thanked them for coming with tears in his eyes.[34] Before Inukai left Shanghai on March 26, 1912, he was honored by Sun with a farewell dinner.[35]

Japan was thus well represented in China. The War Office sent several officers to observe and advise, leading priests were in evidence, Inukai lent the prestige of officialdom, jurists like Terao and Soejima lent academic respectability, and Tōyama and his men were well equipped to inform and inspire public opinion in Japan. In general, all these people wished the revolution well. Certainly none of them favored the coöperation with Yuan Shih-k'ai which proved Sun's undoing. Some, of course, assumed that the rebels would not extend their grasp to North China. But in any case their first concern was to prevent pro-Manchu intervention and financial support. Inukai visited Saionji before leaving Japan, and he was assured that the government did not contemplate intervention.[36]

d. Purposeful loans

The two plans which the Japanese pursued with greatest vigor and which they assumed would be most welcome to the revolutionaries brought them only suspicion and dislike from the Chinese. The *shishi* helped Sun to get large loans from Japan. They also urged him not to compromise with Yuan Shih-k'ai, but to hold out for an independent regime, even if it did not control the Peking area held by Yuan's troops. The loans brought suspicion of Japanese commercial exploitation, and the advice, which seemed evidence of bad faith, speeded the compromise it was meant to avoid.

The financial problem saw Japanese adventurers, businessmen, and politicians working smoothly together to further republicanism in China and big business in Japan. The revolutionists controlled the Yangtze valley, an area in which Japan was vitally interested. Almost from the time of its establishment in 1896, the great Yawata works in Kyushu had relied on ores from the Tayeh mines some eighty miles from Hankow. Beginning in 1899, officials of Mitsui Bussan Kaisha and of the Government Iron Works at Yawata had been at work on a series of loans to the Chinese works to guarantee their supply of iron ore. After the Tayeh mines were incorporated into the Hanyehping Company in 1908, larger loans were necessary, and on the eve of the revolution of 1911 contracts for loans totalling eighteen million yen had been negotiated. Following the disturbances of the revolution and the resulting damage to the Hanyehping Company equipment, the ores stopped coming to Japan. Mitsui and Yawata executives and their friends in the Tokyo government were not slow to consider steps that might be taken to remedy the situation.[37]

Sun Yat-sen was able to procure three loans from Japan. The first could be traced largely to the enthusiasm of his friends and to quick action on the part of Mitsui officials in Shanghai. The second reflected more careful planning in Tokyo. The third, only partly completed, represented a major attempt at control of the Hanyehping Company.

Yamada Junsaburō, a minor Mitsui official and an old friend of Sun's, was among the Japanese who met the revolutionary leader at Hong Kong in December 1911. On their way to Shanghai, Sun urged Yamada to arrange for a loan from Mitsui. Thanks to quick action on the part of the Mitsui branch manager in Shanghai and to the encouragement of Mori Kaku, a high-ranking Mitsui executive with experience in China, Kayano Chōchi was given one hundred and fifty thousand yen to use for arms.[38] The next loan was for double this amount. Among those who worked on its behalf was Uchida Ryōhei. On finding that the great firms in Japan were selling and shipping weapons to the Peking government, Uchida brought pressure to bear on them by wiring his army friends. Also, at Uchida's urging, Miyazaki had Sun Yat-sen send telegrams to Katsura Tarō and Inoue Kaoru. By this means, the Mitsui leaders became convinced that it would not be wise to affront the potential leaders of new China. The loan was negotiated in January 1912. And, in addition, early in February 1912, three million yen of the loans for twelve million which had been negotiated in 1911 were made available to Sun Yat-sen's Nanking government.[39]

In the meantime ambitious plans were prepared to give Japanese interests joint control of the entire Hanyehping Company. The capitalization of the firm was to be increased by new Japanese loans, from which large amounts would be available to Sun Yat-sen. The president of the board of the Hanyehping Company, Sheng Hsüan-huai, had, as minister of communications, directed the centralization of railway construction under government control which had brought on the Szechwan risings of October 1911. When the revolution broke out, Sheng fled to Japan with the Japanese adviser who had been stationed at the Hanyehping Company to safeguard Japanese investments there. With Sheng's industries as security, it was possible to plan larger loans to Sun Yat-sen. Both Sun and Sheng were willing to discuss such plans, and contracts were drawn up to allow for complete reorganization of the Hanyehping Company. The board of directors, made up of six Chinese and five Japanese, was to be headed by a Chinese president with a Japanese assistant. The agreement, however, required consent of the stockholders of the Hanyehping Company and of the Chinese government. In February 1912, Sheng sent out explanations of the plan to his stockholders. He assured them that by this means China could become as strong as Japan, and that he would look out for their interests. On February 14, however, Sun Yat-sen retired in favor of Yuan Shih-k'ai, who was sworn in as provisional president on March 10. The North-South compromise ended all such plans, for Yuan Shih-k'ai was partial to neither Sun nor Sheng, and he preferred to advance national bonds to the Hanyehping Company. And Sheng's stockholders, in any event, rejected the proposals.[40]

Kita Ikki felt that such deals played an important part in the distrust of Japan on the part of the revolutionaries. He claimed that the *shishi* became "running dogs" of Japanese imperialists, and that idealists like Tōyama and Inukai were confused with the selfish, aggressive capitalists of Mitsui. Japanese activity, which should have had as its goal the rebuff of aggressive world capitalism in China, instead substituted Japanese for European exploitation. Kita felt that Sun Yat-sen, who regarded these loans as useful temporary expedients, thereby betrayed his shallow understanding of the issues in China. How could a movement which had its immediate origin in opposition to such abuses have approved these loans? [41]

While there was some basis for this opinion, however, Kita's verdict overlooked the unfortunate fact that such help was precisely what Sun Yat-sen wanted from his Japanese followers. Lacking sources of support among "idealists" of their own stripe, the *shishi* could otherwise have offered little more than encouragement. As far as the possibilities of Japanese help were concerned, the 1911 experience could thus do little more than reinforce the gloomy conclusions which derived from the Amoy incident of 1900.

e. Unwelcome advice

However suspicious the Mitsui loans, it is almost certain that Japanese advice against compromise with Yuan Shih-k'ai incurred far more distrust among the Chinese. Their advice seemed tantamount to advocacy of a partition of China into North and South, for the revolutionaries did not have the armed force with which to overcome Yuan. Uchida Ryōhei wrote a little book entitled the *Reconstruction of China (Shina kaizōron)* in which he urged the Manchus to hand over all of China to the revolutionaries and to return to their native Manchuria. This little booklet was soon translated into Chinese, and it had a considerable circulation. It was followed by other pamphlets which pressed for a "fundamental solution" to the problem.[42]

Inukai advised concentrating more military power to oppose Yuan, and he suggested overtures to the former governor of Szechwan, Ch'en Ch'un-hsuan. The idealistic Sun, however, refused to countenance a deal with a notoriously reactionary Manchu servant.[43]

For a time it was planned to have Sung Chiao-jen go to Tokyo to convince Japanese leaders of the reliable character of the future Chinese government in order to secure early recognition. Although Uchida arranged for Sung's reception in Japan, the trip with its anticipated benefits never took place. Sun Yat-sen was among those who opposed it. He argued that Sung could not go as a minister plenipotentiary, for if he left Nanking with his authority eight-tenths complete, it would diminish to five-tenths by the time he reached Shanghai, and to three-tenths before he reached Nagasaki. The situation was much too fluid to enable an important leader to leave. As confusion grew within the revolutionary camp, distrust of Japan increased. In the midst of these discussions, a telegram came from Japan with the news that the *genrō* were considering the advisability of intervention to put down the revolution. When Kita Ikki showed this to Sung Chiao-jen, the latter's face turned ashen gray; it is not hard to imagine the effect of such news on persons less intimate with the Japanese.[44]

Amid such Japanese fiascoes, the Chinese naturally felt impelled to accept the best agreement they could get with Yuan Shih-k'ai. He still had the only disciplined, well-armed army in China. Sun Yat-sen was inclined to accept his overtures in good faith.[45] The revolutionaries were less united than ever; Huang Hsing had been ready to coöperate with Yuan for some time.[46] It seemed more and more likely that Yuan might get financial help from abroad. Because of all these factors, last minute Japanese efforts to block the compromise proved futile.

When news of the compromise got to Uchida in Tokyo in January 1912, he sent Kuzuu to Nanking to check on the story and to urge Sung Chiao-jen once more to come to Tokyo before making any final arrangements. Kuzuu was amazed to find Tōyama completely uninformed of the compromise plan, and Sung Chiao-jen evasive as to the reasons Tōyama had not been informed. The revolutionaries were obviously not telling their self-appointed advisers very much. Sung would not heed the warnings Kuzuu and Kita gave him of Yuan's probable treachery. He felt that Yuan had greater resources than the revolutionaries. He explained that it did not really matter who headed the new republic. Yuan was old and patriotic, and no longer ambitious. Sung himself was too busy to come to Tokyo.[47]

Tōyama then went to Nanking to remonstrate with Sun Yat-sen. Miyazaki, Kayano, and other Japanese were with him. Incredibly, the China specialists claim that language barriers prevented their success. The interpreter, a Dr. Lin, proved quite inadequate to convey their warnings.[48]

The Shanghai peace talks thus continued in spite of all the Japanese could do, and by February it was evident that Yuan had won. Japan joined with the other powers to back the new government with a loan, and the adventurers in China found themselves thoroughly defeated.

There were many reasons for their failure. Most obvious was the lack of unity among factions in Japan. The contradictions between government actions in North China, statements from Tokyo, and the promises of the adventurers in Nanking would have sufficed to disturb less suspicious men than the Chinese revolutionaries. Yuan Shih-k'ai helped those suspicions by skillfully exploiting the Japanese menace through agents and newspapers. These hinted that Japan and Russia were going to divide Manchuria,[49] they emphasized the predatory nature of the Japanese loans, and they implied that Inukai and Tōyama were directing a vast network of espionage to sabotage Chinese unity.[50] When the Japanese advised that Nanking become the capital of the new republic, the same sources pointed out that Peking would be uncomfortably close to Japanese activities in Manchuria.

Finally, the very enthusiasm of the ubiquitous adventurers in South China lent substance to fears that they were out for more than friendship. No one criticized them more severely than Kita Ikki. Kita decried the concentration of the Japanese effort upon Sun Yat-sen, who represented such a shallow mixture of Western democracy and idealism. Instead of helping the revolutionary movement, the Japanese concentrated on personality. This contributed to distrust of Sun, and when he finally agreed to the compromise with Yuan he erased the work of decades. The *rōnin* were so busy toadying to Sun Yat-sen, the equivalent of the Goddess of Reason of the

French Revolution, that they alienated themselves from the real nationalist movement in China. Thus the adventurers did Japan more harm than good. "They neglected the duties appropriate to a Japan which should lead the development of a backward country, and instead they followed the mob psychology of the revolution." Their obsequiousness knew no bounds. Ike went to Japan to give lectures explaining the revolution. When Sun Yat-sen heard that the lectures were not crediting him with much of a part in the actual events, and expressed discontent with them, Ike rushed back to China to straighten things out. The Japanese were better servants of Sun than the Chinese, and they were more confused than even Sun himself. In fact, Kita concluded, Japanese interference and stupidity in both North and South China did much to frighten the Chinese into the compromise settlement of 1912.[51]

Whatever one's explanation, there can be no question that the aim of the adventurers in helping the revolution and strengthening bonds with the leadership of the new China had failed completely.

4. THE GOVERNMENT POLICY

The conservatives in the Tokyo government were the only ones that contemplated putting down the revolution. Their influence has been seen in each of the previous narratives, and so it can be summarized briefly in chronological sequence.

Saionji himself favored a policy of non-intervention in China, and he withstood pressure from Yamagata to intervene.[52] As disorder increased in the Yangtze area, and as Yuan Shih-k'ai returned to Peking, Ijuin favored helping him in the North. Ijuin did not rule out support for the rebels in the South, but he tended to favor Yuan more and more. Foreign Minister Uchida, who felt Ijuin was too partial, sent a special emissary, Matsui Keishirō, to judge the situation.[53] There was little reason for Japan to support Yuan Shih-k'ai, her long-time adversary. Japan had been well pleased when Yuan was dismissed in 1908, and support for him could not have been justified easily.[54]

But Yamagata Aritomo was very worried about the situation in China. He felt that it was too late to watch and wait, and he pressed for action. In November, Saionji acquiesced reluctantly in a message to Yuan through Ijuin saying that the Japanese government hoped for a constitutional monarchy in China.

Japan was also hampered by the Anglo-Japanese alliance. The *genrō* felt more *rapport* with Tsarist Russia. Tokyo and St. Petersburg agreed to maintain accord on measures in China, and at one stage Japan's policy makers were encouraging Russia to go ahead on a loan to the Peking government without waiting for the Consortium group to organize.[55]

Yamagata thus forced several moves on the government which made it thoroughly suspect abroad. He showed a unique lack of timing and perspective. As early as October, Secretary of State Knox in Washington had received a note from Japan requesting an expression of confidence in Japan's sincerity. This back-handed compliment was duly expressed.[56] American suspicions of Japan seemed confirmed on December 18, when Japan, after an unsuccessful attempt to get English coöperation, sent a note to Washington. This note suggested that since republican government would obviously be disastrous for China, America would surely appreciate Japan's concern in ensuring immediate adoption of the provisional Manchu constitution.[57] This could hardly have had a worse effect. Official Washington and unofficial America had been awaiting the results of the revolution with incredulous but jubilant approbation of the victory of American political institutions in Asia.

It was largely fear of Japanese intervention that prompted the powers, through the British Minister, Jordan, in Peking, to sponsor the Shanghai conferences which led to the coalition government.[58] Foreign suspicions had been further aroused by the reports of the Japanese loans, despite Tokyo's assurance that they were purely unofficial.[59] By February, things seemed so dubious that there were even reports of an offer of alliance the *genrō* had made to Sun Yat-sen.[60] The situation was clearly becoming more and more dangerous. The powers thus used every measure of persuasion to hasten the North-South compromise, and they greeted it with relief when it came.

By February 1912, Japanese policy had suffered a resounding setback. When the revolution broke out five months before, the American Chargé in Tokyo had wired Washington, "Whatever Japan does will be with a view to making herself indispensable to the future Chinese government." [61] Uncertainty as to the eventual makeup of that government had caused a bewildering series of shifts that resulted in suspicion and dislike. Despite all her efforts, Japan had found herself quite helpless in China; instead of providing leadership, each of her groups had done little more than provoke counter-measures. The groups that had first championed the cause of the revolutionary government now found themselves bitterly opposed to the cabinet that took over in Peking because it was headed by Yuan Shih-k'ai. The government, which had opposed the revolution, found itself recognizing and supporting the new regime. The groups that had favored a divided China for Japanese benefits could only mutter dark threats about future disorder in China. Their fears were realized very soon. In the words of the expansionists, Japan had disgraced herself by a course which was first uncertain, then imitative, and always insincere. Fortunately for their hopes, Yuan Shih-k'ai proved to be equally insincere.

7

During the year which followed the formal inauguration of the Chinese Republic, trends toward cynicism which were visible on both sides of the Sino-Japanese friendship in 1912 became more marked. The way was prepared for the disillusioned application of *realpolitik* which Japan and Sun Yat-sen attempted in the Twenty-one Demands of 1915. The Japanese government grew increasingly dissatisfied with the regime of Yuan Shih-k'ai, and it was more and more inclined to resort to subversion or force to unseat it. Sun Yat-sen suffered a calamitous fall from presidential eminence to ignominious exile. When the rest of the world seemed inclined to accept his fate, he was more willing to sacrifice a few points for Japanese support. His contacts in Japan were more often with men of affairs than formerly, and the *rōnin* sank to the status of messengers for their betters.

In Japan, popular displeasure with the government policy which had brought no better result than the regime of Yuan Shih-k'ai grew steadily. Japan had clearly lost ground in China. In the international financial consortium to which she had committed herself, her inferior capital holdings could never give her more than an equal, and more likely a secondary, role. Yuan's hostility to Japan was well known, and it became more evident. Then, when the consortium powers decided on free and equal competition in industrial loans to China, Japan's relative position seemed likely to become even poorer. In this setting, officials and industrialists in Tokyo were more willing to work together with army circles for a special position in China. At the same time, they saw new advantages in promises and agreements with Sun Yat-sen. Japan's participation in the international measures thus became more and more perfunctory in nature.

Sun Yat-sen's shift to opportunism and cynicism was not surprising. In quick succession he had fallen from president, to adviser of the new regime, to traveling functionary, and, finally, to harried exile. He was less able to gather support. The issue of nationalism around which Chinese had united had died with the Manchus. The foreign powers were openly supporting Yuan Shih-k'ai, and the Chinese business men seemed content to follow their lead. Sun was naturally less hopeful, and sooner inclined to deals of practical politics which might regain power for him. As he saw the efforts of a lifetime come to naught, Sun was more convinced of the necessity for his own leadership in China, and he was more willing to make promises to possible allies.

The Japanese friends of the old days played a considerably less important role. When Sun was a social lion in Tokyo, and when he was dealing with Japanese industrialists, their services were little needed. They tended to become messengers, carrying word from the Tokyo center to the China branches of a new revolutionary organization, hopefully preparing for a revolt that might unseat Yuan Shih-k'ai.

1. DISSATISFACTION IN JAPAN

The Japanese who had advocated greater aid to the Nanking provisional government were not slow to denounce their government's adherence to the international backing for the North-South compromise. Inukai led the attack on the government in the Diet, and his speeches in secret sessions were so bitter that the Diet was recessed to avoid further trouble.[1] Inukai urged the government not to regard the present revolution as having settled China's fate; he asserted that China had experienced only a preliminary disturbance. The dissatisfaction Inukai's complaints showed was far more prevalent than the specious optimism of more conservative men like Ōkuma. Ōkuma expressed high pleasure with the new Chinese government; he felt that it fitted China's needs perfectly.[2]

In spite of opposition attacks, the Saionji cabinet lasted until the end of 1912. Even then, its fall was not due to the wrath of the party men but to the opposition of the militarists who were unable to procure Saionji's approval for larger budgets and more divisions.[3]

Six months earlier, the death of the Meiji Emperor had brought home to all the fact that the old leadership was gone. The *Asahi* carried a long interview with Tōyama under the title, "You must commit spiritual *hara-kiri*" (*Seishinteki ni junshi seyo*), in which Tōyama called for close emperor-subject relationships and stressed the poisonous nature of official and bureaucratic rule.[4] The sense of renewed dedication and of protest against the departures from tradition was dramatically expressed by the suicides of General Nogi and his wife. The super patriots, as usual, had their day as well. Before long, Nogi Clubs were formed among reserve officers, and the general's memory was enshrined among enthusiasts.

These warnings seemed well taken when Katsura, after the fall of the Saionji Cabinet, reversed his announced intentions of leaving politics for the office of Lord Privy Seal, and, by the use of Imperial Rescripts from the new Taishō Emperor, secured his own appointment as premier for the third time. Party politicians and patriots combined to levy a furious assault against Katsura as representative of the clan oligarchy, militarism, and insincerity. Katsura tried to organize his own political party, but the opposition was far too strong for him. He resigned on February 11, 1913, amid scenes of wild disorder and rioting in the capital.[5]

Katsura was replaced by Admiral Yamamoto Gombei, the Satsuma veteran who, as navy minister, had counseled the abortive invasion of Amoy in 1900. The *Kokumintō,* led by Inukai and Ozaki, were still violently opposed to this government, and it faced persistent attacks in the lower house. The cabinet was never popular, and it fell early in 1914 when exposures of far-reaching scandals in navy contracts enabled all the opposition groups to concentrate on its removal.[6]

In short, the years following the Chinese Revolution saw turbulence and confusion in Japanese politics. A change of Emperors, several cabinet changes, widespread public indignation and disorder, and increasing discontent among politicians made a popular China policy virtually impossible.

Critics of the government's policy found abundant material for abuse in the results of the "coöperative" China policy. The Five Power Consortium, of which Japan was a member, cast its lot with the regime of Yuan Shih-k'ai in the spring of 1912. In May 1913,

Yuan received over a million (Hong Kong) dollars, the first installment of a Reorganization Loan. For the first time, he was now able to act with some freedom. Almost immediately his government became less tolerant of dissent and opposition. The adherents of Sun Yat-sen and Sung Chiao-jen were soon fighting an uphill battle.[7] Tokyo's policy had thus contributed directly to a decrease of influence for Japan in China; the Reorganization Loan encouraged the repression which resulted in revolution.

2. DISILLUSION IN CHINA

Thanks to Yuan's new self-confidence and financial strength, the optimism that had been held for the youthful republic in China was rudely shattered. Inukai's fears for the coalition government proved well founded as difficulties arose between Yuan Shih-k'ai and the group led by Sung Chiao-jen.

While Sun Yat-sen went on tour, giving his program for the new China to enthusiastic audiences, Sung Chiao-jen and his men had organized a new party, the Kuomintang, in August 1912. This was designed to be the real power in the government under a constitution that would severely limit the president's power. Soon a distinct cleavage was evident between the Nanking group with its constitutional ideals and the Peking faction of Yuan.[8] Yuan and his men were used to autocratic despotism as they had wielded it, and they reacted to opposition with bribery, blackmail, and assassination.

In August 1912, Sun Yat-sen went to Peking for talks with Yuan Shih-k'ai. Their discussions seem to have been conducted with considerable cordiality, and the upshot of the meeting was the appointment of Sun as head of railway development for all of China. Sun received a liberal allowance to use for the purpose of attracting foreign investment capital.[9]

As has been mentioned, Yuan received foreign financial aid in the spring of 1913. The terms of the loan were anything but generous, however, and the Kuomintang group of Sung Chiao-jen, Huang Hsing, and Sun Yat-sen opposed the loan terms and the manner of its negotiation by Yuan bitterly. They were thus not long in following the earlier example of their Japanese allies in condemning the new financial structure.[10]

Among the republicans, dissatisfaction and disillusionment led to opposition. The movement was one which developed gradually, however, and it does not seem to have received the united consideration of the former revolutionary leaders. There were only indications and rumors which were made into reality by the arbitrary action and despotic retribution of Yuan Shih-k'ai. There is no question but that the obvious discontent among Sun's friends in Japan worked with this feeling in China, and raised Chinese hopes for joint action. One of the central events in the "Second Revolution" of July 1913 was Sun Yat-sen's visit to Japan in the spring of that same year.

3. Sun's Reception in Japan

Ostensibly, Sun's purposes in coming to Japan were to offer thanks for Japanese help in the revolution and to inspect the railroad system in his new capacity. Sun had obtained a considerable body of knowledge about Japanese railroads during previous visits, however, and it is not surprising that other purposes loomed larger.

The timing of Sun's trip showed the influence of dissenting groups within Japan. In December 1912, Japanese papers had announced that Sun was about to sail for Japan. It was said that he had sent Miyazaki on ahead to get a sampling of public opinion. Then, suddenly, the papers announced that Sun would be unable to come because of ill health. It was hinted that he had insisted on official status and an audience with the Emperor, and that when this was refused he had decided not to come.[11] Akiyama Teisuke's account of all this, however, is quite different. Late in 1912, he met Katsura, who told him that the army, the cabinet, Premier Saionji, and the *genrō* were all opposed to a formal greeting for the revolutionist about to visit them. Katsura was worried about the harm this might do to future Sino-Japanese relations, and he persuaded Akiyama to go to Shanghai to get Sun to delay his trip. Akiyama had a difficult time dissuading Sun, who professed indifference to official honors, and said that he merely wanted another visit with old friends and a look at Mt. Fuji. Akiyama finally persuaded Sun to delay his trip, however, and Sun pleaded illness as excuse for the change in plans.[12]

Sun landed at Nagasaki on February 13, 1913, and he stayed until March 22. Although Katsura had resigned his post three days before Sun's arrival, the succeeding Yamamoto cabinet did not take over until the twentieth, and so Sun was able to have several talks with the premier.[13]

According to Akiyama, Sun's talks with Katsura were devoted to planning future Sino-Japanese policy. Sun was still optimistic about the situation in China. Several anti-Japanese boycotts had broken out in South China, and Sun promised Katsura he would do all he could to stop them.[14]

To judge from the account given by Sun's interpreter, Tai T'ien-ch'ou, however, the talks took a rather different turn.[15] Katsura, we are told, had decided on a fundamental change in Japanese policy to coincide with the apparent betrayal of the revolution by Yuan which had disillusioned Sun. He felt that Japan should give up the Anglo-Japanese Alliance and work for the elimination of England in the Far East in order to free China from British imperialism, just as Japan earlier had eliminated the Russian menace. This done, Japan could work on the liberation of colonial peoples in Southeast Asia and India, leaving continental development for her new and strong ally, China. Thus all of Asia would be freed from white oppression, and a new and brighter day would dawn in the Orient. Sun responded enthusiastically to these suggestions. His war-time writings show that his own ideas at the time were very much along these lines.[16]

Throughout Japan, Sun's arrival was the occasion for a tremendous outburst of popular enthusiasm. His triumphant progress through the country was in startling contrast to his previous furtive movements as the leader of a secret revolutionary movement. Nevertheless, there was much to suggest that his business was not seriously different from what it had been.

At the almost daily dinners and receptions held for Sun, the honored guests were always Sun's old companions, along with politicians like Inukai and Ōkuma, or leading businessmen and industrialists such as Shibusawa, Iwasaki, and Ōkura. Sun's visit brought a great deal of mutual congratulation; at a dinner given by Ōkuma, for instance, he attributed the success of the revolution in large part to students of Ōkuma's Waseda University.[17] With Miya-zaki, Professor Terao, and others, he called on army heads; General Hasegawa, chief of the General Staff, General Kigoshi, minister of war, and General Kawashima, director of ordnance.[18] He also visited the graves of Prince Konoe and General Kodama.[19]

In the speeches at the many gatherings he was asked to address, Sun stressed the pan-Asian theme that his Japanese backers were so glad to hear. "If there were Europeans here tonight," he would begin, "they would not be able to tell the Chinese from the Japanese. Japan is my second home, and I regard this as a family reunion." Japan's help was emphasized: "I undertook the work of revolution relying upon the strong military force and faith of Japan, which I knew would prevent the European powers and America from dividing the melon among themselves." Sun pointed out that Tur-key's experience had been unfortunate because Turkey lacked a strong and unselfish neighbor like Japan. Japan and China should coöperate closely together, thus securing forever Asia for the Asians against European and American imperialism. "The patriots of your country have led and taught me, and I deem Japan my second fatherland and your statesmen my mentors. China awaits your saving help."[20]

In Kyoto, Sun expressed regret that China had extended to other countries the privileges which had been granted to Japan. Sun's hearers must have been well pleased with his assertion that only Japan was entitled to a special position in China.

In Osaka, Sun pointed out that both the Chinese and Japanese civilizations were founded upon the Confucian ideals of brother-hood, peace, and love. Therefore, although Japan had strengthened her army and navy, this should not worry China, since it had been done to counter European and American imperialism. Japan and China should coöperate to maintain peace in the Orient so that it would not be affected by this "imperialism, which may be called the barbarous civilization of Europe and America. Let Asia be governed by Asiatics."[21]

Just before Sun left for China from Kyushu, he visited the Fukuoka home of the *Genyōsha*. It was there that he received news that the political situation in China had taken a decided turn for the worse.[22] On March 20, an assassin hired by Yuan Shih-k'ai had killed Sung Chiao-jen as he was about to board an express for Peking, where he was slated to become premier of the new cabinet. This murder, and the sensational trial which followed it, played an important role in the increasingly acrimonious dispute between Sun's old friends and Yuan Shih-k'ai. Sun Yat-sen's hosts of the *Genyōsha* on that March day were not likely to counsel moderation or caution in responding to such tyranny in China. Surely, by the time Sun returned to a tremendous welcome in Shanghai, the stage was well set for revolt.

The business magnates who entertained Sun Yat-sen were anxious to enlarge and strengthen Japan's interests in China. The contracts which were negotiated for the loans to Sun's provisional government at Nanking had indicated that Sun would have no objection to greater Japanese holdings in China, and such proved to be the case. On February 24, a series of meetings were begun in the Tokyo headquarters of Mitsui Bussan Kaisha for the formation of a new Sino-Japanese firm which was to use Japanese capital in the development of China's raw materials. Sun's interpreter, Tai T'ien-ch'ou, served at these meetings as he had in the interview with Katsura. By June, announcements were forthcoming of the formation of a China Industrial Company (*Chūgoku Kōgyō Kabushishi Kaisha*). Sun Yat-sen was president, Viscount Kurachi, former vice-minister of Foreign Affairs, was vice-president, and the capital was to be provided by the great firms of Mitsui, Mitsubishi, Yasuda, and Ōkura.[23]

It is clear that the visit renewed Sun's bonds with Japanese leaders. In a sense, however, it was a different friendship, for on the whole there were different Japanese representatives. The adventurers and plotters had been replaced by bureaucrats, militarists, and leading industrialists. Inukai was no longer a lieutenant of Ōkuma's, but a party leader. Miyazaki was mentioned less and less. Tōyama, too, was no longer needed to protect and guard the foreign guest, for Sun's was a state visit; private railway trains and the best suites were reserved for him. Sun himself had changed from a youthful, idealistic enthusiast to a man whose signature on a contract as promoter lent it new worth and solidity. It is safe to say that there was less sincerity in the Japanese effusions of friendship than before, and that Sun Yat-sen no longer represented a movement and a party as clearly as he had in previous years.

Upon his return to China, Sun sent telegrams to the Peking government and the various provincial governors telling them of Japanese good will and urging coöperation for prosperity and peace. A speaking tour through China was announced in which Sun was to spread the news that Japan was a friendly, valuable commercial and, possibly, political ally. As Sun told the press, "I have visited Japan for the purpose of ascertaining what foundations these suspicions (of Japanese motives) have, and to my satisfaction I have realized that the protestations of friendly sentiments of Japan are not superficial, but come from the bottom of their hearts." "What Japan wants is not territory in China, but increased trade, and the Japanese are following a peaceful policy — the only means by which they can attain their object." [24]

4. JAPAN AND SUN'S "SECOND REVOLUTION"

Sun Yat-sen had now obtained the support of all but the highest government circles in Japan. As the dissatisfaction of the Kuomintang circles in China grew, Sun's friends in Japan urged their government to withdraw its support of the odious government of Yuan Shih-k'ai. The adventurers, of course, were the first and most vehement to express their feeling. Kita Ikki, who had plotted to avenge the death of Sung Chiao-jen, was ordered to leave Shanghai by the Japanese consul. His *Shina kakumei gaishi* was written upon his return and reflected his extreme disgust with the government policy.[25]

In a sense, Sun Yat-sen set the pace for Japanese efforts, for one of his first tasks upon his return to China was to warn the foreign representatives of the Shanghai-Hongkong Bank that if the Five Power Consortium loan was forced through without parliamentary approval, the provinces south of the Yangtze would almost certainly revolt.[26]

But even before Sun's visit, leading Japanese had begun to express their doubts about the new Chinese government.[27] On May 15, 1913, the *Chronicle* reported that Viscount Shibusawa and other businessmen had called on Premier Yamamoto and asked him not to enter the Consortium. It was said that they had done so at the request of Sun Yat-sen. The government, however, ignored their request.[28]

In June, Ozaki Yukio spoke at a rally. He said that he had approached Foreign Minister Makino, while Inukai had seen Yamamoto, to urge a change in policy. Ozaki argued that since seventy per cent of Japanese trade was with South China it was foolish not to be pro-South politically. In no case should support be given to Yuan. Inukai, who followed Ozaki on the rostrum, reported gloomily on his interview with Yamamoto. He had found the premier partial to Yuan Shih-k'ai, as could be expected of a conservative Satsuma oligarch. Unfortunately, he said, foreign policy was not sufficiently affected by cabinet changes. Inukai assured his hearers that his friendships with South Chinese leaders did not influence his views, but he stated as his opinion that Yuan's brand of centralization was hopeless for China, since it was at variance with her political tradition.[29]

A week later Inukai, Ozaki, Tōyama, and Nakano, head of the Tokyo Chamber of Commerce, announced the formation of the *Tai Shina Mondai Dōshikai,* or League of Those Agreed on the China Problem. They called for neutrality, stricter controls over the five-power loan, and no further payments of that loan until China had solved her domestic problems. Inukai probably betrayed his Mitsubishi leanings in a simultaneous statement denouncing the government for its foolishness in failing to insist on security for the loan in the form of the China Merchants Steamship Navigation Company. He announced that the government's imitative policy was doomed to failure.[30]

Yuan Shih-k'ai vainly tried to avert the increasing hostility of Japan. He corresponded occasionally with Ōkuma, who suggested a loose federalism for China. Ōkuma also warned that unless order was restored Japan might have to move into Manchuria.[31] In July 1913, Yuan sent two representatives, Sun Pao-ch'i and Li Sheng-to, to Japan. The Chinese press interpreted their mission to mean a promised extension of the Liaotung lease to Japan in an attempt to counteract Kuomintang propaganda. Ijuin, in Peking, was said to have suggested the move to Yuan as a means of turning the tide of (Inukai's) *Kokumintō* opinion.[32] Another source reported that the two envoys were trying to stop Kuomintang propaganda, secure recognition of China, and promise Japan special privileges.[33]

The Yamamoto government was finally forced to make concessions to the critics of its China policy. In July 1913, Ijuin was replaced by Yamaza Enjirō. Yamaza, a Fukuoka man, was a member of the *Genyōsha* and a friend of Sun Yat-sen, and the *shishi* rightly hailed him as one of their own. Although he was restrained by Foreign Minister Makino, he did stop the regular conferences with the British Minister, Jordan — meetings which had been denounced as proof of the imitative policy personified by Ijuin. Yamaza regarded Yuan Shih-k'ai as a menace to Japan, and he wrote home to the *shishi* urging them to mobilize public opinion by word and deed against the weak government policy.[34] He himself provided part of the excuse for a different policy; his train was stoned on the way to Peking, and there was no honor guard there to meet him. These were obviously insults to his country.[35]

While his supporters in Japan were securing their first concessions from Yamamoto, Sun Yat-sen seized upon the dismissal of several provincial governors by Yuan Shih-k'ai to issue a manifesto ordering the president to resign. He promised to use his influence to avoid rebellion if Yuan would step aside. When this manifesto brought no result, a "punitive expedition" against the president was announced. Huang Hsing took command of the armies at Nanking, and the provinces of Kiangsu, Kiangsi, Anhui, and Kwangtung declared their independence of Peking.

Yuan Shih-k'ai, secure in financial backing from abroad, was able to crush the revolt quickly. The Chinese people showed remarkably little enthusiasm for the revolution. The best anti-Manchu issue, that of nationalism, could no longer be used. The business classes were content with Yuan's "law and order." Unquestionably, however, the foreign financial backing was Yuan's greatest boon. The rebellion centered in the Yangtze area, in which water communications were vital. When the Navy showed sympathy for the rebels, the Consortium Powers made payments available for the Navy, thereby guaranteeing its loyalty.[36] Later, when the Northern troops

were slowed down in Kiangsu and Kiangsi, the Consortium provided large sums to buy off Southern troops. Yuan's success was
thus quite certain. Fighting began on July 12, and by July 25 the
rebel cause was doomed.[37]

Within Japan, public opinion was strongly favorable to the rebels.
The press reported that numerous Japanese were with the Southern
forces, and Japanese officers were said to be in command at several
strategic points. These stories seemed to have some basis when the
government ordered censorship of all news from China relating to
delivery of arms and military supplies. As before, Chinese students
in Japan marched to the ports to join the revolutionary forces. At
Shanghai, the Japanese admiral who was Senior International Officer
of the foreign fleets refused to assist the volunteer force which had
occupied Chapei in order to keep Chen Chi-mei's troops from
occupying that spot. Highly placed Japanese military and naval
leaders encouraged their colleagues to provide weapons to the
revolutionaries.[38] Yet, while such stories were exploited by German
propaganda sources and by Yuan's officials, it is doubtful that the
direct help given the rebels by Japan was as important as the in-
direct aid which Japan furnished Yuan through the Consortium.
The monthly *Chūō Kōron* dismissed the issue by remarking that
if Japan had helped the revolutionaries they would have fared quite
differently.[39] Indeed, the fighting ended so quickly that there was
hardly time to organize help on any adequate scale.

There was, however, an abortive project which found Sun's recent
partners in industrial and financial enterprises working on a plan
for an outright territorial grant. Mori Kaku, Mitsui executive and
official of the new China Industrial Company, had been conspicuous
in plans for the aid of Sun ever since the murder of Sung Chiao-jen.
His first contribution took the form of assistance in the procurement
of a Japanese chemist who set up a laboratory in Peking. The goal
of this individual's research was the poisoning of Yuan Shih-k'ai.[40]
Then, when the revolution broke out, Mori was quick to devise a
means which should profit both Japan and Sun Yat-sen. He wired
from Tokyo to Nanking suggesting that Sun be offered twenty
million yen and equipment for two divisions in return for the
cession of Manchuria. The bearers of this message were Yamada

Junsaburō, the minor Mitsui official who had helped Sun get his loan in 1911, and Miyazaki. The two found Sun with Hu Han-min. Sun, after asking for thirty minutes to consider the proposition, discussed it with Huang Hsing in an adjoining room. Upon his return he indicated his agreement, and urged speed in arranging the details. Mori now wired that a warship would be sent for Sun Yat-sen; he could arrange the matter in personal talks with Katsura Tarō. Sun pleaded inability to leave China, however, and designated Huang Hsing as his alternate. This substitution proved acceptable to Tokyo, and Yamada waited patiently for the rendezvous with the warship. The ship never came. Soon the revolution had failed, and the revolutionaries who narrowly missed returning to Japan under imperial auspices were forced to flee there as refugees. The project seems to have been a product of enthusiasm shared by Katsura and Mori. It was balked by the opposition of the Yamamoto Cabinet, especially on the part of Foreign Minister Makino. Of the *genrō,* Inoue Kaoru, Mitsui adviser, apparently saw some merit in the proposed deal. Yamagata Aritomo, however, dismissed the enterprise with the observation that there was little point in paying so high a price for an area in which Japanese control was already adequate.[41]

Sun Yat-sen and Huang Hsing fled to Japan early in August. By now the Tokyo government was so determined to back a winner that it seemed doubtful that Sun would be allowed to land. Permission for him to do so was secured by Inukai and Tōyama after strenuous efforts. The press supported them enthusiastically. For a time, Tōyama sheltered Sun in his Tokyo house.[42]

The contrast with Sun's previous visit could not escape the attention of observers. Six months before, he had received a tremendous popular welcome and had been honored by all strata of Japanese officialdom and society. This time his entry had been made possible only by an extended debate. The mournful *shishi* who came to greet Sun reflected somberly on the transitory nature of life. Some, however, felt that Sun's flight had come rather too soon to be heroic; Nanking was still resisting stoutly, and it did not fall until September first.[43]

Those who had favored open support for Sun Yat-sen regarded

Photograph taken on the occasion of a visit by Sun Yat-sen to the graveyard of the *Genyōsha* adventurers in Fukuoka during Sun's visit to Japan in 1913. Principal figures, left to right, are Miyazaki Torazō (bearded), Fujii Tanetarō, Sun Yat-sen, Ho T'ienchiung, and (with top-hat) Tai T'ien-ch'ou (Tai Chi-t'ao).

the whole train of events as proof of their arguments as to the bankruptcy of Japanese policy. While paying lip service to the principle of neutrality and international financial aid to the official government of China, Japan had drifted into a situation in which she was completely out of the political picture in China and thoroughly distrusted abroad. To be sure, the industrialists who had signed with Sun Yat-sen were able to shift their contracts and loans to a new *Chū-Nichi Jitsugyō Kaisha* which differed from its predecessor chiefly in the political affiliations of the Chinese personnel represented among its executives.[44] Yet, a firm of this sort could hardly function under a Yuan Shih-k'ai as it might have under a Sun Yat-sen. Most groups in Japan were thus prepared to agree that the government had disregarded its true interests. Japanese businessmen and propagandists came to interpret "exclusion" from the Chinese market more and more liberally; it became increasingly apparent that the best alternative to such exclusion was force or the threat of force. Provocations for such threats were not long wanting.

5. JAPAN'S POSITIVE POLICY

In the course of suppressing the rebellion, Yuan's troops committed several atrocities against Japanese nationals which were speedily exploited by the super-patriots and adventurers who desired a change in policy. In the first of these, at Kunchow, Shantung, a Japanese army captain was assaulted. In Hankow, on August 11, a second lieutenant was beaten. And when Chang Hsün occupied Nanking in September the city was given over to complete chaos, in the course of which three Japanese shopkeepers or peddlers were killed.[45]

This came at a very bad time for Admiral Yamamoto's government. In California, the state legislature had just passed discriminatory measures against Japanese, once again inflaming resentment against America in Japan. And the dissatisfaction with the China policy had grown steadily throughout the summer. In July, Tōyama, Inukai, and their friends had organized several leagues to try to change that policy. Their groups included such venerable East Asia agitators as Ōi Kentarō. When the situation became more unfavorable in China, many felt that Japan should take stronger steps in

Manchuria and Mongolia. Pamphlets were printed and lecture tours were sponsored to make more people aware of the crisis which Japan's policy had produced. Then, just as these efforts were reaching their peak, Chang Hsün's soldiers provided proof that caution and weakness could reap only scorn and contempt.

With the *Taishi Rengōkai* (United League for the China Question) as core, a huge mass meeting was held in Hibiya Park in Tokyo early in September. After hearing several inflammatory speeches, the gathering adopted a strongly worded petition condemning the government's policy. The leaders then took this to the government officials. Although the meeting broke up at noon, the crowd continued to grow. Fervor mounted; even women made speeches. The crowd gradually headed for the Foreign Office building, and their self-appointed leaders announced that they would not leave until they had heard from Foreign Minister Makino. Police were helpless to disperse the crowd, and only nightfall prevented a serious outbreak.[46]

When the government showed unexpected strength by arresting several of the leading rowdies, the head of the Foreign Office Political Affairs Bureau, Abe Mintarō, was murdered in a spectacular gesture of protest by a young man who then seated himself upon a map of China and committed *hara-kiri* so skillfully that his blood was shed on Manchuria and Mongolia.[47] Abe was not so much a leader in policy-making bodies as a symbol of the career administrative officer whose reactions to national insults had not been sufficiently aggressive. Moreover, his bureau controlled the network of agents who followed the revolutionaries so faithfully. His death, coupled with the continued unrest and disturbance in Tokyo, was the dramatic gesture necessary to change the government policy.[48] The Japanese press, although it deplored Abe's death, pointed out that if the China policy were changed he would not have died in vain. It was probable that any remaining doubts regarding the justifiability of the deed were dismissed by the telegram of condolence which Yuan Shih-k'ai, who had known Abe years before, sent to his family in Japan.[49]

Forced to action by popular demand, Makino handed Yuan's government a stern ultimatum which demanded financial compensation for the Nanking outrage and apologies by the troops concerned. The Chinese yielded on all points, and Chang Hsün's troops dutifully lined up in front of the Japanese consulate in Nanking while the Japanese national anthem was played. More important was a secret treaty secured by Yamaza which granted Japan rights to build five railroad lines in Manchuria and Mongolia. Soon after, Japan joined with the European powers in recognizing the Chinese Republic. Her concessions, however, satisfied only the smallest part of the desires of the Japanese who had hoped for increased trade privileges in South China as well as control of Manchuria.

The government's policy problems were far from solved. The Consortium Powers were usually unable to agree on any measures of importance. When Yuan Shih-k'ai expressed the desire for another loan, it was suggested that Manchurian revenues be pledged as security. This proved equally distasteful to Japan and to Russia, and their vigorous objections stalled that project. Next, the Powers decided to separate loans for industrial development from the Consortium monopoly, in order to allow for international competition in such matters. Once again Japan found herself in a poor position, for she was still a creditor nation, and could not compete on equal terms with the capitalist giants of the West.[50]

The World War solved most of these problems for Japan. For a time, she found herself free from European competition, able to develop industries and accumulate capital in singularly favorable circumstances. These temporary advantages she then tried to perpetuate through the series of political concessions known as the Twenty-one Demands.

But some remained convinced that concessions of special privileges would be more valuable if they were granted by a willing ally instead of being wrested from Yuan Shih-k'ai. From the sources available, we can see such groups resuming the discussions for commercial benefits that had begun during Sun's visit in the spring of 1913.

6. REVOLUTIONARIES AND FINANCIERS

In Tokyo, Sun Yat-sen was less able to select his backers and to exercise his judgment of personnel than he had been in earlier years.

By and large, his sources of support had dwindled until the few Japanese who now harbored him were completely essential to him. The overseas Chinese who had been paying toward the revolution for so long were considerably less hopeful and generous than they had been. Many of them sided with groups of Kuomintang members in China who felt that the July Revolution had been foolhardy and unjustifiable.[51] With less money at his disposal, Sun traveled less; he did not make a single trip to Southeast Asia for several years. Even the Tokyo government had granted him shelter with considerable reluctance. Perhaps as part of the bargain whereby he was allowed entry into Japan, Sun seldom left the lodging which Tōyama Mitsuru provided for him. To be sure, he was somewhat less subject to the police as long as he was under Tōyama's care. But he was also a good deal less independent.

The daily reports of the secret agents of the Foreign Office make it clear that Sun was no longer in undisputed control of the revolutionary movement. The agents report loud arguments with even so faithful a follower as Hu Han-min.[52] For months at a time Sun Yat-sen and Huang Hsing do not see each other. Occasionally, Miyazaki and Kayano, faithful couriers, visit Sun one day, and Huang the next. But even they tend to see more of Huang than they do of Sun Yat-sen.[53] The younger and newer group of revolutionary stalwarts see Sun constantly. Tai T'ien-ch'ou, the personal secretary who speaks Japanese fluently, is either with Sun or carrying messages for him. Chiang Kai-shek begins to figure in the police reports.[54] Ch'en Chi-mei maintains an unquestioning loyalty to Sun.[55]

Aside from the visits from Miyazaki and Kayano, most of Sun's Japanese visitors were more interested in business concessions than they were in republican government. Within a week of Sun's arrival in Japan, a Mr. Mikami, "of the well-known trading firm with South China," called on Sun.[56] Ōi Kentarō, whose early radicalism and Pan-Asianism seems to have mellowed into a judicious interest in Japanese trade, visited Sun in December. Ōi asked Sun's help in starting industries in China under the auspices of the *Nikka Jitsugyō Kyōkai* (Japan-China Business Association) and was told by Sun that his help would have to be confined to providing introductions to some Shanghai industrialists.[57] Relations with Yasukawa Keii-chirō, Tōyama's Fukuoka mine operator and patron, continued close.[58]

For a time it seemed possible that the next revolutionary outbreak would take place in North China, and the revolutionaries sent frequent emissaries to Dairen.[59] In Manchuria, Japanese interests were of course a good deal more important than Chinese republicanism. In fact, one of Sun's couriers here was a Yamada Junsaburō, now identified as an official of the South Manchurian Railway Company to whom all doors in Kwantung were open.[60] Activities in Shantung were directed from Dairen.

In February, the *Gaimushō* agents appended a diagramatic chain of command for the revolutionary organization. From Sun's headquarters in Tokyo the line led to nine chief lieutenants who delegated funds and directed activities. Tai T'ien-ch'ou, Ch'en Chi-mei, Ho Hai-ming and their colleagues were joined on that roster by Yamada, Tōyama, Professor Terao, and Miyazaki Tamizō.[61] The organization did not extend to Southeast Asia. The Japanese representation had never been stronger, but it is significant that the early Japanese allies were on the whole conspicuous by their absence from positions of authority.

The Japanese government's liberality to political refugees improved after grudging concessions to Sun Yat-sen in August. By September the treaty-port papers were aghast at the discovery that Japanese steamers were granting asylum to conspirators at Kiukiang on the Yangtze.[62] The next month Ike Kyōkichi explained to one agent that the sensible policy for Japan would be to help the revolutionaries quietly without letting the press get word of it. That way the official correctness could be maintained without injuring the revolutionary cause.[63] Shortly thereafter the Japanese treatment of Ho Hai-ming, a "notorious conspirator" who was safely in Nagasaki before the Japanese authorities in Shanghai began promising to turn him over to Chinese police if he were found in Shanghai, left little to be desired along the lines Ike had suggested.[64]

In January 1914, the Japanese Consulate in Shanghai forwarded to Tokyo a series of letters which Yuan Shih-k'ai had submitted to the foreign powers in a vain attempt to secure a more effective policy toward revolutionary "terrorists." One of the letters, by Ch'en Chi-mei, read in part

Of late the country has been full of Northern and Southern spies, and we should be careful to keep our actions secret. All arms and correspondence are being kept in the hands of Japanese firms. The members of our party at Shanghai have now decided that one half of them should go to a conference at Nagasaki, and should unite with Japanese in finding funds and purchasing weapons; Formosa to be used as a base, and operations to begin from Chekiang and Fukien.[65]

The worried officials in China reported that the revolutionaries were apparently preparing to burn Japanese buildings while dressed in the uniform of Yuan's troops, thereby expecting to give the Japanese an excuse for intervening against Peking.[66]

Early in 1914, the Foreign Office agents felt that a new revolt was near. Some reported that Sun Yat-sen had conferred with Tōyama on plans for assassinating Yuan Shih-k'ai.[67] Tai T'ien-ch'ou and Ch'en Chi-mei made frequent trips to Dairen and Shanghai. The Royalist Party at Dairen, still led by Kawashima and Prince Su, was also the subject of numerous reports. Apparently a joint strike might remove Yuan's shaky centralization in favor of a Manchu state to the North and a republic to the South.

As spring continued a steady crescendo of revolutionary activity was clear. Anxious to keep up with developments, the agents frequently compiled charts giving the whereabouts and activities of the leading revolutionaries. But in August, 1914, a discouraged Ike Kyōkichi told friends that plans for a third revolution had failed completely. He blamed the failure on several factors. Too much had been expected from Japanese help, and the participants had talked too much to reporters.[68]

Sun Yat-sen was thus as far from power as he had ever been. His desperate need for support was to result in some extremely ill-advised bids for full Japanese support during the negotiations for the Twenty-one Demands. But none of his offers to Japanese firms was stranger than a scheme he developed with an admirer in San Francisco, a Mr. Dietrick of the Palace Hotel, on the eve of the Demands. Sun sent Dietrick papers granting him powers of attorney to organize a "department store trust."

The most important of all is to look for expert organizers and managers of department stores, for I want to put up a system of such stores all over the country. This will follow the step of the Revolutionary Army. At such time goods can be gotten very easily by the Government, in form of taxation, contribution and exchange for other goods. The people will be only too glad to dispose of their over-productions or stagnant goods. So we can run a government without asking the people for money. This will be a great blessing to all the people.[69]

Certainly none of Sun's Japanese friends ever received more sweeping grants:

If, owing to the disturbed financial conditions, you find it inconvenient to secure said sum, then you will use your own judgment as to disposal of districts to various persons and for such sums as may be deemed prudent and fair. For example, say the district around Hankow or Nanking or Shanghai, etc. In case of cash transaction you will have the money deposited in a bank in my name.[70]

In case you cannot find such a party willing to undertake this department at once, you are authorized to close up a deal with said party to undertake work in such industrial lines as Mining, Iron and Steel Works, Transportation, etc. The scope of the powers sent you are large, but I believe in your tact, wisdom and good judgment. . .[71]

Actually Sun's main purpose was to obtain money with which to buy off the troops of the "arch murderer," Yuan, and the scheme collapsed quickly as the letters from Tokyo began dunning Dietrick for advance payments beginning with ten million dollars and becoming so low as to request, "Can you do anything to get from a few hundred thousand to half a million?" By the time Sun ended a letter with a scolding, "Now I hope that you will do *your best*," the partnership was wearing thin; it collapsed when Sun sent an agent to retrieve the powers of attorney.[72]

As this desperate scheme suggests, Sun Yat-sen was not even confident of Japanese support any more. The Japanese were preparing to take matters into their own hands. Not that they had lost interest in their Chinese guests. Professor Terao opened a new law school for Chinese students in Tokyo which included such noted scholars as Yoshino Sakuzō and Minobe Tatsukichi.[73] But activities of this sort could offer little immediate profit. They certainly offered no outlet for the restless and discontent. Great opportunities were at hand, and something still had to be done about Yuan Shih-k'ai.

8

The Twenty-one Demands of 1915 marked the last decisive step by Japan in her attempt to dominate China until the Manchurian Incident of 1931. Since 1911, Japan had been following a vacillating policy of drift. The Tokyo government had been unable to pursue either intervention or non-intervention in China. Failing both, it had combined the more unfortunate features of each. Help for the revolutionaries had been too small to affect the course of events, and yet sufficient to alienate the established government of China and arouse the suspicions of the powers. After each attempt the Japanese government had ended with formal support of the Peking regime, surprised and a little hurt to find that its actions had been taken amiss.

By 1915, Japan's position vis-à-vis the China of Yuan Shih-k'ai was considerably less fortunate than it had been in the last days of the Manchu Dynasty. Yuan's German advisers were in charge of his armies, and his Consortium backers enabled him to be independent of Japanese blandishments. Then the World War furnished Japan with an opportunity for removing German influence from China. Japanese occupation of Shantung posed new problems that demanded solutions. With Japan's rivals fully occupied in Europe, there could be no threat of foreign interference. It was clearly a propitious time for settlement of all disagreements with China in a single dramatic stroke.

How could this best be done? A great many Japanese had become convinced that constitutionalism and republicanism did not fit the Chinese scene. Some of the adventurers thought that Japan should try to turn the clock back in North China and Manchuria by re-instituting Manchu rule there. If this was to be the policy, the Manchu Prince Su was still available at Dairen for Japanese sponsorship. Others thought that Sun Yat-sen should be backed in South

China. They never had better reason for helping him. Sun, who was now without support of any proportions, encouraged Japanese hopes by making elaborate promises of guarantees and privileges in letters to the premier and Foreign Office. Not a few thought that support to Prince Su in Manchuria should be combined with help to Sun in South China.

But many Japanese had tired of the attempts to influence Chinese politics. They noted that Sun Yat-sen was farther from power than he had ever been, and they concluded that the chaos in China was so great, and the opportunity so inviting, that only force and threats of force would achieve the things they wanted. Such exponents of a vigorous policy were most influential in the War Office, but they were to be found in the business world as well.

The cabinet which had to decide on these matters was no ordinary collection of officials. The *genrō,* discouraged by the failures of Katsura and Yamamoto, had turned to one of their own generation and experience for leadership in the hope of achieving a strong and popular government. Ōkuma Shigenobu thus achieved power in the twilight of his life. His, it was hoped, would be a "Taishō Restoration." Long acclaimed as an authority on the Chinese problem, Ōkuma had consistently favored the encouragement of moderate, constitutional government in both Japan and China. Instead, his cabinet presented China with the most drastic demands that had yet been made.

But Ōkuma was by no means a free agent. Japan had entered the World War in order to profit from the enforced inactivity of her European competitors in Asia. The military naturally exerted constant pressure on the cabinet's policies. More particularly, Ōkuma's colleagues of Restoration days, the aging *genrō,* were ever at his side. They urged him to undertake negotiations with China. Failing in their attempt to direct those negotiations, they attacked them bitterly. They were dismayed by the international opprobrium which resulted from the Twenty-one Demands, and forced the dismissal of the foreign minister.

Ōkuma and his foreign minister succeeded in satisfying none of their self-appointed advisers. They never contemplated help for Sun Yat-sen, and they used his pleas merely as threats in extorting privileges from Yuan Shih-k'ai. They blocked the military who sought a resort to force. They called off an attempt in Manchuria after it was well launched. In order to ensure Chinese acquiescence, they moderated their demands sufficiently so that they could be assailed as indecisive in Tokyo.

The resulting compromise satisfied no one. The army would have preferred recourse to force, and the adventurers felt that little had been gained at a tremendous cost in unpopularity and ill will in China. The Chinese government was no more dependable than it had been. Once again the government in Tokyo had preferred to deal with duly constituted authority in Peking.

The Twenty-one Demands mark a definite break in Japanese relationships with China. The Demands were the logical fruition of previous policies, and they marked a type of attempted solution that was not to reappear for almost two decades. Within a year of the negotiations with Japan, Yuan Shih-k'ai was dead. In his place a series of governments lost ground steadily in the face of the growing power of the regional warlords. Japan, in a stronger financial position because of war-time profits, was able to barter and deal with many of these regimes. Very soon, however, her favorite puppets, the Anfu warlords, were out of power. Large sums of money had thus been wasted on discredited regimes. The Tokyo government gradually realized the impossibility of selecting China's leadership. The minimum demands had been gained in 1915. Under the influence of post-war internationalism and party government, Japan was content for a time to pursue a policy of relative neutrality in China's chaos.

For the Chinese revolutionaries and their Japanese friends, the year 1915 also marked a definite terminus. Slogans of guidance and leadership had little place in the tactics which the Ōkuma cabinet followed. Sun Yat-sen, in occasional interviews, showed a realization of this, and a reluctant readiness to consign Japan to the list of imperialist powers. More often, however, opposition to Yuan Shih-k'ai exceeded for Sun any other motivation. To achieve his goals he promised Japan better terms than could be wrested from his rival. His adventurer friends helped provoke government action by forwarding suggestions that were curiously prophetic of the ultimate demands. And since these adventurers still sheltered Sun Yat-sen, their influence on his offers cannot be overlooked.

The two decades of coöperation with the Chinese revolutionaries thus ended with each side in the alliance trying to use the other for its own purpose. Among the Japanese adventurers, the nationalists of the *Kokuryūkai* were far more prominent than Sun's earlier friends. The logic of power, of support, and of profit had passed the others by. Among the Chinese, disillusioned and hardened opportunists were now willing to surrender economic independence for political advantage.

1. BACKGROUND OF THE TWENTY-ONE DEMANDS

The cabinet discussions and international diplomacy relative to Japan's entry into the World War in August of 1914 have no relevance to this study. It is sufficient to note that after the decision for war had been reached public opinion manifested its usual wartime unanimity in Japan. Large budget increases were passed without dissent by the Diet. Once the military excitement had died down so that normal politics could be resumed, however, several contentious issues awaited Ōkuma's critics. Although Ōkuma was a popular figure, his cabinet and his policies reflected so many compromises that he was never certain of Diet support.

a. The genrō

Ōkuma's appointment as premier had been the work of Inoue Kaoru. Inoue had persuaded Yamagata, Matsukata, and Ōyama that Ōkuma would be preferable to a party politician. Before his candidate took office, Inoue made sure that he was properly informed in problems in politics, finance, and foreign policy.

Inoue envisaged Ōkuma's regime as the beginning of a new Taishō Restoration, and he was insistent that the cabinet should reflect more than a partisan selection. The cabinet that resulted was safe, conservative, and respectable.[1] Among its members, Ozaki Yukio was perhaps the only popular figure; Inukai, long a friend and supporter of Ōkuma, refused to serve as home minister.[2] This had an important effect, for the popular and articulate Inukai continued to serve as head of the *Kokumintō*. He combined with Hara

Kei, *Seiyūkai* head, to attack the government's policy. Ōkuma's foreign minister, Katō Kōmei, was chief of the *Dōshikai,* the party Katsura had formed shortly before his death. Inoue was not content with this choice, and he warned Ōkuma that Katō was likely to be bureaucratic and narrow-minded. Inoue would have preferred Gotō Shimpei, Kodama's assistant on Formosa in 1900. Gotō and Katō were political rivals.[3]

Inoue was particularly insistent upon Ōkuma's agreement on foreign policy. It will be remembered that Inoue's mediation as a Mitsui adviser had helped to bring about the abortive agreement for Sino-Japanese control of the Hanyehping enterprises in 1913. He now reminded Ōkuma of the importance of economic interests in determining foreign policy. Inoue wanted better promotion of Japanese commercial interests in China, and closer relations with England and France in order to use their money in the development of China.[4]

The World War provided a perfect opportunity for the development of such plans. Once Japanese troops had captured the German installations on Shantung, Japan had excellent bargaining power. The Shantung holdings, which were ultimately to be returned to China, had a long period to run. Japan's Manchurian grants, however, were of relatively brief duration. The agreements covering Port Arthur and Dairen, for instance, were due to expire in 1923. Japan had strengthened her position in Manchuria by a series of secret treaties with Russia which staked out zones and interests. Russia, however, seemed to be making better progress toward the incorporation of areas within her zone.[5]

The World War also offered a unique opportunity to redress by special benefits and promises the more general difficulties which lack of capital had imposed upon Japan in China. Without special economic privileges Japan was unlikely to gain the dominant position which she felt her proximity warranted. Yawata was still dependent upon Hanyehping, but the reverse was not the case. It was quite certain that upon the conclusion of the World War Japanese capital would again take a secondary role. The Open Door meant a closed door for Japan's dreams of economic mastery.[6]

After the Japanese occupation of Shantung the *genrō* were therefore quick to suggest ways of exploiting the situation. Inoue suggested sending Gotō Shimpei to China as a special emissary to negotiate an over-all settlement.[7] Matsukata too suggested sending an outstanding leader, possibly a *genrō*, as evidence of Japan's sincerity. Kiaochiao, Germany's base on Shantung, should not be handed back without some suitable settlement.[8] Yamagata forwarded a lengthy memorandum to Ōkuma and Katō. He urged attempts to improve relations with China. It was still not too late, he felt, to undo the work of the pro-revolutionary clique in the Foreign Office which had encouraged Sun Yat-sen. Manchuria and Shantung represented Japanese blood and Japanese money, and the Chinese government, if properly approached, could surely be made to see that Japan was its true friend. Yamagata felt that it was essential to secure China's good will for the racial war which he felt was approaching. At the same time, he warned against antagonizing the United States.[9]

The opinions of the *genrō* thus represented a conviction that there was needed a new agreement with China which should strengthen Japan's economic position. Toward this end special political agreements were required. Nevertheless, nothing should be allowed to antagonize Japan's commercial competitors; foreign gold was essential to Japanese plans. Indeed, Inoue and Yamagata were eager to accept offers of alliances when they came from France and Russia.[10]

b. Uchida Ryōhei and the Kokuryūkai

The nationalists were less worried about foreign opinions, and their agitation envisaged a plan which would remove Yuan Shih-k'ai from power. The *Kokuryūkai* was probably at the most influential stage in its history. It had played a leading role in the agitation over the Nanking outrage, and it had clamored for the removal of Yamamoto. Uchida's contacts in the government were more numerous than ever before. He and his followers had decided that the pseudo-republic under Yuan Shih-k'ai could satisfy neither Japanese needs nor Chinese problems, and he was convinced that Japan should seize the unique opportunity which now presented itself for an over-all agreement. Uchida thus took it upon himself to enlighten the nation's leaders.

On November 29, 1914, he presented to Premier Ōkuma, Foreign Minister Katō, and other leaders his opinions in a lengthy "Memorandum for a Solution of the China Problem" (*Taishi mondai kaiketsu iken*). This interesting document has been much discussed and doubted by writers who generally assume that its contents are of interest even though its authenticity is uncertain. Actually, it fits perfectly into the pattern of unsolicited advice which the society heads had set up, and the Japanese sources leave no doubt whatever of its reliability and importance.[11]

Uchida's document surveyed the probable effects of the war in Europe and concluded that the uncertainty demanded a foolproof position for Japan within China as well as an iron-clad alliance with China in which Japan would accept her moral obligation to protect China from all other powers. Uchida was uncertain as to the degree of opposition this would arouse within China, but he was convinced that Yuan Shih-k'ai's had to be replaced by a more reliable government in Peking. He warned that insurrection was inevitable in China, and he felt that Japan should plan now to support the groups that would succeed Yuan. Uchida emphasized the fact that Yuan could not be trusted. Yuan had lost the confidence of the people, and even though he might last a little longer with Japanese help the ultimate effect would only be treachery and failure. China's ultimate good depended upon a Sino-Japanese alliance which would repel all foreign aggression.

In order to bring about such an alliance Uchida felt that Japan should support the friendly, reliable revolutionaries who were impeded only by a lack of funds. Nevertheless, Japan should not confine her support to the rebels, for the supporters of legitimacy, the *Tsung-she-tang* (Royalist Party) of Prince Su were popular in North China and Manchuria. Uchida had, however, decided that republicanism was basically incompatible with China's traditions. Once Yuan was overthrown, Japan should devote her energies to the construction of a stable, friendly constitutional monarchy in China. Sun Yat-sen might be allowed a role in South China, but it could hardly be a very important role. No time should be lost in implementing such an independent foreign policy. It would lead to an independent Asia, free from white oppression.[12]

Uchida's program was worked out in considerable detail, and it anticipated most of the Twenty-one Demands. Nevertheless, there were two basic differences between the memorandum and the Demands. Uchida's plan was premised on a change of government in China, and it envisioned a definite political tie with China's future government. The Demands, on the other hand, achieved only concessions from a hostile Peking government.

Uchida's document was intended for few readers, and its accidental discovery by foreigners resulted in the indignant denials by responsible Japanese that resulted in the doubts of its authenticity.[13] It illustrated clearly that Uchida's group, who had acted as intermediaries in the help to Sun Yat-sen and the revolution, were now prepared to regard that movement as no more than a possibly necessary transitional and destructive phase preliminary to the establishment of a monarchy under a Manchu puppet.

c. The Diet

The action groups were rarely as united and formidable as they were at the end of 1914. In December *Seiyūkai* and *Kokumintō* members joined with Uchida Ryōhei to form the National Foreign Policy Association (*Kokumin gaikō dōmeikai*). As usual, the general program called for an independent foreign policy, national unity, and a fundamental solution of the China problem. Behind these hackneyed phrases lay a program much like Uchida's; the Association desired a close alliance with China and a change in Chinese government in which Yuan would be replaced by a dependable monarch.

In its more specific "Fundamental Policy," the Association called for the integrity of China, an alliance with China, help toward self-strengthening for China, and guarantees for Japan in return for that help. The guarantees were to take the form of equal rights for Japanese and Chinese in Mongolia and Manchuria, temporary rights in Kiaochiao and along the Shantung railroads, and a concession for the construction of a railway from Fukien to the Yangtze valley.[14]

Ōkuma and Katō were thus well supplied with advice. Not all of it was welcome. The Diet was dealt with first. When that body failed to approve an expansion of the army by two divisions, Ōkuma dissolved it. The elections of the following spring saw the same interference and bribery which Ōkuma had attacked so often when he had been victimized. The government's tactics were successful, however, and pro-government parties received a comfortable majority. The new Diet did not convene until May 1915. From December 1914, the time of dissolution, until the following May, the cabinet was able to consider its policies without Parliamentary obstruction. Unfortunately, the *genrō* and the nationalists could not be dismissed as easily, and they disapproved loudly of Ōkuma's methods in establishing what he termed the "lasting peace and equity in East Asia." [15]

2. Japanese Opinion and the Twenty-one Demands

The Twenty-one Demands were presented to Yuan Shih-k'ai by Minister Hioki on January 18, 1915. They were arranged in five groups which covered concessions in Shantung, South Manchuria and Eastern Inner Mongolia, the Hanyehping industrial works, general non-alienation of Chinese territory, and, in group five, a series of sweeping agreements for military and governmental advisers which would very nearly have reduced China to the status of a Japanese protectorate. The story of the proposals and counter-proposals which extended up to the final treaties of May 25 is of little concern here.[16] In considering the setting of Sun Yat-sen's desperate appeals to the Ōkuma government, however, it is of interest to note how general was the discontent with the policy of Katō Kōmei. As might be expected, the cabinet took steps to ensure secrecy during the negotiations, and only the *genrō* and the nationalists were fully aware of their consequences.

Katō showed a novel disregard of even *genrō* opinion. He did not acknowledge Yamagata's memorandum of policy suggestions, and he did not refer important decisions to the *genrō* as his predecessors had done. The elder statesmen were not fully aware of the content of the original demands, and they did not become conscious of what was at stake until Yuan Shih-k'ai sent Ariga Nagao, a distinguished jurist who had been working as constitutional adviser in China, back to Japan to intercede with them. Ariga aroused the elder statesmen to the dangers to Japan's position and Japan's trade in China as a result of indignation against the demands.[17] As the *genrō* learned more about the negotiations, they denounced Katō indignantly for his "secret diplomacy" and his incompetent management. After the foreign press learned of the sweeping nature of the concessions at stake, the chorus of opposition was sufficient to shake the confidence of the Tokyo government. Foreign disapproval, the influence of Ariga, and the natural conservatism of the elder statesmen combined to render Tokyo more cautious. The fifth group of demands became listed as "desires" which could be postponed for future discussion. Even then, it required a threat of force to secure China's acquiescence. At the final conference with the *genrō* at which the ultimatum was discussed, Yamagata angrily berated Katō for his clumsiness, and suggested that the foreign minister should either go to China himself (as Ōkubo, Inoue, and Itō had done in earlier days) or else resign.[18] Inoue and Matsukata too criticized Katō sharply for his aggressive and crude diplomacy; they pointed out that Japan's prestige had suffered irreparable harm and that the friendship with China was now impossible.[19]

It is probable that these charges reflected more pique than justice.[20] The *genrō* had urged negotiations on the government, and their criticisms concerned chiefly the manner and not the content of those negotiations.[21] Nevertheless, it is worth remembering that in their early days they had usually set a pattern of reasonableness and accommodation when they were entrusted with negotiations with China. Their influence was now waning. But it was still sufficient to block Katō's ambition. They never forgave Katō for his independent attitude. His resignation was secured shortly after the treaties were signed,[22] and he did not become premier until Yamagata, Inoue, and Matsukata were dead.[23]

The military, who had been held in check by the *genrō* during their tenure, showed signs of doing better in the future. During the negotiations over the demands, General Oka, minister of war, had invoked his prerogative of access to the Emperor to try to secure the use of greater force. Foreign Minister Katō narrowly averted this threat to civilian control.[24]

By and large, the opinions of the business community can probably be equated with that of Inoue Kaoru, whose Mitsui ties were very close. It is worth noting, however, that among the Japanese businessmen in China there was vigorous support for a strong and resolute stand. Mori Kaku, who was in Peking as an official of the development company that had been formed with Sun Yat-sen in 1913, kept in close touch with officials of the Japanese lega-tion in Peking. His office became a propaganda headquarters from which he and a group of reporters urged their friends in Japan to work against the moderation of the original demands. Mori ap-parently felt that the negotiations had already harmed Sino-Japanese friendship and that there was no point in giving up the fifth group of demands. In fact, with bad blood on both sides, he felt that those final grants were now more important than ever.[25] In this, Mori reflected the opinions of the nationalists in Japan.

Uchida Ryōhei and his men did all they could to counter the conservative influence of the elder statesmen. The sweeping con-cessions outlined in the original demands of January seemed to coincide with many of Uchida's suggestions. "At that time the con-tents of the articles under negotiation became known to our group," the *Kokuryūkai* chronology relates, "and they were almost exactly like those previously forwarded by us to the government circles in our 'Memorandum for a Solution of the China Problem.'"[26] It was thus natural that when the difficulties of the negotiations grad-ually became known the nationalists did all they could to support the government. In April, several public meetings were held to encourage the government by a new association, the *Taishi mondai daikonshinkai* (Great Friendship Society for the China Problem). Among those present were such men as Tōyama, Uchida, Professor Terao, and several Diet members.[27]

But when it became obvious that the negotiations were arousing great opposition among Chinese nationalists, and when the Japanese Foreign Office appeared to be hopelessly trapped in its self-contrived web of denials, the *Kokuryūkai* decided that Katō's diplomacy was thoroughly unskillful and clumsy. This feeling apparently made them sympathetic toward Ariga Nagao. They realized that Ariga harbored the correct feelings toward Japan's rightful sphere in Man-churia and Mongolia. His role as Yuan's emissary to the *genrō* brought him much opprobrium; some labeled him "Yuan's Foreign Minister," and Foreign Minister Katō termed him a traitor. Nevertheless, if Uchida Ryōhei and his firebrands had shared this opinion it is not difficult to imagine that Ariga's mission would have come to a speedy and violent end.[28]

a. Expressions of dissatisfaction

Consistency was a virtue not attained by the professional patriots. When Katō, as a result of much bickering and argument, agreed to modify the demands and class the fifth group as mere "desires," the *Kokumin gaikō dōmeikai* shifted from condemnation of Katō's technique to support of his earlier draft. They warned that it would never do to let the world see that Japan could be intimidated by foreign displeasure or by Yuan's use of barbarians to rule barbarians; Japanese honor was now at stake. Moreover, the adventurer's friends in Peking had reported that China was ready to give in to all the demands.[29]

Uchida and his stalwarts resented bitterly the final form of the Sino-Japanese treaties. They felt that irreparable harm had been done to Sino-Japanese relations and that relatively little had been gained in the treaties. Renewed scrambles for gain in China would come after the European war ended. Japan had bungled her one great chance. No revolutionaries had been supported. Yuan had stood as a bulwark of Chinese nationalism against Japanese imperialism, gaining in strength as his opposition to Japan became more obvious. Instead of the coördinated program Uchida had presented, a series of minor concessions had been taken up piecemeal with great rancor and lasting bitterness. The Foreign Office stood exposed before the world in its duplicity and equivocations, and Japan, instead of gathering unto itself a properly grateful and appreciative Chinese constitutional monarchy, had been the object of the first great, united show of Chinese nationalism. Uchida's dislike was as lasting as Yamagata's; in 1925 he was arrested for complicity in an attempt on Premier Katō's life.[30]

The *shishi* never did things by halves, and their resentment at the diplomatic blunders was expressed vividly in Tokyo upon conclusion of the negotiations. On May 9, 1915, when a group which had backed the government stand organized a meeting to express approval of the course events were taking, Uchida decided people should be able to know the true story. *Kokuryūkai* members infiltrated the meeting and collected at key points throughout the auditorium in a manner their ideological opposites have made common practice in recent years. While the resolution of approval of the government's policy was being read by the chairman of the meeting, the *Kokuryūkai* men rose as one with the cry, *"Igi ari!"* (We disagree!) and precipitated a riot. In the confusion the previous resolution was destroyed. Several members rushed to the rostrum to harangue those who could hear them, and others showered pamphlets from the balcony which explained the error of the government's ways and policies. At the appearance of the police, the rioters melted away, confident that the government had derived little support from the meeting.[31]

The general line of attack taken by Uchida was also followed by his fellow members of the *Kokumin gaikō dōmeikai* Inukai and Hara Kei, as leaders of the opposition in the Diet, attacked the government vigorously. They condemned the removal of Group V, and they criticized the extraordinarily clumsy diplomacy that had resorted to an ultimatum for so little profit.[32]

In the face of such criticism, Ōkuma contented himself with assertions that the preservation of peace constituted a triumph for Japanese diplomacy. Ozaki Yukio said that the negotiations were neither a failure nor a success, but constituted agreements for natural and essential needs in China. Group V, he pointed out, had been merely postponed, and not dismissed.[33]

Inukai's *Kokumintō* then went on record with a lengthy resolution which accused the government of having jeopardized the peace of Asia. The government had bullied, it had used force, it had misjudged the timing, and it had shown great clumsiness. In June the *Kokumintō* and *Seiyūkai* tried to unseat the government.[34] Although their frontal attack on the cabinet did not succeed, charges of corruption which involved Home Minister Ōura forced a reshuffle which offered an opportune time for Katō Kōmei to resign.

Inukai's split with Ōkuma, his former mentor, was thus complete and striking. He did not escape editorial criticism for irresponsibility, however, since he had presented no alternative line of action.[35] Moreover, the alliance with Uchida Ryōhei certainly absolves Inukai of exaggerated idealism in his opposition to the government policy. In the words of a biographer of Ōkuma, the opposition of Inukai and Hara was motivated "not by a conviction that the Demands were fundamentally wrong, but that Katō's methods had been wrong." [36] The Demands evidently appeared to Inukai as a crystallization and a formalization of the position of guidance that was rightly Japan's in China. They represented a different method for exerting the guidance that had formerly been sought through help for the Chinese revolutionaries. How did those negotiations appear to Sun Yat-sen?

3. THE CHINESE REVOLUTIONARIES AND THE DEMANDS

In considering Sun Yat-sen's relations to the Twenty-one Demands, we must focus attention upon two letters by Sun. One, to Ōkuma, offered sweeping concessions in return for Japanese help. The second, to the Foreign Office, offered more favorable terms than Yuan Shih-k'ai was willing to grant in return for Japanese support. Of these letters, the first has been much doubted and little discussed. The second remained hidden until the Foreign Office files were opened after World War II. Taken in their setting, the documents give convincing evidence of the discouraging situation that the revolutionaries faced in Japan. Committed to the cause of Chinese nationalism, they needed help so desperately that they contributed to Japan's insistence on sweeping concessions from China.

a. Sun's letter to Ōkuma

Shortly after Ōkuma took office in 1914, Sun Yat-sen addressed to him a plea for help in terms so startling that they suggest ghost writing by Uchida or hypocrisy by Sun.[37] Taken in conjunction with the later propositions to Mr. Dietrick of San Francisco, the letter establishes the desperation with which Sun Yat-sen sought backing. In the case of the American, however, that backing would have been economic in nature. Ōkuma was promised a good deal more.

Sun pleaded for Japanese help to drive Yuan Shih-k'ai from office, and guaranteed a lasting Sino-Japanese alliance thereafter. In addition, he promised the most elaborate commercial benefits: rights of unrestricted residence for Japanese in China, a customs union, and over-all commercial domination. Sun pointed out that England's greatness depended on India, for which she had had to fight. But Japan had at hand a potential India for which she did not need to fight; she had only to arm and help the *Kuomintang* forces. France, he said, had aided America for reasons of chivalry and idealism; England helped Spain in order to defeat her enemy Napoleon, while America had freed Panama for commercial benefit. But Japan could achieve all these goals simultaneously by helping Sun Yat-sen against Yuan Shih-k'ai. By doing so, she would earn the undying gratitude of the Chinese people.

Until this remarkable letter was found among the papers of Ōkuma after his death, there seemed good reason to doubt its authenticity. It could perhaps be held that Sun Yat-sen, by offering such encouragement to Japan's leaders, had as much to do with the Twenty-one Demands as did Uchida Ryōhei. Sun could not know that Uchida planned support for the revolution as a prelude to the establishment of a safe, constitutional monarchy. Nor could Uchida know that Sun anticipated Japanese guidance as a transitional stage of tutelage toward a truly independent China. Nevertheless, it is not surprising that Sun's role during the negotiations was a contradictory one. He became, at times, an apologist for Japanese expansion, and even an instrument of that aggression. Sun's promises to Ōkuma were used as a threat to Yuan Shih-k'ai prior to the presentation of the Demands, and the fear of Japanese support for his enemies was much with Yuan all during the negotiations.[38] Certainly correspondence of this sort more than balanced out the occasional public statements Sun made criticizing Japanese policy as imperialistic.[39]

b. Discouraged revolutionaries

During the negotiations Japanese newspaper files showed a growing weakness and division among the Chinese revolutionaries in Japan. They were torn between disapproval of Japanese aggression and pleasure at the discomfiture of Yuan Shih-k'ai. As it became more evident that Japanese support was not going to be available for Sun Yat-sen, Sun's followers were more susceptible to the arguments of Chinese spokesmen who held that all Chinese should stand together in the face of Japanese aggression. In particular, Sun's old rival Liang Ch'i-ch'ao waged a most successful propaganda campaign using this theme. Sun Yat-sen was forced to resort to contradictory measures to maintain his standing. To rally his followers, he suggested that the Demands were actually instituted at the instigation of Yuan Shih-k'ai. To get Japanese support, he offered better terms than were included in the Demands themselves.

It is not surprising that the Chinese in Japan became discouraged. In January 1915, the *Mainichi* reported that only three or four hundred of the several thousand who had fled after the second revolution were still in Japan. It described this remnant as poor and dispirited and quite incapable of action. Huang Hsing had gone to America, and many others had gone to Singapore. A group of revolutionaries in Nagasaki were so hard pressed for funds that they had been caught counterfeiting. Revolutionary work had become secondary to raising money for personal needs. The men were organizing protective agencies for Chinese shops, and they were even trying their hand at such things as raising chickens.[40]

Yuan Shih-k'ai was not slow to take advantage of this progressive demoralization among the revolutionaries. He issued numerous proclamations which pleaded for national unity to prosper the new republic, and condemned the revolutionary leaders as hungry for power.[41] At the same time, he was able to use threats of force. Early in 1915 *Mainichi* readers learned that there were many secret Chinese agents in Tokyo who had been sent by Yuan to watch revolutionaries and students. All students, fearing assassination or reprisals at home, had to be wary and discreet.[42]

As anti-Japanese feeling grew in China, Yuan's position became stronger. In February 1915, the *Mainichi* reported an offer of pardons for all members of the revolutionary party who would return to China to help resist Japanese aggression. It was soon evident that many of the indigent rebels were taking advantage of the offer.[43] There were rumors that Yuan was offering more than pardons. In March, the *Hōchi Shimbun* reported the departure of one Chin

Pang-p'ing, whom it described as a special agent of Yuan's. He had bought off many of the leading revolutionaries in an attempt to organize a united front against Japan. The paper reported that he had offered Sun Yat-sen and Huang Hsing five hundred thousand *yuan* each.[44]

By March 13, over one hundred and fifty revolutionaries had returned or planned to return to China. Among them were Huang Hsing and many other important leaders. Only Sun Yat-sen, Ch'en Chi-mei, and their immediate circle remained to advocate Sino-Japanese coöperation.

The revolutionaries who remained tried to fight back by invoking the Japanese bogey against Yuan. Shanghai papers often carried letters from revolutionaries in Japan pointing out that Yuan's position was quite hopeless because Japan had committed herself to support for Sun Yat-sen. Other letters pointed out that the Demands were no more than just retribution for Yuan's misgovernment.[45]

Sun Yat-sen tried several expedients to stop the return to China. He announced that most of those returning were military men who were discouraged by the failure of the Second Revolution. They lacked the long view, and did not realize that the future of China was one of imperialist domination unless China and Japan could coöperate. Sun expressed his sympathy for the patriotic emotions of those men who had returned, but he warned that they were courting disaster for China.[46] Then, as the battle continued, Sun no longer contented himself with the argument that Yuan had brought the Demands upon himself through insincerity. In a letter to Peking students, Sun proposed the thesis that Yuan had invited the Japanese to present him with their demands in return for Japanese help in his own imperial aspirations. Sun buttressed his points with quotations from the Japanese press which explained that the fifth group had been kept secret at the request of the Chinese government. If this were so, then the manner and content of the Demands represented considerable restraint and good will on the part of the Japanese. By this unique device, Sun was able to condemn both the Demands and the enemy. They were, in fact, one — Yuan Shih-k'ai. For selfish reasons, the scoundrel was willing to sell the country.[47]

Yuan's counter-attack was no less personal. He made good use of a document which purported to be a secret agreement to finance Sun's revolution by a syndicate calling itself the Europe and Asia Trading Company. Although the authenticity of this agreement has yet to be established, its guarantees and terms are not inconsistent with other offers and agreements Sun had made with Japanese financiers in the past.[48] By May, a series of defamatory booklets about the traitor Sun Yat-sen were circulating in China.[49]

Sun's position during this duel was at best compromising, and he fared poorly in the struggle against the pen of Liang Ch'i-ch'ao and the politics of Yuan Shih-k'ai. In his attempts to even the struggle, Sun once again sought Japanese help with a letter which would have given Yuan's propagandists an easy victory if they had known of its existence.

c. Sun's letter to the Foreign Office

On March 14, Sun addressed a letter to Koike Chōzō, head of the Political Affairs section of the Foreign Office.[50] Sun expressed his concern at the news of negotiations with Yuan Shih-k'ai's "evil government." He explained that he did not yet know the full details of the negotiations, but he warned that they must inevitably fail because of bad faith on the part of Yuan.

Sun agreed, however, that a settlement of outstanding issues was essential to the peace of Asia, and that a Sino-Japanese alliance was the only path to freedom from European imperialism. He assured Koike that the revolutionaries desired nothing more than cordial relations with Japan. All they needed was Japanese support. With Europe preoccupied at home, the present was the perfect time to overthrow Yuan Shih-k'ai. Then, as a foretaste of what might be done, Sun enclosed a sample treaty for consideration. It included eleven articles:

1. Japan and China to consult together before either concluded important agreements with a third power on matters relating to Asia.
2. To facilitate military cooperation, China to use Japanese style arms, ammunition, and equipment for both army and navy.
3. For the same reason, China to give priority to Japanese officers when employing foreign military advisers for army and navy.

4. To effectuate political coalition, China to give priority to Japanese when employing foreign specialists in the central and local governments.

5. To develop economic cooperation between China and Japan, a Sino-Japanese Bank, with branches, to be established in all important cities of both China and Japan.

6. For the same reason, China to consult Japan first if outside help and capital is needed for mining, railroads, and coastal trade, and outside help to be invited only if Japan cannot supply it.

7. Japan to provide the necessary help for removing the evil government of China.

8. Japan to help China reform her government, adjust her military system, and establish a sound nation.

9. Japan to support China in the changing of the treaties regulating customs independence, extraterritoriality, etc.

10. The contents of the foregoing articles having been agreed to by the proper authorities in China and Japan and by those initialing the treaty of alliance, neither party to form an alliance with any other power.

11. From the day this treaty is signed until its expiration cooperation is to extend, and thereafter it can be renewed according to the desires of the two parties.[51]

A consideration of these documents and their possible effect on Japanese policy makers leads to the inescapable conclusion that Sun Yat-sen had seriously compromised himself with the revolutionary and nationalistic movement in China. His presence in Japan made it relatively easy for his opponents in China to vilify him, and it certainly provided Tokyo with a convenient threat to use against Yuan Shih-k'ai. It may well be that it was a realization of Sun's weakened position on the part of the Japanese that resulted in their steadfast refusal to lend him aid thereafter. It certainly fortified the natural inclinations of the Tokyo government to work with the recognized government in Peking. Nor should it be forgotten that all parties had reason to be slightly skeptical of the promises which Sun Yat-sen was so quick to make.

4. THE JAPANESE AND THE "THIRD REVOLUTION" OF 1915–1916

When the revolution did come, neither Sun Yat-sen nor his Japanese friends had a leading part in it. The Japanese army was not inclined to leave things to the adventurers, and it was more interested in a plan to restore Manchu rule in Manchuria than it was in returning Sun Yat-sen to China.

After the treaties had been signed with Yuan Shih-k'ai in May 1915, it appeared that Japan had acquired many of the rights in name alone. Chinese obstruction and delay prevented capitalizing on the new gains. Foreign Minister Katō left the cabinet, and no strong hand was available for help. Education Minister Takada then asked Uchida Ryōhei for his advice, and that worthy was once again glad to oblige with a document in which he advocated aid to the many dissatisfied groups in China to foment revolt.[52]

Yuan Shih-k'ai himself was not long in providing the stimulus for such opposition. He was in thorough agreement with the Japanese theorists who advocated a constitutional monarchy as best suited to Chinese tradition. By the end of 1915, a Peking-fostered campaign to have Yuan ascend the Dragon Throne was in full progress. This unfortunate attempt resulted in general agreement that Yuan's government must be overthrown. For the Japanese, the thought of Yuan as Emperor was completely untenable, and many considered the present an opportune time to try Uchida's policy. According to the *Kokuryūkai* history, however, the war minister, General Oka, wanted to have the General Staff in complete charge throughout; he had no confidence in the *rōnin*. As a result, the upper hand passed from the skilled intriguers to the militarist leaders, and the situation was not exploited to the full advantage of Japan.[53]

a. The minor role of the Japanese

Just as the *rōnin* were less important on the Japanese side, Sun Yat-sen counted for less in the campaigns in China. In the propaganda battle Liang Ch'i-ch'ao led the way against Yuan, and in the military campaigns the future warlords predominated. The field campaigns were spearheaded by General Tsai Ao, a man who had had his military schooling in Japan and who had many Japanese friends.[54] Aside from a few individuals, however, Japanese did not contribute very much to those campaigns. In part, this may have been due to the ease of the victory, for Yuan gave up his plan as soon as he saw the preponderance of feeling and power which was arrayed against him.

Sun's old friends did participate in a few minor incidents in Shantung and Shanghai. Kayano's account of one such attempt in Shantung may serve to illustrate the ambiguity of government policy and individual status that now prevailed. Kayano, nominally opposed to Ōkuma, could approach him readily; Ōkuma, officially holding to neutrality, was not averse to adventurism.

Kayano, hoping to get arms for a rising in Shantung, approached Itagaki Taisuke. The latter expressed sympathy with the project, but explained that he had no influence with the government. Itagaki was able to arrange an interview with Ōkuma for Kayano. When Kayano explained his plan for releasing captured German stock at Tsingtao to the revolutionaries, Ōkuma's refusal was brusque and emphatic:

That's completely out of the question. Tsingtao is an international port with foreign consuls there. If we did that it would become a serious problem. If we helped the revolutionaries, England, America, and France would object. I'm responsible for the government, and it would be serious if the Diet found out about it. I want you to tell no one that you came to see me; this is really most awkward.[55]

A week later Kayano returned to Tsingtao, and was called in by General Ōtani, commandant of the area. Kayano was understandably surprised and pleased when the general told him he had received secret orders from Ōkuma to help Kayano as much as possible.[56] But despite such connivance, there is little indication that the Japanese help and arms made much difference in the events that followed.

By and large, the revolutionaries were reduced to sensational feats which did them little good. Japanese were well represented in a comic-opera battle waged for Shanghai, where Ch'en Chi-mei tried to capture several warships and take the city by sea as a prelude to the return of Sun Yat-sen. In this operation several Japanese officers were present, as well as many young and enthusiastic Chinese soldiers like Chiang Kai-shek. The revolutionaries managed to get aboard the cruisers while the ships' officers were at a banquet on shore. The narrative of their exploits may best be left to the indignant editors of the *North China Daily Herald:*

The would-be heroes . . . get on board by a ruse, threaten to take the life of the lieutenant in command of the vessel unless he hands over the keys of the magazines, succeed in overawing some 150 men after killing 4 of them and force the ships' gunners to open fire. The gunners, with an excusable eye to the main chance, fire at an elevation that ensures their missing everything the buccaneers want them to hit and endangering the life and property of a neighboring foreign settlement not in the least interested in either side. Then well placed shots absorb the oozing courage of the desperadoes, who take to boats quietly and quickly disappear in the mist and though hotly pursued are able, through getting a good start, to show clean pairs of heels.[57]

Little long-range gain for Japan could be expected from such heroics. By this time most responsible quarters in Japan were inclined to agree with the unflattering estimate the treaty-port editors had made of Sun Yat-sen and his partisans. The Japanese army was more inclined to experiment with support for Manchu rule to the North.

b. The second Manchukuo

Ever since the abortive attempt of 1911, Prince Su had remained at Dairen, ready to coöperate with the Japanese if they should decide to reinstitute Manchu rule in Manchuria. There were frequent rumors that such an attempt was due.[58] When Yuan Shih-k'ai tried to ascend the throne, conditions seemed opportune for sponsoring Prince Su. There was no difficulty in recruiting the experienced Kawashima Naniwa, who still felt that legitimacy was the key to Chinese stability.

Funds came from many sources. The Prince parted with some family heirlooms to do his part in financing the venture. The Japanese army provided arms that had been captured from the Germans in Shantung. The Ōkura Trading Company contributed two million yen.[59] Ammunition was smuggled in with Mitsui connivance.

Despite General Oka's disapproval, several *shishi* went to Manchuria with junior army officers. The presence of Chang Tso-lin posed a major problem, and the *shishi* and officers failed in several attempts to kill him. According to the *Kokuryūkai* history, the project occupied almost three thousand men, and at its height they had mastered about two thousand miles of territory in Manchuria. The death of Yuan Shih-k'ai in 1916 brought a change in policy in Japan, however, and when the Japanese army withdrew its support the project collapsed. The rebel forces retreated toward the South Manchurian Railway zone, and there they disbanded. They had accomplished nothing of value.[60]

This renewed demonstration of the Ōkuma cabinet's predilection for halfway measures in China stirred the patriots to wrath, and one was sufficiently exercised to throw a bomb at Ōkuma's car. This resulted in some repressive measures, but the cabinet continued in office until its replacement by one headed by General Terauchi in October 1916.

5. PARTING OF THE WAYS

The confusion that followed the passing of Yuan Shih-k'ai from the Chinese political scene ended all hopes for a unified, strong China indebted to Japan for her administrative and military system. The kaleidoscopic changes that featured the era of the warlords made an ideal setting for intrigue and double-dealing. It was less than ideal for business interests, and it was hopeless for those who sought to bring about unity on a basis of peace and democracy. Sun Yat-sen had no illusions as to the source of power in those days, and in Canton he tried his own hand at the arts of war and power politics, usually with disastrous results.

The Terauchi Cabinet, which held office until 1918, devoted all of its efforts and much of Japan's war profits to political, military, and administrative loans to the pro-Japanese warlords who controlled the Peking area.[61] By this means they won temporary advantage for short-sighted policies, and incurred the cordial contempt of the Chinese nationalists. The May 4, 1919 movement and the wave of nationalism that followed were in large measure directed against Japan. Hara Kei, who followed Terauchi in 1918, brought to an end the more reckless features of Terauchi's financial dealings, and Hara proved willing to make cautious concessions to Chinese opinion on questions relating to Shantung. During these years Japan's attention was drawn to the North, where Japan through military intervention in Siberia tried to guarantee Manchuria and Japan itself immunity from communist contamination. Even after

Japanese troops withdrew from Siberia in 1922, the regime of Marshal Chang Tso-lin in Manchuria was considered the principal Japanese interest in China. Under the circumstances Foreign Minister Shidehara of the Katō cabinet could be relatively objective about the Northern Expedition of the Chinese Nationalists in 1926. This by no means implied favor for that movement or approval of Sun's turn to Russia for aid, but it contrasted so favorably with the reaction of the Western European imperialist powers that Chinese nationalism became for a time more anti-British than anti-Japanese.[62] For most Chinese, however, Japan had become the personification of a particularly persistent and dangerous imperialism, and it was permanently disqualified as an ideological model.

The adventurers and patriots became less and less important in the Chinese scene. Some, of course, were little more than hirelings for the army, and they continued to find employment in forwarding arms to figures like Chang Tso-lin. The Manchurian wing of *rōnin,* which had worked with Kawashima, spent much time and energy on a plan for Manchu restoration that was to be made .possible by the armies of the reactionary Chang Hsün, the perpetrator of the Nanking outrages a few years before. This project was managed by one Tsukuda Nobuo. When the "Restoration" came in 1917 it proved a complete failure, however, and the Japanese officials were quick to disavow the plot.[63]

The old China hands were also less in evidence in Japan. Miyazaki and Ōi Kentarō died in 1922. The professional patriots turned their attention to combatting the new currents of internationalism and liberalism that pervaded Japan under the party governments of the 1920's. On every hand western fads — jazz, the movies, the flapper and her counterpart — seemed to be upsetting the traditional Japanese virtues for which the *shishi* had lived. Worse still, the industrial proletariat had grown to such proportions that a new variety of international socialism and communism entered the list of evils. Thus, figures like Uchida and Tōyama came to be connected with a series of right-wing, nationalistic societies which abjured all the new evils and fads as traitorous. Their youthful followers found outlets for their enthusiasm in frequent assaults on liberals and liberal journals.

The nationalists were naturally much perturbed by Sun Yat-sen's *entente* with Moscow in the closing years of his life. Inukai deplored this search for a "red short cut," and Tōyama and his followers were particularly disturbed by this fresh proof that Sun was a poor representative of Oriental virtues and ideals.

Late in 1924, Sun Yat-sen, on his way to Peking to seek an understanding with Chang Tso-lin, made a last visit to Japan. Once again the adventurers saw their former friend. Akiyama was shocked to see Sun in such obvious ill health, and tried to get him to stay for a rest.[64] Tōyama reproached Sun for his demands for treaty revision and warned that Japan's rights in Manchuria and Mongolia must be safeguarded.[65] Sun's last speech, in Kobe, however, tried to relate his Russian ties to the broader principle of Asiatic freedom from imperialism.

When Sun fell ill upon his arrival in China, Kayano sped to see him once more. He reached his bedside in the Rockefeller Hospital in Peking, and found a few of Sun's most faithful followers — among them Wang Ching-wei — gathered about the patient. With great effort, Sun rose from his pillow, and asked, "Are Inukai and Tōyama well?" On receiving an affirmative answer, Sun asked about the reception of his Kobe speech. He seemed relieved when Kayano assured him that it had received wide distribution in press and radio. The doctors then entered to stop the conversation, and a few days later Sun Yat-sen was dead.[66]

The adventurers had a final flurry of activity when Chiang Kai-shek visited Japan in 1927. Tōyama was his host, and he met with the *shishi* to discuss the proper role of Sino-Japanese relations. Chiang was bitterly resentful of the hostile policy of the Tanaka Cabinet, and it took some persuasion to get him to come to Tokyo. When he did, Tsukuda Nobuo acted as chief Japanese spokesman. He assured Chiang that the Japanese no longer contemplated a Manchu restoration, and urged him to return to China to finish the task of unification. Chiang met Inukai, Uchida, Akiyama, and many others of the old circle that had worked with Sun. Despite these promising developments, however, the Tanaka Cabinet's policy continued to harass Chiang, and the *Kokuryūkai* history blames the Japanese militarists and Kuomintang extremists for the hostilities that finally ended their hopes of coöperation with Chiang Kai-shek.[67]

Two years later Kayano, Inukai, Tōyama, and Miyazaki's son stood together at the tomb of Sun Yat-sen in Nanking. The Tanaka Cabinet had fallen, and under party government the moderate policies of Foreign Minister Shidehara seemed to presage a possible return to friendship with the China of Chiang Kai-shek, whose government was dominated by men who had been students in Japan in former years. Yet the bases for friendship and coöperation were no longer strong. Manchuria seemed to be coming into the Kuomintang orbit, and in Japan political differences could no longer be bridged by personal friendships like that between Tōyama and Inukai.

The great depression swept parliamentarianism out of power in Japan. Under the pressure of economic discontent theorists like Kita Ikki argued for a complete renovation of national life. The whole parliamentary structure itself, and the business interests which supported it, now became objects of searching scrutiny. The business interests seemed akin to those cosmopolitan centers of thought in the West which had produced subversion, and by their control of the Diet they were interposing a screen between the Emperor and his subjects. The *Kokuryūkai* leaders sponsored society after society designed to stimulate nationalistic feelings, strengthen national unity, and preserve national ideals. They thus coalesced with the rising fanaticism of the younger officers and brought about what was proudly termed a "Shōwa Restoration."

The external corollary of the victory of the military in Japan was the Manchurian Incident of 1931. In turn, the foreign victories which followed the Incident encouraged the fascist terrorists at home. Inukai, who had changed parties to succeed General Tanaka as head of the *Seiyūkai* in 1929, won an election campaign shortly after the Incident began by assuring the voters that his experience in the Chinese situation was needed for the formation of a policy stronger than the moderation of Shidehara Kijurō. After taking office, Inukai sent Kayano Chōchi to Chiang Kai-shek to try to settle the Manchurian and Shanghai incidents. At the army's insistence, Kayano—who had been making good progress—was recalled.[68] Shortly afterward, the aged premier was cut down by naval officers whose creed derived from Kita Ikki and Tōyama Mitsuru.

As crisis followed crisis, Tōyama's position became ever stronger in Japan. And, under military rule, Japan adopted an increasingly intransigent policy of aggression in China. Territorial mastery of China posed once again the old questions of form and personnel of government for China. The quandary was never fully resolved. In Manchuria, the Manchus were enthroned. At Peking, elderly Confucian reformers issued injunctions to morality and condemned the radicalism of the Kuomintang. Their authority overlapped with that of Nanking, where Wang Ching-wei reproduced the flag and government of the Kuomintang and claimed that he, not Chiang, was following Sun Yat-sen's wishes for alliance with Japan. Curiously, the Japanese never comprehended the fact that their actions by now belied their words; as late as 1941, a plan was on foot to send Tōyama to see Chiang Kai-shek to arrange for a settlement by appealing to their old friendship.[69]

Even after allowance is made for the blindness of those who will not see, this refusal of the Japanese to believe that their former Chinese guests no longer esteemed them requires explanation. Ultimately, that refusal must derive from the logic of coöperation between China and Japan. The Chinese revolutionaries turned toward Japan a face which the West did not see: Pan-Asianism. It is this aspect which underlies the entire history of Japanese relations with Sun Yat-sen. For the Japanese, it was a theme which was basic to the thought of Sun Yat-sen, one to which he adhered throughout a long series of intellectual changes.

Sun Yat-sen was central to the whole pattern of Japanese coöperation with the Chinese revolutionaries. When he was in Japan, relations between the two groups were most intimate. When Sun was away, jealousies and doubts replaced friendship and confidence. Of all Sun's followers Wang Ching-wei alone reproduced fully the tendency to look first to Japan for help. It is true that for Sun Yat-sen other help, when it was available, was most welcome, but Western businessmen could never have convinced him so readily of their good will as did their Japanese counterparts. The reasons for this are to be sought in a process of motivation in which Sun Yat-sen's experience was somewhat complementary to that of Japan.

The Japanese rationale for giving help to neighboring revolutionaries has been considered at some length. Psychological motivations for that policy derived from both external and internal factors. They were external in that Western imperialism threatened to deprive Asia of all self-determination, and Japan of any economic or political *lebensraum*. They were also internal; a conviction that Japan's tested synthesis of East and West was the surest path to modernization for all Asia blended imperceptibly with historic beliefs of divinity and destiny.[1] This unfortunately rendered most Japanese immune to suggestions of error and deceit, and by the time the militarists had overcome the external dangers there were too few voices raised to protest an extension of the same technique to Asia. Sun Yat-sen and his cause were then unceremoniously discarded for more direct and more promising means. In this process, the Japanese alienated most Chinese. It should be stressed, however, that the break with Sun Yat-sen himself was never so complete as to remove the possibility of a reconciliation. The presence of Inukai and Tōyama at the Nanking ceremonies in 1929 testified to that possibility. What, then, were the sources of Sun's reluctance to think ill of his Japanese benefactors?

Like the Japanese, Sun's attitude derived psychological support from external and internal factors. Externally, Japanese imperialism never affected him as directly and as critically as did Western imperialism. Except for his release from the Chinese Legation in London in 1896 and his brief flurry of popularity and respectability in 1911, Sun Yat-sen had bitter and increasingly acrimonious relations with the official channels of the Western governments. These altercations at times hindered his plans, as did the British refusal to let him land at Hong Kong in 1900; at times they affected him personally, as when the Portuguese revoked his permit to practice medicine at Macao in 1893, and at other times, as in the Shanghai community's reception of him in 1924, they infuriated him. Despite Sun's cordial relations with and sincere affection for many individual westerners, those men were never able to persuade their governments or parties to commit themselves to Sun's causes. Moreover, as Japanese imperialism became more obvious and more dangerous, Sun's relations with the West grew increasingly tenuous. These factors played an important part in his continued reluctance to think the worst of his second homeland.

Internally, Sun's actions derived from a sense of destiny only slightly less intense than that of his chosen allies. The conviction of consecration to the task of liberating China that came upon Sun in his London prison in 1896 never left him. Despite the many dagger men available to the Manchus and to Yuan Shih-k'ai, Sun never doubted for a minute that he would be spared to finish his proper task. In this sense of security, the charismatic charm that won him support and sanctuary so often must have played an important though unconscious role.

Sun's sense of destiny naturally bred the conviction that what was good for him was also in the best interests of China. Once he was able to associate the fate of China with his personal lot, the various compromises and adjustments he made with Japan and the Japanese could all be interpreted to China's gain. By an understandable corollary, what was bad for Sun's enemies was good for China. Thus the many obvious Japanese moves against the Manchus and against Yuan Shih-k'ai could seem merited by the recipients and, curiously, advantageous for the broader aims of the Chinese revolution.

All these assumptions then reinforced Sun's acceptance of the Pan-Asian ideas of his Japanese friends. That acceptance, however, went through several periods of emphasis and nuances of meaning. What kind of an Asianism was it that included Filipinos and excluded Manchus? What sort of nationalism prompted Sun to accept Japanese aid against the Manchus?

This unfortunate plight of the Manchus probably derived from Sun's pro-Western ideological orientation and his fervent hatred of Western imperialism. The Manchus, in all their inefficiency and weakness, he regarded as the negation of Western progress and a stimulus to Western imperialism. In the drive to rid China of their misrule, Sun's nationalism approached racism. Japan, meanwhile, could appeal to Sun's love of the modern and the progressive, and in her Asia policy she resisted and weakened both Western imperialism and Manchu oppression.

And yet, without this Western imperialism and the safety zones it established on the Chinese circumference, Sun's activities and success would have been unthinkable. In his appeal for British aid in 1900, and in his probable promises to Japanese that same year, Sun showed that on this issue of imperialism he could hate the sin while befriending the sinner. Evidently, however, the Manchu sin was so great as to remove its perpetrators from grace forever.

Until the Revolution of 1911, Sun Yat-sen was usually in a most tolerant and idealistic mood. He was sanguine of foreign motives and fearless for his person. He had only contempt and hatred for the Manchus, but he felt certain that they were about to fall. China could and would arise overnight, accomplishing in fifteen years what Japan had required thirty to achieve.

It was in this optimistic mood that he wrote his little preface to Miyazaki's autobiography in 1902:

It is told that during the Sui there was a chivalrous man of Tunghai called Ch'iu Jan. He had travelled all over China and visited all the great heroes; in Lingshih he met Li Ching, and in Taiyuan he met Li Shih-min. Together they discussed all important matters. Since Li

Shih-min had a superior nature, Li Ching had resolved to help him to bring about his great work. Afterwards Li Shih-min rose in revolt to put an end to the confusion of the Sui, and founded the house of T'ang, becoming known as T'ai Tsung. It is said that in the fulfillment of these intentions the efforts of his chivalrous friends were of great effect.

Miyazaki Torazō is a present day chivalrous hero. His knowledge is extensive, his ideals are out of the ordinary; he is one who hastens to help another's need, his heart warm with benevolence and righteousness. He always laments the oppression of the yellow race by barbarians, and grieves because of China's increasing weakness. He often visits the mainland to visit the valorous comrades, and it has been his heartfelt desire to bring about together the great achievement of our age, the raising up of Asia. When he heard that I was planning the building of a new China by starting a republican movement, he hastened to join us, planning together with us in closest harmony and energetically urging us on. In comparison with that Ch'iu Jan, he has done even more.

Unfortunately, however, I have not the character of T'ai Tsung, and lack the masterly strategy of Li Wei; it is a grievous imposition on his kindness that the activities of the years up to now have brought no results.

Upon ending his recent travels, he has returned to his country and set down his experiences for the consideration of those who shall in the future feel concern for the rise or decline of Asia and the existence of the yellow race. I approved of the idea, and in view of his unparalleled efforts, add this preface to show my respect.[2]

During the excitement of the Revolution of 1911, however, Sun's cordiality for the Japanese diminished markedly. He had received far less hospitable treatment in Japan after 1907, and he had turned more to France and the overseas Chinese for help. He was also restrained by a situation not of his making. The thousands of students who had imbibed nationalism and little else from their stay in Japan were keenly suspicious and wary of any and all Japanese. Their distrust was given new emphasis by the threat of Japanese intervention to put down the revolution. Sun remained convinced of the friendly feelings of the Japanese people, as distinguished from their government. But in the need of allies to counter that government's possible intervention he relied more and more upon the giants of imperialism. English and French money, English warnings, and American enthusiasm for the republic did more to restrain the Japanese government than the work of Tōyama or Uchida.

Then it became evident that the humiliating conditions attached to foreign loans were not merely a particularly odious result of Manchu misrule, but that the imperialist powers would even feel impelled to attach them to loans for the new republic. Moreover, Yuan Shih-k'ai was obviously in high favor with the foreign masters. In Sun Yat-sen's eyes, the two were soon inextricably bound together. Appeals to Europe to deny Yuan the funds fell on deaf ears, as did warnings to Yuan that the loans could not be validated by presidential fiat alone.

As distrust increased in China, Sun's reception in Japan in 1913 convinced him anew of the preferability of Japanese loans and aid. The Japanese had apparently become convinced of the errors of their policy. Their military leaders were restive under the British tie, and their financiers realized that they could not compete with European capital on equal terms in China. Sun was once more in a poor bargaining position, for his opponent again had the full support of the imperialist powers. Sun had seen his highest ideals and fondest hopes betrayed by his antagonist. Yuan was a scoundrel, and he was bolstered by British gold.

Investigation into Sun's meager writings during the World War shows that his anti-British feelings were steadily on the increase. It will be remembered that Katsura, in his talks with Sun in 1913, had pointed out to him the likelihood of a switch in Japanese policy from a pro-British to a pro-German course. At times it seems that Sun was more consistent in following such a policy than the Japanese were. It is true that in his letters to English friends he portrayed Yuan Shih-k'ai as pro-German and therefore condemnable.[3] Nevertheless, Sun's irritation with England rose steadily, and this must soon have been evident even to his English friends. "In the past our people have always looked upon England as a friend and have reciprocated whenever possible. Unless such persecutions are stopped and policy changed, henceforth the Chinese peoples cannot help but look upon England in another light."[4]

To this must be added the evidence of a conviction that Asia would fare better if England lost the war. According to Inukai, Sun disapproved strongly of Japan's action in joining the war against Germany. In several letters to Inukai Sun argued that Japan should have allied with Germany to drive England and America from China.[5] And to a Japanese journalist who interviewed him in Canton in August 1917, Sun echoed the Japanese nationalists in deploring Japan's imitative policy:

Your country is acting like a marionette on the British string. You did not have to declare war on Germany on account of your alliance with England; you should have bided your time, extending your assistance, in the meantime, not to the minions of the allied Powers at Peking, but to us of the South — the only real patriots in China.

It is not to the advantage of Asia, especially of China and Japan, that this war in Europe should end in the crushing defeat of Germany — that the allied Powers, under British domination, should come out victorious from the conflict — because such an eventuality would tighten the British hold upon Asia in general, and upon China in particular.[6]

Earlier that same year, Sun wrote a little booklet called the *Vital Problem of China* which argued against China's entry into the war.[7] Here he developed his theme of the identity of Chinese and Japanese interests.

He saw three alternatives. In the case of an Allied victory, England, although she would have lost her financial strength, would use her matchless guile to remain in the rank of great powers. But she would have to share her spoils with Russia. Either China or India would have to be sacrificed. Obviously, China would be bargained away. But should Germany win, England could still placate the Kaiser by concessions; "to gratify Germany's desire, Britain must offer China as an inducement." Thus, "Whether Britain will choose Germany, or Russia, for an ally, China will be the first to suffer at her hands." [8] Since the Russians would probably treat the Chinese more cruelly than the Germans would, an Allied defeat was on the whole preferable.

Sun vastly preferred a third alternative, one that would call for an independent neutrality for China, abjuring entangling alliances with nations whose reliability was uncertain. The only true criterion of alliance was mutual interest. With Japan, China's community of interest was so close as to be obvious. America might become a secondary ally.

The relationship between China and Japan is one of common existence or extinction. Without Japan, there would be no China; without China, there would be no Japan. . . China should rely on these two friendly states for capital and technical advice as well as raw materials. Japan, because of her similarity in language and race with China, can be of even greater assistance to China than America, and on the reconciliation with Japan depends the welfare of China, peace in the Far East, and the very civilization of the world.[9]

Although the remaining years of Sun Yat-sen's life lie outside the scope of this study, his continued professions of belief in Pan-Asianism deserve brief comment, for both Japanese and Chinese collaborationist leaders made good use of them.

Sun Yat-sen became less idealistic, increasingly disillusioned, and far more bitterly resentful of British imperialism than ever before. The sordid struggles for position and power of the warlords kept China in constant turmoil. Sun's political organizations featured an increasingly rigid central control. In his thinking, the period of "party tutelage" which should precede "democracy" loomed ever more important. The young idealist who had organized the project to help Aguinaldo in 1899 could now refer to the wisdom of America's decision to educate and civilize the Filipinos before giving them self-rule.[10]

When Sun tried to show the way by establishing a "model" regime at Canton, he was repeatedly the victim of his own political ineptness and inability to work constructively with others as equals. What disturbed him most, however, was the discovery that he was to be greatly limited by British control over the Canton customs receipts. His dislike for the Western imperialists hardened. To the denizens of the Treaty Ports he came to seem a virtual Bolshevik. In 1923 and 1924 Canton merchants organized to subvert Sun's plans for the reorganization of the city. Sun, fearing another setback, put them down at the cost of considerable fighting and destruction. At the same time, Sun's new relations with Russia drew Western fire. Sun had changed his mind about Russian imperialism since the advent of the Soviets, and from 1923 on he was in increasingly close touch with advisers who aided and superintended the reorganization of the Kuomintang. Western business circles, who had seen in Sun's struggle with the Canton merchants proof of his radicalism, found their worst fears confirmed by his new alliance.

At the same time, Sun won new favor among a younger student generation which had organized in response to foreign insults. During the Canton customs difficulties, Sun's vigorous anti-British statements had helped increase his stature among those students. To be sure, after the Versailles settlement Sun also issued several strong statements against Japanese policy. Nevertheless, his bias against the West remained too strong to admit a forthright anti-Japanese stand. In a letter he wrote Miyazaki in November 1920, this was dramatically brought home. After reminiscing about some of the stirring events they had experienced together, Sun remarked that at present British and American policy seemed to be more favorable to the revolutionary cause. He assured Miyazaki, however, that they could not repose ultimate trust in the whites; if Japan would depart from her militarist ways, reconciliation was still sure, for in the final analysis "we cannot be friendly with England and America and become anti-Japanese." A change in Japanese policy could still result in amity and a hundred years' peace for Asia.[11]

Sun had become a symbol of resistance to Western imperialism in the years when that imperialism was most detested by Young China. When he arrived in Shanghai in 1924 on his way to Peking for the final conference that preceded his death, Sun's popularity among Chinese was unquestioned. The treaty ports watched his progress wrathfully. According to one writer, "Dr. Sun, arriving in Shanghai with his hands still stained with the blood of his fellow citizens, was surrounded in the eyes of those urchins with all the glamour of triumph. It was above all the protagonist of the hate against the foreigners whom they applauded." [12] There was even doubt that Sun would be allowed to land; the *North China Daily News* took a firm stand against him. "Now we would plainly say that Shanghai does not want Dr. Sun Yat-sen, that it has no business to admit him and that it is to be hoped the authorities will prevent his landing here." [13]

It is important to contrast this reception with that Sun received in Japan. As has been mentioned, he saw the comrades of the former years, and was invited to give several lectures. His presence and treatment was that of an honored guest.[14]

Before leaving Canton, Sun had addressed a futile request for aid to the American minister. The Shanghai situation proved England was now his enemy. Russian assistance was uncertain in extent, and so it behove him to keep from alienating the Japanese. He made no demands for a change in policy, but stressed again and again the community of interests China shared with Japan. The Japanese papers were delighted to print Sun's anti-British statements.[15] Sun urged the Japanese not to follow the bad example the British had set. "If Japan in particular wishes to gain the real friendship of her neighbor, she must return all she has taken from her, like Russia and Germany have done." [16]

Sun's last major address was delivered to a large audience in the Kobe Prefectural Girls School on November 28, 1924. He took as his subject Pan-Asianism. As on previous Japanese trips, Tai T'ien-ch'ou was his interpreter. The English *Mainichi* editor was obviously stirred by the talk.

Dr. Sun delivered in Chinese a thundering address on "Great Asia." He completely carried his whole audience off the floor. Warmed by his own enthusiasm and that of his audience, Dr. Sun, in the course of his address, was obliged to take off one of his coats. When the meeting came to an end, the whole house rose and spontaneously gave three deafening *Banzai's* for the Chinese leader.[17]

Sun's speech was, in the main, a restatement of his beliefs about the basic superiority of Asian culture and virtues. He pointed out that Asia was the source of the world's civilization, and that the Greek and Roman civilizations had been transmitted from Asia. Despite Asia's historic role, however, it had grown weaker at the very time that Europe had gained in strength. As a result a steady decline had set in for all Asian nations. Out of this decline they had been newly awakened by the rise to independence of Japan; "the day when the unequal treaties were abolished by Japan was a day of regeneration for all Asiatic peoples." Japan's victory over

Russia had indebted Asia further to her. "We regarded that Russian defeat by Japan as the defeat of the West by the East."

Sun then turned his attention to westerners who considered the rising of the East as a revolt against civilization. He refuted them by pointing out that Western civilization was based upon scientific materialism which resulted in a rule of force. This cult of Might was far inferior to the Oriental culture which was based on virtues of benevolence, justice, and morality — the Kingly Way. The problem of Pan-Asianism was a cultural problem of the conflict of the Occidental rule of Might with the Oriental rule of Right. There was, for Sun, no question of their intrinsic strength. Nepal, for instance, had sent tributary missions for centuries to China of her own volition. But if England should fall, all her contact with Nepal would cease overnight.

Benevolence alone, however, would not conquer the West; Asia was indebted to its two sentinels, Japan and Turkey, who had armed themselves. Similar measures should also be taken by China. Together with those progressive forces in Western countries that had begun to see the primacy of benevolence, Asian arms would then ensure Asian liberation. Already, progressive forces were to be found in most Western nations; one entire country had already reoriented her policy to insist on the rule of right and advocate the principles of benevolence and justice. For this reason, Russia was now being shunned by Europe. She had subscribed to the Oriental values.

Sun's final words were addressed to his hosts of the evening:

We advocate the avenging of the wrong done to those in revolt against the civilization of the rule of Might, with the aim of seeking a civilization of peace and equality and the emancipation of all races. Japan today has become acquainted with Western civilization of the rule of Might, but retains the characteristics of the Oriental civilization of the rule of Right. Now the question remains whether Japan will be the hawk of the Western civilization of the rule of Might or the tower of strength of the Orient. This is the choice which lies before the people of Japan.[18]

It was primarily in this speech that Wang Ching-wei claimed to find the justification for his coöperation with Japan.[19] The Japanese felt that it constituted a fitting conclusion to Sun Yat-sen's years of friendship with them. According to Kayano, the speech was a final legacy to Japan; [20] Pan-Asianism thus stood forth as Sun's real ideology.[21]

Actually, the speech was not the blanket endorsement of Japanese policies that Wang made it seem. But it is clear that at the end of his life Sun Yat-sen was still not convinced that Japan had chosen a course unfavorable to China. And if Sun, at that late date, was still so reluctant to abandon the dream of his revolutionary years, it is evident that during the Meiji Period those ideas and ideals of Asiatic coöperation were more than the contrivance of Japanese imagination. They represented a reasonable and probable solution to a very present problem, and they were abandoned only gradually and reluctantly as the Chinese revolutionaries saw Japan try to justify a rule of Might with Oriental maxims of Right.

CONCLUSION

Despite the optimism with which Sun Yat-sen had continued to regard Sino-Japanese coöperation, it was evident by June 1929, that the small contingent of Japanese who stood before his tomb on Purple Mountain were symbols of a hope and a period that had passed. They and their countrymen had had little contact with the Northern Expedition. Already their presence and their reception seemed in rather anomalous contravention of the increasing acrimony that had marked the relations of the Chinese Republic with its most powerful neighbor. As years passed, and as acrimony hardened into warfare, the earlier friendships of Sun Yat-sen with the Japanese seemed increasingly incongruous. It has been attempted here to survey those friendships and activities from the perspective of the earlier years, thereby to remove anachronism and lessen incongruity. Sun's friendships with Japanese, and his collaboration with them, were far more logical and natural than they have since appeared. The Japanese that aided Sun Yat-sen were not always of one mind, and their intentions were not solely those of aggrandizement. To point out, in closing, the significance of that diversity of opinion, it will be useful to recapitulate briefly the gist of what was discussed previously.

The close coöperation of the Chinese revolutionaries with the Japanese nationalists was conceivable only within the broader context of Western imperialism. To that physical and ideological aggression Pan-Asianism seemed the logical answer. In the face of the new, unprecedented power of the West which could be met only through mimesis and adaptation, the ancient superiority of the Chinese over their Japanese neighbors was replaced by a willingness to avail themselves of the ready-made synthesis of Western tools and Eastern values which Japan professed to offer.

The awareness of this need on the part of the Chinese coincided with a moment of history in Japan in which the Tokugawa restrictive military rule which had eschewed all foreign influence was replaced overnight by a group of eager young planners. They had studied under teachers whose chief grievances against the military feudalism had been its refusal to seek adventure, trade, or expansion abroad and its resulting betrayal of the imperial mission; Japan was, as a result, likely to come under foreign control. The facts of their case — the actual intention of Europe regarding Japan at that period — were irrelevant to the emotional drive they built up. Certainly their fears seemed well justified by what they had heard of China and what they saw of the early traders and merchants.

For the first decades of the new regime in Japan, however, any sort of ideological or sympathetic link with China was likely to be emphatically rejected. Fukuzawa Yukichi's joy at his liberation from the "dregs of Chinese philosophy" expressed the feelings of his age. "China" was compounded of misgovernment such as Japan had never known, an intellectual stultification that the Tokugawa regime had barely approached, and shameful weakness which was made the more obvious by the need to placate the foreign masters. For Japan, freedom lay in an identification with those masters and not with their servant. The early Meiji leaders therefore did their utmost to prove their worthiness to join the parade of Western powers demanding ever greater rights in China. To do this was to gain their liberty at home and freedom of action abroad. Japan's early treaties with China were accordingly worded with caution, and the phrases calling for mutual friendship and aid were inserted out of Chinese desire and not from Japanese expressions of amity.

At the same time, the Meiji leaders had to guard against domestic chauvinists and warmongers who were impatient with delay and who sought immediate satisfaction abroad for the frustration they felt in being removed from the social and political pinnacle at home. The leaders opposed those chauvinists with arguments that the West would not permit the use of force by so crude and immature a rival as Japan then was. A period of tutelage in the political arts, techniques, and, above all, the laws of Western nations was necessary. The oligarchs were able to win out over their opponents, and, by grudging compromises and reluctant concessions, they maintained internal unity while government, industry, and the military were developed and strengthened. This policy received its crown of success when the turn of the century found Japan with a constitution Europe could respect, a victory over China which proved her military worth, and tariffs that allowed her industries a chance to develop independently.

Despite the evident reasonableness of the government's procedure in conciliating and imitating the Western powers, formidable groups had continued to assert their belief in an immediate Asian orientation of policy instead of further appeasement of Europe. In small discussion groups, in patriotic societies, in demogogic activities, in newspaper work, and among the small political parties, they did all they could to impeach the government's course as cowardly and ignoble. These men now decided that Japan's mission could best be advanced by sponsorship and cultivation of the various reforms and nationalist groups that were trying to bring about a renovation in the outmoded government and society of Korea and China. Their activities have been the subject of this study.

There were numerous points of contact for these groups and their Chinese and Korean wards. They impressed upon them the similarity of the struggle taking place in Korea and, more particularly, in China, with that which had gone on in Japan. The Manchus were representatives of "feudalism"; they were tradition-bound and inefficient; they stood for weak, ignoble compromise with the foreign aggressors. The same things had been true in Japan when the hapless Tokugawa Shōgunate had had to shoulder blame for the numerous evils then prevailing. Opposition to such a regime was required by every rule of courage, morality, and loyalty to the best of the past.

So it was that Tōyama and his cohorts, who felt themselves in the political tradition of Saigō Takamori and the ideological heirs of Yoshida Shōin, could urge their assistance upon Chinese nationalists. Their case could quite easily be rendered more convincing and less menacing than the use of names like Yoshida and Saigō would suggest. Yoshida was an opponent of narrow exclusion and a backer of Western technology, as Saigō was a friend and sometimes a mentor of several of the new liberal leaders. Both had been fearless fighters for their cause. These men stood for more than mere militarism.

But of course the issue of Pan-Asianism was not purely, or, one is tempted to say, even primarily, one of ideas. Social change and economic distress had combined in the formation of the patriotic societies and the early political parties. The government-sponsored industry, which had grown and prospered, had played an important role in allaying the social and financial malaise of many of the ex-samurai. In the face of the tremendous population rise and meager natural resources of Japan, this industry could survive only by finding raw materials and markets abroad. For all such purposes, China inevitably loomed more and more important. The industrial firms which owed their life and prosperity to government favors could hardly risk giving all their support to determined opposition forces, but they did find it possible to have close connections with the main figures of the political parties. The shipping and coal empires of the Mitsubishi firm were early allied with the numerous activities and enterprises of the party of Ōkuma Shigenobu. The early *Jiyūtō* group of Itagaki had less urban and more rural support, and the extremism to which its less sophisticated base rendered it subject largely vitiated its early influence as an effective instrument. When it was resurrected anew after a dissolution forced by this extremism, it soon assumed the character of a foil to the Ōkuma group, for it was financed by and represented competing industrial and financial interests. The struggle of the parties and of the financial firms, however, was not a mortal one. Their highest figures could usually be conciliated or checked by judicious expenditure of funds, privileges, or posts. Their basic aims were too similar to allow permanent rifts. Those aims centered around a desire for some moderate say in government through the parties they sponsored, and a foreign policy that would give their industries tariff freedom and provide a market for their products.

It is easy to over-emphasize the importance of the business groups in policy levels. They were too much the creatures of their government, and too dependent on its favor, to exert a particularly striking independence. Nevertheless, they were a central element in Japanese society. Money gained through their enterprises was essential for every project of strengthening and modernizing the country. The business leaders amassed huge fortunes, as did the political leaders.

Each of the oligarchs became wealthy; such projects as Ōkuma's Waseda University and the political parties set up by Itō and Katsura gave sufficient proof of their relation to the enterprises government subsidies had held together.

The main contribution the industrialists and financiers were able to make toward the ends of Pan-Asianism was their support of the dissatisfied groups who agitated for an increased emphasis on Asia. They could provide such circles with financial help, with occasional government contacts and interviews, and with protection against the harsh police repression that would ordinarily have attended unauthorized or subversive political agitation. The strangely even tenor of the life of Tōyama Mitsuru could only have derived from such a double base of financial and ideological integrity. Of these, the latter was certainly the more important. With a long and honored career as exemplification of all traditional virtues, Tōyama was a symbol of old-line simplicity and honesty that no government would have attacked without serious reflection. But in addition to this prestige, Tōyama enjoyed cordial friendship with many a moneyed baron. His Kyushu background and his widespread contacts combined with his great prestige to make him a valuable ally in several phases of the coal industry.

Tōyama's mine operator friends very probably shared many of his affirmations and prejudices, but their main interest in China was certainly the iron interests which Japan lacked. These could have been combined with their own coal for the development of the heavy industry complex of modern Kyushu. Thus one of the three most important independent mine operators in Kyushu, Yasukawa Keiichirō, was from the first an admirer of Tōyama. He furnished funds for the early *Genyōsha* activities, supplied the funds for Tōyama's trip to China in 1911, and entertained Sun Yat-sen as his guest in 1913.

And yet, it would be a serious oversimplification to conclude that Tōyama and his men were mere hirelings of such capitalists. There is, of course, no difficulty in seeing why Tōyama's Kyushu mine operators should have responded with enthusiasm to his appeals for help in his many projects of aid and comfort for Sun Yat-sen. Numerous other Asian projects, such as the China Trade

Research Bureau of Arao Kiyoshi, had an evident value for the business interests. But on the whole, semi-official and large-scale financial support for Sun Yat-sen was limited to the brief period between his return to Japan in 1898 and the events of 1900. Thereafter, official circles in Japan were increasingly unfriendly to Sun's radicalism and republicanism. Sun's difficulties extended to his Japanese friends, and their persistence in his behalf showed a decided independence of action. Their actual help, however, was largely limited to moral support. On the few occasions when Sun's friends could approach him with concrete suggestions, their proposals were transparently opportunistic. The drawbacks of such assistance were illustrated by the offer Mori Kaku extended to Sun for the purchase of Manchuria in 1913 — an offer that was made through Miyazaki.

When all this has been granted, however, we remain confronted by the acceptance of the sentiments and expressions of Japanese Pan-Asianism by Sun Yat-sen and his closest friends. Today, Tōyama and his cohorts seem patently unworthy of inspiring confidence in the minds of Chinese nationalists, no matter how hard-pressed the revolutionaries may be for help. It is the more surprising that they should have convinced Sun Yat-sen, a man with a Western education and numerous foreign friends.

It seems clear that the protestations of Tōyama and his men would have been futile if it had not been for the efforts and personalities of a smaller group of men who served as the actual intermediaries and personal friends of the Chinese leaders. In using the word "idealist" for persons like Miyazaki Torazō, one courts the danger of implying a complete lack of idealism in the other figures and a corresponding lack of nationalism in Miyazaki himself. Moreover, it would be erroneous to impute elaborate thought processes to any of the *shishi*. They *felt* more than they *thought,* and they acted before they reasoned. All that can be safely maintained is that the radical liberals, instead of capitalizing on and profiting by social distress in Japan as Tōyama did, were revolted by it. They wanted a different solution to the agrarian hardships and national inequality than that offered by military strength and diplomatic maneuver. A rebirth for oppressed peasantries elsewhere in Asia was, for them, a necessary adjunct and stimulus to amelioration of the peasant's lot in Japan. Hence Ōi Kentarō, with his Quixotic schemes for Korean reform, and the Miyazaki brothers with their dream of applying Henry George's theories to China could offer a Kim Ok-kiun or a Sun Yat-sen a genuine friendship that must frequently have been worth more than the gold of the industrialists.

In men like Ōi, Miyazaki, and Kayano the Chinese leaders recognized kindred spirits. They shared a hasty and imperfect philosophical position in which the bases of their traditional culture had been removed without having been adequately replaced by Western substitutes. Midway between two societies and traditions, they tried to use the one to overthrow the other. Historically and intellectually, they were comrades in arms in a cause whose goals were but dimly visible. Indeed, the discernible goals were seldom more explicit than the destruction of Western imperialism. In this cause Chinese and Japanese were partners, and the revolutionaries could relate their struggle to the political battles in Japan. "We," said Sun, "are the *shishi* of the Meiji Restoration of fifty years ago."

The constituency of the Japanese group Sun knew and liked was as unstable as the individual world view presented by Miyazaki. This lack of a stable base of support nevertheless increased its influence as much as it weakened its ability to carry through on promises. This was so because the *shishi,* representing no fixed group or interest, were necessarily dependent upon outside support from government or private interests. The funds provided to Miyazaki by Inukai and Tōyama, and their obviously close association with him, inevitably extended to them the ideals which Sun felt in Miyazaki. And since Miyazaki, Kayano, Tōyama, and Inuki all represented opposition to the oligarchy, they could blunt Chinese suspicions of Japanese imperialism by identifying that imperialism with the workings of an unfriendly government. And since even that imperialism weakened a government Sun Yat-sen was determined to overthrow, it is not surprising that Sun was slow to think evil of his Japanese allies.

This, in outline, was the Japanese society that received Sun Yat-sen. To Sun, that society seemed capable of generous and far-sighted action, and he never fully resigned himself to the harsh fact that a rapacious imperialism would destroy the broader and earlier dreams of Japanese friendship. In this reluctance to credit his hosts with violating the canons of enlightened self-interest, Sun was a true child of the nineteenth century. But he was not alone in his conviction, for the Japanese too were so convinced that it was ultimately to China's best interest to coöperate with them that they refused to believe that the awakened national consciousness of aroused Chinese students was more than a temporary gesture of ingratitude. Those failings on both sides thus transcended the immediate political issues, and reflected more fundamental frames of psychological and philosophical conviction. This being so, we may conclude this study by advancing four rather sweeping, though interrelated, morals which suggest themselves.

First of all, a common enemy provides only the most negative and temporary basis upon which to construct a party of alliance. The Western danger was the strongest element which impelled neighboring Asiatics to unite in coöperation. Nevertheless, that danger was rarely as acute as it was pictured, and at its worst it hardly approximated the new Japanese imperialism that replaced it. Again, the Manchu Dynasty served as common foe to Sun and the Japanese, but Sun miscalculated in thinking that the Japanese opposition to that rule was as implacable as his own. Among the Chinese leaders, hatred of the Manchus was essential to the formation of the *T'ung-meng-hui,* but the realization of the revolution showed how slight such a negative bond could be. The same was true in the last days of Tokugawa Japan, when samurai who sought adventure combined with others who sought change, and in the days of Meiji, when all hues of political opposition rallied to attack the government.

In the second place, a consideration of the use to which the words of former leaders can be put by self-styled followers serves as a reminder of the need for considering those words in their historical context. By this means, figures like Sakuma Shōzan and Yoshida Shōin regain their original prestige as daring radicals, and those who seem to resurrect their thoughts without their setting stand exposed as obscurantists. There may have been little distinction to be drawn between the actual feelings of Yoshida Shōin and Tōyama Mitsuru — although even that is open to debate — but in their chronological, contemporary importance, they must be considered to stand at opposite poles. The same is true, of course, of those who sought to keep inviolate the words of Sun Yat-sen, in disregard of the obvious temporal factors that conditioned those words. Thus it was that Wang Ching-wei, Chiang Kai-shek, and Mao Tze-tung could each claim to be a follower. For each, proper quotations can be produced, but it must be evident after a consideration of Sun's personality that he would have parted with each of them.

A third observation is that national and factional movements can be used and directed to serve secondary ends only with the greatest difficulty and danger. Sun Yat-sen and the Japanese were each bitterly disappointed in their expectations of the other. Within China, the attempt to use Yuan Shih-k'ai permanently disillusioned Sun Yat-sen, and within Japan the ill-starred coalition of liberals and chauvinist reactionaries ended with Inukai's murder by army officers who considered themselves spiritual followers of Tōyama. For the Japanese, attempts to arouse Chinese national spirit to overthrow the Manchus ended when success in the secondary aim doomed their ultimate goal. The new Chinese nationalism could best be directed against Japan, and it grew the more as Japan tried to retreat to a policy of conservatism by backing Manchu rule in Manchuria.

Finally, the conviction of destiny and historical justification was a key element in the extended coöperation and complete failure of the projects of Japanese aid to Sun Yat-sen. The Japanese, secure in the logic of their position, did not realize that they could destroy the principle of coöperation with China by their actions. Despite the sincerity of individual Japanese and despite the logic of a general union of Asiatic nations against Western imperialism, Japan was the victim of her own sense of destiny. The conviction of Japanese sincerity and righteousness was a guiding thread that made possible the varied careers of adventurers from Tokugawa to modern days. Their drawback, however, was a fundamental inability to grasp the fact that tutelage implied eventual maturity for the tutored, and that guidance should result in ultimate arrival at modernization. Moreover, any appeal based upon traditional Chinese virtues overlooked the probability that the blissful harmony of international relations pictured would find the satellites revolving about the Middle Kingdom, and not its neighbor. A similar self-imposed guidance was also the bane of Sun Yat-sen. It rendered him intolerant of competitors in China, and it produced uncritical reliance upon Japanese aid which, since it helped him, could not but help China.

It is not difficult to see the possible ends to which Sun Yat-sen's legacy of Pan-Asian sentiment can be put by the Chinese Communists as they choose to promote the common bond of Asiatic and world communism. In their propaganda, America has already assumed a more frightening aspect of rapacious imperialism than ever England had for Sun Yat-sen. The Communists, however, are the possessors of a new sense of destiny and historical justification which, under the name of Science, contains many of the same flaws which weakened Japanese claims to righteousness. The basic incongruities of destiny, infallibility, and tutelage that rendered Japan incapable of leading Asia will again combine to plague the newer dialectic.

A NOTE ON SOURCES

This study lies midway between two well-established fields of study, those of modern Japanese and Chinese history, and it concerns itself in part with a third field, that of diplomatic history. While it would be impractical to attempt to do justice to this coverage in a well-rounded bibliography, some comments on the character and limitations of the Chinese and Japanese sources which have been used most heavily may be of help for those who plan to read farther.

In recent years we have had several new and workable bibliographies. For modern China, John K. Fairbank and Kwang-chin Liu, *Modern China: A Bibliographical Note to Chinese Works 1898–1937* (Cambridge, 1950) will prove of great help. Nothing as comprehensive exists in English for Japanese sources. The bibliographical essays appended to E. H. Norman's *Japan's Emergence as a Modern State* (New York, 1940) and Nobutaka Ike's *The Beginnings of Political Democracy in Japan* (Baltimore, 1950) contain good surveys of some of the materials available in Japanese. Most recently, Robert E. Ward's *Guide to Japanese Reference and Research Materials in the Field of Political Science* (Ann Arbor, 1950), and John W. Hall's *Japanese History: A Guide to Japanese Reference and Research Materials* (Ann Arbor, 1954) have become essential guides to Japanese sources.

a. General Works

For recent Japanese history, Tōyama Shigeki's *Meiji Ishin* (The Meiji Restoration; Tokyo, 1951), 358 pp., is an invaluable guide. Mr. Tōyama treats the period from Tempō (1830) to the Satsuma Rebellion (1877). His work is footnoted carefully and it contains a helpful bibliography. For Tokugawa expansionist patriots, the fifty volume set of Tokutomi Iichirō (Sohō), *Kinsei Nippon kokumin shi* (A history of our country in recent times; Tokyo, 1934), is extremely useful. See especially volumes 25 and 30, which treat the Tokugawa decline and the situation before the coming of Perry. Tokutomi, whose intellectual hegira mirrored the national experience, began as an enthusiastic young Christian, conducted the progressive school in which Miyazaki first met the heady doctrines of liberty and people's rights, and then ended securely in the nationalist and conservative fold. This work, which dates from his mature years, reflects his nationalist zeal. It attempts to establish the late Tokugawa patriots as true prophets of their militarist successors.

For the political developments of the Meiji and Taishō periods, Ōtsu Junichirō, *Dai Nihon kensei shi* (A constitutional history of Japan; Tokyo, 1927–8), 10 vols., although somewhat dated, has not been surpassed. Ōtsu was a participant in the struggles for constitutional government, and he treats the liberal movement sympathetically. A work of encyclopedic proportions, this set includes highlights of Diet orations, excerpts from government papers, and memoranda; it is studded with long quotations from participants in the political battles.

During the 1930's, younger Japanese historians turned away from political history to problems of economic analysis. Since World War II there has been a new interest in reinterpreting political history in the light of previous economic findings. One of the more interesting attempts at this is that of Shinobu Seisaburō, whose *Taishō seiji shi* (Political history of Taishō; Tokyo, 1952), 4 vols., while not closely documented, relies heavily upon some of the biographies noted below for political details. It presents an interesting and readable account.

For Sino-Japanese relations, Wang Yün-sheng, *Liu-shih-nien-lai Chung-kuo yü Jih-pen* (Sixty years of Sino-Japanese relations; Tientsin, 1933), 6 vols., is a basic source. The author, a former editor of *Ta Kung Pao,* has used unpublished Chinese documents as well as Japanese sources. Liu Yen, *Ou-chan ch'i-chien Chung-Jih chiao-she shih* (A history of Sino-Japanese negotiations during the European war; Shanghai, 1921), is also useful. In Japanese, Watanabe Ikujirō, *Nihon kinsei gaikō shi* (Diplomatic history of modern Japan; Tokyo, 1938), remains a useful summary. It has many post-war competitors.

The history of the Chinese revolution of 1911 is to be found in the compendious work of Chou Lu, *Chung-kuo kuo-min-tang shih-kao* (Draft history of the Kuomintang; Shanghai, 1929), 2 vols., 1262 pp. This work includes a good deal of primary material. It is a convenient source for platforms, manifestoes, and even occasional articles, letters, and other writings of leading revolutionary figures. Feng Tzu-yu, a participant in the revolution who spent much time in Japan, has several anecdotal histories. *Chung-hua-min-kuo k'ai-kuo-ch'ien ko-ming shih* (History of the revolution before the founding of the republic; Shanghai, 1928), 322 pp., and *Ko-ming i-shih* (Reminiscences of the revolution; Chunking, 1945), 3 vols., contain illuminating stories of the close liaison with the Japanese. Feng is almost the only one of the Chinese participants in that movement who has written at length about his life in Japan. I have not used a postwar, four volume edition published in Shanghai.

There are several good histories of the revolution in Japanese. Hatano Kenichi, *Chūgoku kokumintō tsūshi* (A history of the Chinese Nationalist Party; Tokyo, 1943), 639 pp., gives a carefully documented and reliable account. The author, long a reporter in Peking, later served in the Japanese Foreign Office, where he helped edit some of the monumental histories of political movements in China which that bureau compiled. Yoshino Sakuzō, a pioneer student of recent Japanese history and a leading liberal, wrote his *Shina kakumei shōshi* (A short history of the Chinese revolution) in 1917. Yoshino had served as one of the Japanese advisers to Yuan Shih-k'ai, and he knew China well. He later collaborated with the great Japanese sinologue Katō Shigeshi to write *Shina kakumei shi* (A history of the Chinese revolution; Tokyo, 1922), 457 pp., far and away the best and most convenient history of that movement which I have found.

b. Japanese Organizations

For studies of the Japanese liberal movement and its relations with Asian causes, one should first consult the official history, Itagaki Taisuke, ed., *Jiyūtō shi* (A history of the Liberal Party; Tokyo, 1910), 2 vols. More recently, Hirano Yoshitarō has interested himself in this problem. His *Minken undō no hatten* (The course of the movement for people's rights; Tokyo, 1948), 340 pp., focuses chiefly on Ōi Kentarō. Hirano's "Nisshi kōshō shi" (History of Sino-Japanese relations), in *Shina mondai jiten* (Dictionary of the China problem; Tokyo, 1942), pp. 592–601, gives a quick sketch of the relations with Sun Yat-sen. Tōyama Shigeki has contributed some penetrating studies on the contradictions which resulted from the expansionist tendencies of the Japanese liberal-democratic leaders. Especially valuable are his "Seikan ron, jiyūminken ron, hōken ron" (Discussions of a punitive expedition against Korea, liberty and people's rights, and feudalism), in *Rekishigaku kenkyū* (Historical Research, Tokyo), Nos. 143, 145 (January, May 1950), and "Jiyūminken undō to tairiku mondai" (The liberal-democratic movement and the problem of the continent), *Sekai* (June 1950).

The histories of the nationalist societies and the memoirs of their members have been used heavily for this study. Those interested in the development of Japanese nationalism will find especially valuable the books of Kinoshita Hanji, *Nihon kokka shugi undō shi* (A history of the Japanese nationalist movement; Tokyo, 1940), 557 pp., and his more recent three-volume history of Japanese fascism, *Nihon fascism shi*. Another useful work is that of Kada Tetsuji, *Nihon kokka shugi no hatten*

(The development of Japanese nationalism; Tokyo, 1938), 390 pp.

The official histories of the patriotic societies are invaluable sources of information for the activities, programs, and personnel of those groups. Far from attempting to conceal the activities of those groups, they tend to exaggerate their role. They must therefore be used with caution and checked against other sources. The first of these, the *Genyōsha shashi* (The society's history of the *Genyōsha;* Tokyo, 1917), 731 pp., is particularly good for the period through 1911 and for the Japanese figures who led the *Genyōsha.* More ambitious is the official history of the *Kokuryūkai,* Kuzuu Yoshihisa, *Tōa senkaku shishi kiden* (Stories and biographies of pioneer East Asian adventurers), cited here as *TSSK* (Tokyo, 1933–1936), 3 vols., total, 2588 pp. This set begins with late Tokugawa expansionists, and it carries on an extraordinarily full account of activities up to the enthronement of Henry Pu Yi in Manchukuo. Most of volume 3 is devoted to biographies. Kuzuu, who was head of the *Kokuryūkai* in the 1930's, also included in the society's *Nikkan gappō hishi* (The secret history of the Japanese annexation of Korea; Tokyo, 1930), 2 vols., 634 and 778 pp., a sixty-page chronology of the society's activities at the end of Volume I. This is frequently helpful in checking dates. Also by Kuzuu and from the *Kokuryūkai* press is a two-volume *Nisshi kōshō gaishi* (An unofficial history of Sino-Japanese relations; Tokyo, 1935), which traces relations between Japan and China from early Meiji through the China Incident of 1937. It is, however, not always reliable.

Of a different order is a publication of the *Dōbunkai* edited by Nakajima Masao, *Taishi kaiko roku* (Memoirs about China; Tokyo, 1936), 2 vols., 781 and 1520 pp. This work, compiled by the "Society for the compilation of writings about men who have rendered conspicuous service in regard to China," is particularly noteworthy for its coverage of societies which sought to further cultural bonds with China. Its coverage of incidents is more judicious and more official, and it includes accounts of commercial ventures and personnel as well as the political story. Volume 2 is given over to biographies. The Supplement, *Zoku taishi kaiko roku* (Tokyo, 1941), 2 vols., 588 and 1316 pp., includes, in Vol. 1, accounts of diplomatic wrangles and commercial developments of the thirties, and in Vol. 2, biographies of persons who failed to be included in the earlier volume of biographies.

For cultural contacts between Japan and China, there are the excellent works of Professor Sanetō Keishū of Waseda University, *Meiji Nisshi bunka kōshō* (Cultural relations between Japan and China in the Meiji

Period; Tokyo, 1943), 394 pp., which includes excerpts from the diary of Ambassador Ho Ju-chang, notes on early cultural organizations, and the diary of a Chinese student. More detailed is the same author's *Chūgokujin Nihon ryūgaku shikō* (Draft history of Chinese students in Japan; Tokyo, 1939), 368 pp. This excellent volume carries the student movement into the 1930's.

c. Personal Accounts

For the writings of participants, Sun Yat-sen's collected works, *Tsung-li ch'üan-chi* (Complete collected works of the Leader), edited by Hu Han-min (Shanghai, 1930), total 2442 pp., are of course basic. This collection includes speeches, writings, and letters. Practically all of it is also available in Japanese in the Foreign Office publication *Son Bun shugi* (Sunism; Tokyo, 1936), 2 vols., which includes some items not available in the other. In addition, Mr. Miyazaki Ryūsuke, in Tokyo, kindly made available nine letters from Sun Yat-sen to his father as well as the notes which Sun and the elder Miyazaki scribbled on the occasion of their first meeting. Some of Wang Ching-wei's essays written for *Min Pao* can be found in *Wang Ching-wei wen-ts'un* (Collected essays of Wang Ching-wei; Canton, 1926), 258 pp. Also worthy of note is a collection of Sun's pro-Japanese writings which were issued in Shanghai in 1941 under the title *China and Japan: Natural Friends — Unnatural Enemies,* edited by T'ang Liang-li and with a foreword by President Wang Ching-wei. Another follower of Sun's, Tai T'ien-ch'ou, has, in his *Jih-pen-lun* (Discussion of Japan; Shanghai, 1928), 176 pp., included personal accounts of talks with Prince Katsura, Admiral Akiyama, and General Tanaka along with a historical sketch of the Meiji Restoration and an enthusiastic chapter on Itagaki Taisuke.

Among the Japanese adventurers, Miyazaki Torazō (Tōten), *Sanjū-sannen no yume* (The thirty-three years' dream; Tokyo, 1926, 1943), has been used heavily. This is a highly personal account which traces the author's intellectual development from childhood. Also of note for Miyazaki's change from Christianity is his anti-Christian polemic, *Kyōjin ron* (Discussion of madmen; Tokyo: 1902). Unfortunately, Miyazaki is rather difficult to document for the later period. His rival for the role as Sun's confidant, Kayano Chōchi, has written *Chūka minkoku kakumei hikyū* (Private sources for the Chinese republican revolution; Tokyo, 1940), 431 pp. This volume is well written with many personal touches as well as a history of the revolution, and it is copiously illustrated. Besides pictures, the illustrations include over five hundred photographs of the loyalty oaths Sun demanded from the members of his organization in 1913. Hirayama Shū's account can be found in an article, "Shina kakumeitō oyobi himitsu kessha" (The Chinese revolutionary party and the secret societies), in *Nihon oyobi Nihonjin* (Japan and the Japanese; Tokyo), pp. 75–108 (November 1911). This article is not signed, but it is clearly Hirayama's. It is particularly good for the early work of the Japanese with the secret societies in China and for the attempt to help Aguinaldo in the Philippines. Akiyama Teisuke's account was given to a friend, Muramatsu Shōfū, who published it as *Akiyama Teisuke wa kataru: Kane, Koi, Hotoke* (Akiyama Teisuke talking: Money, Love, Buddha; Toyko, 1948), 260 pp. This work is of value for descriptions of money-raising activities and for the arrangements for the talks with Katsura in 1913. Kita Ikki's *Shina kakumei gaishi* (Unofficial history of the Chinese revolution; Tokyo, 1931), 435 pp., is an invaluable first-hand account which includes analyses of revolutionary forces and personalities as well as accounts of the political and military events in which the author participated.

Among personal accounts of those more highly placed in Japanese government and society, mention should be made of the breezy memoirs of Ambassador Hayashi Gonsuke, *Waga shichijū nen o kataru* (Telling the story of my seventy years; Tokyo, 1939), 403 pp., for some of the dealings with the warlords, and Prince Higashi-Kuni's *Watakushi no kiroku* (My memoirs; Tokyo, 1947), for the desperate plan to send Tōyama Mitsuru to China during World War II. Finally, Hara Kei's diary, *Hara Kei nikki* (Tokyo, 1950), 9 vols., is a mine of important information and comment for the greater part of the Meiji and Taishō periods. Entries run from 1890 to 1921. It has been used heavily by Professor Shinobu for his *Taishō seiji shi*.

d. Biographies

The *Lives* of important Japanese figures have been used extensively for this study. They are inexhaustible mines of information of every kind, and they require a word of description. These works are usually commissioned by the subject's family or by his political associates, and they are repositories of his writings, speeches, and letters. A frequent feature is the assembling of contemporaries of the subject for sessions of discussion and reminiscences. The comments so passed, recorded by secretaries, are then inserted at appropriate points in the narrative, accredited to the appropriate speaker. The biographies are thus compilations of raw material for a proper study of each figure, and their value varies with the nature of the editing that has been done. When properly checked against each other to allow for bias, they become excellent sources for recent Japanese history, policy, and thought.

Tokutomi Iichirō has to his credit a three-volume set devoted to Yamagata, *Kōshaku Yamagata Aritomo den* (Tokyo, 1933), 1226, 1236, and 1230 pp., two volumes on Katsura, *Kōshaku Katsura Tarō den* (Tokyo, 1917), 1131 and 1051 pp., and two volumes on Matsukata, *Kōshaku Matsukata Masayoshi den* (Tokyo, 1935) 1201 and 1187 pp. These three sets are about equal in value; Tokutomi resolved all problems of selection by ruling in favor of material and comment which would shed the greatest credit on his hero. Considerably better are the sets devoted to Itō, *Itō Hirobumi den* (Tokyo, 1940), 3 vols., 1030, 1059, and 1059 pp., compiled by the society formed to "eulogize the Prince," and the excellent *Life* of Inoue, *Segai Inoue Kō den* (Tokyo, 1933–1934), 5 vols., of which I have here used chiefly vols. 3, 944 pp., and 5, 860 pp. Somewhat less satisfactory is the set devoted to Ōkuma, *Ōkuma Kō hachijū-gonen shi* (Tokyo, 1926), 3 vols., edited by Ichijima Kenkichi. There is, however, a good work by Professor Watanabe Ikujirō of Waseda University, *Ōkuma Shigenobu* (Tokyo, 1943), 444 pp.

Probably because its contents bear so largely on foreign relations, the set on Katō, *Katō Kōmei den,* by Itō Masanori (Tokyo, 1929), 2 vols., 816 and 786 pp., has been used more widely in the West than any of the other sets listed here. Works like Lafargue's *China and the World War* (1937), and, more recently, Mario Toscano's excellent study of the Twenty-one Demands, *Guerra diplomatica in Estremo Oriente* (Turino, 1951), 2 vols., have used material from this set. Toscano's work has also made use of some of the material in the Ōkuma set. But while the Katō biography is on the whole a good one, it needs to be checked against those of the *genrō* whom it denounces.

Excellent too is the set devoted to Gotō Shimpei, *Gotō Shimpei,* by Tsurumi Yūsuke (Tokyo, 1937), 4 vols. Shinobu Seisaburō has excerpted from this material for his *Gotō Shimpei* (Tokyo, 1941), 392 pp.

Sun Yat-sen figures much in the *Life* of Inukai, *Inukai Bokudō den,* Washio Yoshitsugu, ed. (Tokyo, 1938–1939), 3 vols., especially in volume 2, of which pp. 705 to 819 are entitled "East Asian Concerns."

An extremely important figure in financial and industrial enterprises in China was Mori Kaku, whose biography, *Tōa shintaisei no senku: Mori Kaku* (Herald of the new order in Asia: Mori Kaku; Tokyo, 1940),

1124 pp., contains numerous details of Mitsui attempts to underwrite Sun Yat-sen and, through him, the Hanyehping works. The Inoue biography is also of help on this point.

Considerably less reliable is Fujimoto Shosoku, *Kyojin Tōyama Mitsuru Ō* (Grand old Tōyama Mitsuru; Tokyo, 1922), 890 pp., published by the *Kokuryūkai*. This is less a biography than a collection of tales which do Tōyama honor.

Hirano Yoshitarō's *Bajō Ōi Kentarō den* (Tokyo, 1938), 476 pp., is the best study available of this important figure. Much of this book reappears in the same author's post-war *Minken undō no hatten,* but the biography is more detailed, and it gives more generous excerpts from Ōi's writings. Unfortunately this work appeared in an issue of only 300 copies, and it has become quite rare.

The above biographies have been those which I have found most useful for this study. It should be understood that they represent only a fraction of the biographical literature of this sort which is available for recent Japanese history.

There are many biographies of Sun Yat-sen, but none is completely satisfactory. Suzue Genichi, *Son Bun den* (Tokyo, 1950), 555 pp., is useful, but marred by the author's attempt to give a complete interpretation of the Chinese revolution in Marxist terms. Sun frequently drops out of sight. The author originally published this under a pseudonym, Ō Su-shi (Wang Shu-chih; Tokyo, 1931), 438 pp., to avoid police investigation of his Marxism. Of the many works in English, Lyon Sharman's *Sun Yat-sen: His Life and its Meaning* (New York, 1934), 418 pp., has proven the most careful and most useful. Also of note is the early work of Karl A. Wittfogel, *Sun Yat Sen: Aufzeichnungen eines Chinesischen Revolutionärs* (Berlin, n.d.), a Marxist account which, although occasionally in error, is stimulating. It has had a good deal of influence in Japan. Mario Ponce's *Sun Yat-sen, El fundador de la Republica de China* (Manila, 1912), 71 pp., is of some help for the Philippine imbroglio, but not as good as Enrique J. Corpus, "Japan and the Philippine Revolution," *Philippine Social Science Review,* VI: 249–298 (Manila, Oct. 1934).

The great majority of the actors of this piece have not been deemed sufficiently important by their countrymen to receive full biographical treatment, and it is therefore fortunate that the *Kokuryūkai* and *Dōbunkai* publications listed above include a total of three volumes of biographies of minor figures. Those in the *Dōbunkai's Taishi kaiko roku* and its supplement tend to be longer and better than those in the

Kokuryūkai set. Some, but not many, of these men are listed in the basic Japanese biographical dictionary, *Shinsen dai jimmei jiten* (Tokyo, 1937), 9 vols. Their Chinese counterparts appear in *Tōyō rekishi daijiten* (Tokyo, 1937), 9 vols.

Finally, the recently microfilmed files of the Tokyo Foreign Office open up a multitude of new problems and possibilities for the student. I have used the volumes devoted to refugee revolutionaries, but they constitute only a small portion of the storehouse of official documents now available. A forthcoming catalogue to be issued by the Library of Congress will itemize the reels and their contents for interested users. It is ironic that these records have not yet been made available to Japanese historians.

NOTES

INTRODUCTION

1. Descriptions of the ceremonies can be found in the *North China Herald*, June 6, 1929, and by Shimizu Ginzō, a man who accompanied Inukai and who wrote a daily column for the Japanese paper *Shōwa nichi nichi shimbun*, in *Inukai Bokudō den* (Life of Inukai; Tokyo, 1939), II, 743–767.

2. *Tsung-li ch'üan-chi* (Complete works of the Leader), compiled by Hu Han-min (Shanghai, 1930), I, 6. Kayano Chōchi, however, feels that Sun was at fault in not acknowledging Japanese help more extensively in his writings. *Chūka Minkoku kakumei hikyū* (Private sources for the Chinese Revolution; Tokyo, 1940), p. 59.

3. Inukai Ki, preface to K. Kawakami, *Japan Speaks* (New York, 1930), pp. v, vii. Inukai continued by expressing grief that Sun had chosen a "Red short cut."

4. R. K. Hall, ed., *Kokutai no hongi* (Cardinal Principles of the National Entity of Japan; Cambridge: Harvard University Press, 1949), pp. 175–179.

5. R. d'Auxion de Ruffe, *Chine et Chinois d'Aujourd'hui* (Paris, 1926), pp. 171–208, contains a scathing indictment of Sun.

6. For such a view, see R. M. Roy, *Revolution und Konterrevolution in China* (Berlin, 1930), pp. 206–236. For a different Marxist appraisal, see Karl A. Wittfogel, *Sun Yat Sen: Aufzeichnungen eines Chinesischen Revolutionärs* (Berlin, n.d.), whose opinion of Sun is far more favorable.

7. For example: Wang Yün-sheng, *Liu-shih-nien-lai Chung-kuo yü Jih-pen* (Sixty years of Sino-Japanese relations; Tientsin, 1934), Vol. 6, p. 1, "The general policy of Japan towards China was to promote internal disruption and destroy China's unity." Similarly, one of many journalists: A. M. Pooley, *Japan's Foreign Policies* (London, 1920), p. 56: "To keep the undercurrent of Chinese unrest always on the move, and the Central Government always in hot water, was a most desirable object in the view of Tokyo."

CHAPTER 1. THE IDEOLOGICAL AND POLITICAL CONTEXT OF MEIJI EXPANSIONISM

1. Tokutomi Iichirō, *Kinsei Nippon kokumin shi* (History of our country in recent times), Vol. 25, *Bakufu bunkai sekkin jidai* (The period approaching the decline of the Shōgunate; Tokyo, 1936). For Hayashi, pp. 23–47; for Takayama and Gamō, pp. 403–514. Honda Toshiaki (1734–1821), pp. 71–85, advocated developing Japanese commerce. He thus went farther than Hayashi, but escaped punishment because he was not so well known.

2. Sir George Sansom, *The Western World and Japan* (New York, 1950), pp. 261–266, gives a sympathetic account of the career of Watanabe, with less attention to Takano.

3. D. C. Green, "Osada's Life of Takano Nagahide (1804–1850)," in *Transactions of the Asiatic Society of Japan*, Part III, p. 429 (1913).

4. Tsuchiya Takao, "Bakumatsu shishi no mitaru Shina mondai" (The prob-

lem of China as seen by patriots at the end of the Shōgunate), in *Kaizō,* p. 159 (Tokyo, 1938). Among the plans proposed were those of Aizawa Hakumin (1782–1863), who advocated joint defense of the Amur line with China against Russia, and Satō Shinen (1768–1850), who argued for a gradual conquest of China by way of Manchuria, North China, and South China, and then moves on India and Siam.

5. The famous Dutch scholar Sugita Gempaku was particularly scornful of the samurai. He wrote that "Seven out of ten look like women; their will is depraved, like that of merchants." Tokutomi, *Bakufu bunkai,* p. 336. Sansom, *Western World,* p. 234.

6. Tokutomi, Vol 30, *Perri raikō izen no keisei* (The situation before the arrival of Perry), p. 147. Also Sansom, *Western World,* pp. 253–260. There is also a lengthy biography in *Shinsen dai jimmei daijiten* (New biographical dictionary; Tokyo, 1937), III, 85–87.

7. Among Sakuma's students were important Meiji figures like Katō Hiroyuki and Katsu Awa as well as the famous Hashimoto Sanai (1835–1859), who worked out a plan for conquest of Manchuria, Korea, India, and America. Yoshi S. Kuno, *Japanese Expansion on the Asiatic Continent* (University of California Press, 1940), II, 93–94.

8. Kumura Toshiō, *Yoshida Shōin no shisō to kyōiku* (The thought and teaching of Yoshida Shōin; Tokyo, 1942), *passim;* Heinrich Dumoulin, "Yoshida Shōin (1830–1859). Ein Beitrag zum Verständnis der Geistigen Quellen der Meijierneuerung," in *Monumenta Nipponica,* Vol. 1, No. 2: 58–85 (Tokyo, 1938). See also Sansom, *Western World,* pp. 269–274.

9. Fukumoto Yoshisuke, *Yoshida Shōin no junkoku kyōiku* (The patriotic teaching of Yoshida Shōin; Tokyo, 1933), pp. 475–479, gives a list of Yoshida's famous pupils.

10. Feng Tzu-yu, *Ko-ming i-shih* (Fragments of the history of the revolution; Chungking, 1945), III, 2.

11. Thomas C. Smith, "Government Enterprise and the Initial Phase of Japanese Industrialization, 1850–1880" (Unpublished Doctoral Dissertation, Harvard University, 1948), p. 118. It should be noted that high agricultural taxes were made possible by larger harvests which can be explained through technical improvements, especially in fertilizers and improved strains of rice, and the new motivation that accompanied private landholding rights for the peasants. See, for the increased yields, Bruce F. Johnston, "Agricultural Productivity and Economic Development in Japan," *Journal of Political Economy,* LIX. 6: 498–513 (December 1951). But while the peasants were undoubtedly better off in Meiji than in feudal days, the substitution of new taxes for the old understandably seemed to them of dubious benefit.

12. Kada Tetsuji, *Nihon kokka shugi no hatten* (The development of Japanese nationalism; Tokyo, 1940), pp. 11–13. Sansom, *Western World,* p. 367, discusses an essay by Sada entitled "On lamps as a national disaster."

13. Smith, "Government Enterprise," quotes a sample survey of Hiroshima in 1883 which showed that of some 6000 samurai over 4000 were living at the level of bare subsistence.

14. Ariga Nagao, "Diplomacy," in Alfred Stead, ed., *Japan by the Japanese* (London, 1904), p. 165.

15. F. C. Jones, "Foreign Diplomacy in Korea, 1866–1894" (Unpublished Doctoral Dissertation, Harvard University, 1935), p. 93. Based on British documents.

16. Kuzuu Yoshihisa, *Tōa senkaku shishi kiden* (Stories and Biographies of Pio-

neer East Asian Adventurers), the official *Kokuryūkai* (Amur; "Black Dragon" Society) history (Tokyo, 1933), I, 88. Hereafter, cited as TSSK.

17. *TSSK*, I, 36.

18. *TSSK*, I, 18–25.

19. *TSSK*, I, 49. Etō believed that Japan should take China in order to extend progressive government throughout Asia.

20. *TSSK*, I, 38.

21. *TSSK*, I, 38–39.

22. *TSSK*, I, 29–33. Maruyama later became an important figure in government circles. He founded a pro-government political party, and served on Prince Itō's constitutional committee.

23. Ōtsu Junichirō, *Dai Nihon kensei shi* (A constitutional history of Japan; Tokyo, 1927), I, 571–677, includes an excellent and heavily documented account of the debates. Hereafter, *Kensei shi.*

24. Ōtsu, *Kensei shi,* I, 853. Itō, in explaining his approval of the expedition later, said that the government had had to choose between the expedition and civil war within Japan.

25. One of the long term effects of the expedition was the alliance between Ōkuma and Iwasaki Yatarō, founder of the firm of Mitsubishi. Ōkuma was able to delegate all transport to Iwasaki, and arranged for government-owned ships to be given to him in return for his services.

26. T. F. Tsiang, "Sino-Japanese Diplomatic Relations, 1870–1894," in *Chinese Social and Political Science Review,* 17, No. 1, p. 5 (1933).

27. See, on this point, a valuable study by Oka Yoshitake, "Meiji shoki no jiyū-minken ronsha no me ni eijitaru tōji no kokusai jisei" (The international situation as seen by the democratic spokesmen of early Meiji), in *Seiji oyobi seijishi kenkyū* (Studies in politics and political history), 471–514 (Tokyo, 1935). A volume of essays dedicated to the memory of Yoshino Sakuzō. A recent work by Robert A. Scalapino, *Democracy and the Party Movement in Prewar Japan* (Berkeley: University of California Press, 1953), p. 58f, treats these expansionist trends of the democratic movement.

28. Ōtsu, *Kensei shi,* I, 794.

29. Ōtsu, *Kensei shi,* I, 836–837. This time the manifesto made no specific mention of Asia, but it denounced special privileges, called for equality, and pointed to the political institutions of Europe and America as the source of success and wealth. Nobutaka Ike, *The Beginnings of Political Democracy in Japan* (Baltimore: Johns Hopkins Press, 1950), p. 61, points out that the *Risshisha* was also something of a mutual-aid society for samurai in economic difficulties.

30. Ōtsu, *Kensei shi,* I, 842.

31. Ōtsu, *Kensei shi,* II, 36–60, feels that because of these "liberal" features the revolt should not be grouped with the frankly reactionary and anti-foreign samurai revolts that took place in Kumamoto, Akitsuki, and Hagi.

32. Some Japanese writers credit Sun Yat-sen with a great admiration for Saigō. Yamakawa Yoshiro, "The First President of China," in *Independent,* LXXII, 76 (New York, 1912), claims that Sun modelled his dress and life on that of Saigō, whose biography he read often. No other writers substantiate this dubious theory.

33. A. H. Mounsey, *The Satsuma Rebellion* (London, 1879), pp. 86–87. Ōtsu, *Kensei shi,* I, 844–845.

34. T. F. Tsiang, "Sino-Japanese diplomatic relations," p. 62.

35. Mounsey, *The Satsuma Rebellion*, p. 161.

36. Ōtsu, *Kensei shi*, II, 112.

37. Ōtsu, *Kensei shi*, II, 494f. Itagaki had beeen lured back into the government in 1875, but he had withdrawn again because of his disgust with the weak Korean policy and the lack of domestic reforms.

38. *Loc. cit.*

39. Ōtsu, *Kensei shi*, II, 520. The original *Kaishintō* platform made no mention of Asian problems, but simply called for a strong and resolute foreign policy and for the advancement of trade and commerce.

40. Ōtsu, *Kensei shi*, II, 522.

41. Watanabe Ikujirō, *Kinsei Nihon gaikō shi* (Diplomatic history of modern Japan; Tokyo, 1938), pp. 301–306.

42. Inukai and Ozaki were close friends and allies throughout the period of constitutional government, and even complemented each other in their popular names, with Ozaki using "Gakudō" to Inukai's "Bokudō."

43. Ōtsu, *Kensei shi*, II, 540.

44. Fujii Jintarō and Moriya Hidesuke, *Meiji jidai shi* (History of the Meiji Period), XII, *Sōgō Nihon shi taikei* (Synthesis of Japanese history: Tokyo, 1934), pp. 851–853. The party was founded by Tarui Tōkichi, a man later active in the socialist movement and in numerous schemes for the reform of Asia.

45. Ōtsu, *Kensei shi*, II, 504–505.

46. Fujii and Moriya, *Meiji jidai shi*, pp. 857–862.

47. Itagaki Taisuke, ed., *Jiyūtō shi* (History of the Liberal Party; Tokyo, 1910), II, 495. In 1887, Itagaki and Gotō attacked the Inoue treaty revision plan which permitted unrestricted residence to foreigners and the use of foreign judges for foreign trials. Ōkuma, the only effective public speaker among the leaders, joined this attack. When he had his own chance as Foreign Minister in 1889, the opposition party berated Ōkuma's plan, and a nationalist's bomb cost him a leg.

48. Sansom, *Western World*, p. 414, quotes a celebrated work, *Kajin no kigū* (Strange Encounters of Elegant Females): "Your August Sovereign has granted political liberty to the people, the people have sworn to follow the Imperial leadership. . . Korea will send envoys and the Luchu Islands will submit to your governance. Then will the occasion arise for doing great things in the Far East. Your country will take the lead and preside over a confederation of Asia. . ."

49. For analyses of contradictions that resulted in the early liberal movement, see Tōyama Shigeki, "Seikan ron, jiyūminkenron, hōkenron" (Discussions of a punitive expedition against Korea, liberty and people's rights, and feudalism), in *Rekishigaku Kenkyū* (Historical Research), No. 143: 1–12 (January 1950); No. 145: 19–34 (May 1950); and, by the same author, "Jiyū minken undō to tairiku mondai" (The liberal-democratic movement and the problem of the continent," *Sekai*, pp. 27–38 (June 1950).

CHAPTER 2. PERSONALITIES AND PRECEDENTS

1. Mounsey, *Satsuma Rebellion*, p. 162.

2. For a graphic first hand description see Shidzue Ishimoto, *Facing Two Ways* (New York, 1935), pp. 161–163.

3. E. H. Norman, "The *Genyōsha*: A Study in the Origins of Japanese Imperialism," *Pacific Affairs*, XVII, 3, 266 (1944).

4. *Genyōsha shashi* (The Official History of the *Genyōsha*: Tokyo, 1917), p. 223.

5. Kuzuu Yoshihisa, *Nikkan gappō hishi* (Secret history of the annexation of Korea), a *Kokuryūkai* publication (Tokyo, 1930), I, Appendix, "Thirty Year History of the *Kokuryūkai*," p. 4.

6. *TSSK*, I, 58.

7. Biography in *Shinsen dai jimmei jiten*, V, 261.

8. Kojima Kazuo, "Ichi rō seijika no kaisō" (An old politician's recollections), *Chūō Kōron* (Central Review; November 1950). Kojima (1865–1952), who edited the paper for Hiraoka, later entered politics as a follower of Inukai, and at the time of his death in 1952 was a confidential adviser to Premier Yoshida.

9. *Genyōsha shashi*, pp. 613–624, and personal communication from Matsumoto Kaoru, grandson of Yasukawa Keiichirō, mine operator, sponsor of Tōyama, Yamaza, Hirota, and close friend of Hiraoko. Kojima, "Ichi rō seijika," Installment 5, *Chūō Kōron* (January 1951), p. 161, tells of jokes about the possibility of naming Hiraoka Minister of War and Tōyama Minister of the Navy in this cabinet.

10. Biography in *Shinsen dai jimmei jiten*, VI, appendix, p. 17.

11. Fujimoto Shōsaku, *Kyojin Tōyama Mitsuru Ō* (Grand Old Tōyama; Tokyo, 1922), pp. 707–714.

12. Introduction to Seizo Kimase, *Mitsuru Toyama Kämpft für Grossasien* (Munich, 1941), pp. 10–11. Kimase also quotes Inukai:

> Ohne irgen etwas zu tun,
> erreicht er ein Vollendetsein der Natur.
> Ohne irgen etwas zu wollen,
> hat er eine gottliche Wandelbarkeit.

13. Fujimoto, *Kyojin Tōyama*, p. 57. Stories of Tōyama's youth are replete with instances in which he illustrates courage, naturalness, and a laconic abruptness reminiscent of Zen heroes. To the outsider these tales are more suggestive of rudeness and ill temper. See Kimase, *Mitsuru Toyama*, pp. 32–40.

14. Biography in *Shinsen dai jimmei jiten*, VII, 366.

15. Fujimoto, *Kyojin Tōyama*, p. 94.

16. See Chapter I, note 45.

17. For the mine rights, Matsumoto Kaoru, pers. comm., for labor force, E. H. Norman, pers. comm., who adds that Uchida Ryōhei performed similar services for Japanese operators of Korean mines. Kojima, "Ichi rō seijika," No. 6, *Chūō Kōron*, p. 193 (February 1951), cites the Fukuoka miners' prosperity after the Sino-Japanese War as explanation for the amount of help given Sun Yat-sen immediately thereafter.

18. Ogata Taketora, "Mitsuru Toyama," *Contemporary Japan*, p. 818 (July 1940), tells of the Tōyama largesse. In 1954 Ogata, a Fukuoka man, was minister of state under Premier Yoshida.

19. For the American loan, Kimase, *Mitsuru Toyama*, p. 19; for the conversion experience, Fujimoto, *Kyojin Tōyama*, p. 266.

20. Biography in *Dai jimmei jiten*, III, 466.

21. *Genyōsha shashi*, p. 416.

22. Fujimoto, *Kyojin Tōyama*, p. 266.

23. Kimase, *Mitsuru Toyama*, p. 124.

24. Fujimoto, *Kyojin Tōyama*, p. 367.

25. Fujimoto, *Kyojin Tōyama*, p. 857.

26. Norman, "The Genyōsha," p. 283, says, "The societies were . . . the cement

which [held] together the whole edifice of Japanese aggression — the army, big business, and the key sections of the bureaucracy."

27. For a fuller account of Ōi, see Marius B. Jansen, "Ōi Kentarō (1843–1922); Radicalism and Chauvinism," *Far Eastern Quarterly* XI, No. 3 (May 1952).

28. Katayama Sen, "Nippon rōdō undō" (The Japanese labor movement), in Yoshino Sakuzō, ed., *Meiji bunka zenshū* (Works on Meiji Culture; Tokyo, 1930), 21, p. 166. See also Hirano Yoshitarō, *Burujua minshu shugi undō shi* (History of the bourgeois democratic movement), Iwanami Kōza, *Nihon shihon shugi hattenshi kōza* (Lectures on the development of Japanese capitalism; Tokyo, 1932), Part III, 40.

29. Hirano Yoshitarō, *Bajō-Ōi Kentarō den* (Tokyo, 1938), and the same author's *Minken undō no hatten* (The development of the movement for people's rights; Tokyo, 1948), contain the best accounts of Ōi's thought, with excerpts from his writings and speeches.

30. Hirano Yoshitarō, "Nisshi kōshō shi" (Sino-Japanese relations), in *Shina mondai jiten* (Dictionary of China problems; Tokyo, 1942), p. 592. By "Feudalism," of course, they meant little more than "corrupt" or "old fashioned."

31. Hirano, "Nisshi kōshō shi," p. 594.

32. *Loc. cit.*

33. *TSSK*, I, 60–61.

34. Biography of Kim in *Tōyō rekishi daijiten* (Dictionary of Oriental History; Tokyo, 1937), II, 294.

35. Ōtsu, *Kensei shi,* II, 705.

36. *TSSK*, I, 69.

37. Ōtsu, *Kensei shi,* II, 708. The *Jiyūtō shi,* II, 345, however, stresses that this was to be done as an unofficial loan through private sources in France. Neither account is dated very carefully, and there may have been two attempts, with the Japanese government safeguards requested by the French for the first attempt.

38. *Jiyūtō shi,* II, 349. The liberals claim that Inoue, jealous of their probable success, wanted to try the *putsch* under his own auspices through Minister Takezoe's plot in 1884. Ōtsu, however (11, 718), feels that Takezoe's plot was the work of Gotō, Fukuzawa, and the Jiyūtō group. The *Kokuryūkai* explanations (Biography of Takezoe, *TSSK,* III, 302–304) seem more likely. Takezoe was a good scholar and Confucian, but a poor choice to send to the anti-Confucian reformist party in Korea. After much hesitation, he informed the Kim faction that the Japanese government would support them in their efforts. Anxious to act while the Japanese were favorable, Kim showed himself much too rash. Itō, in negotiating with Li Hung-chang at Tientsin, disclaimed all government responsibility. If the *putsch* had succeeded, of course, all factions in the government would have claimed credit for it. It seems, however, to represent more bungling and confusion than malicious direction.

39. Here we have all three opposition groups working closely together with Kim, as they later worked with Sun.

40. Sakatani Yoshio, *Segai Inoue Kō den* (Biography of the immortal Marquis Inoue; Tokyo, 1930), III, 741–743. Kim took the name Imata Shinsaku. Again, a precedent for Sun.

41. Good accounts of the incident can be found in *TSSK*, I, 92–116; Ōtsu, II, 725–737; *Jiyūtō shi,* II, 357f., and Hirano, *Minken undō,* pp. 49–94. Also involved in the plot was Tarui Tōkichi, who had formed the *Tōyō shakaitō* mentioned earlier. *TSSK*, II, 32.

42. Yamamoto fought with Saigō in 1877, and later befriended Liang Ch'i-ch'ao. His proclamation can be found in each of the three accounts of the incident mentioned above.

43. For a girl of 21 to aid in the fund collections and act as go-between for such determined roughnecks probably justifies the *Kokuryūkai* praise for her as an Oriental Joan of Arc. *TSSK*, I, 100.

44. *Jiyūtō shi*, II, 360.

45. All sentences are given in Ōtsu, II, 732–733.

46. *TSSK*, I, 110. Tōyama had been planning a filibustering expedition of his own to Korea, but he cancelled his plans when Ōi's was discovered. *Ibid.*, p. 120. The prisoners were released in 1889 under an amnesty granted political prisoners to mark the granting of the Meiji Constitution. In 1890 Ōi and Yamamoto set up a private school for Chinese, English, and French. *Meiji hennen shi* (Annals of Meiji newspapers; Tokyo, 1940), VII, 363, art. dated January 9, 1890.

47. Tsiang, "Sino-Japanese Diplomatic Relations," p. 95.

48. *Segai Inoue Kō den*, III, 758. The Japanese government put Kim on Ogasawara in the Bonins, and later moved him to Sapporo on Hokkaido.

49. *Inukai Bokudō den* (Life of Inukai), II, 775–881, quotes Inukai's high praise for Kim. Kim was a Zen believer, spoke Japanese fluently, and was a scholar. When he was killed he had with him a volume of Inukai's copy of the *Tzu-chih t'ung-chien*.

50. During the Sino-Japanese war, a last attempt to "reform" Korea was made. Arao Kiyoshi served as adviser, and Gotō was to be ambassador. Instead, Itō sent Inoue, who alienated the Koreans instead of winning them over. This is the view of Ōtsu, IV, 493–506, 588.

51. Jones, "Foreign Diplomacy," p. 219, quotes an English writer in 1890: "Any supposed offence by a Corean is summarily dealt with by the first policeman or by any Japanese who cares to assume the task of beating the offender. (They) buffet and kick them as they would beasts." This seems to have been pretty common practice for all foreigners in Korea, but it was not likely to help the cause of Pan-Asianism.

52. Watanabe, *gaikō shi;* especially 135–142, "Nisshi dōmeiron" (The discussion of a Sino-Japanese alliance). See, however, Tsiang, "Sino-Japanese Diplomatic Relations," pp. 105–106, for his opinion that the conciliatory policy was temporizing until Japan would be strong enough to become aggressive. Nevertheless, the nationalists certainly accepted that policy as genuine.

53. Tsiang, *loc. cit.*

54. Kishida (1833–1905) worked with Dr. Hepburn in Yokohama. With Joseph Hiko, he started the first foreign style newspaper in Japan, and he was a war correspondent during the Formosan Expedition. Norman, "The Genyōsha," p. 279; Biography of Kishida in *TSSK*, III, 659–660, and in *Dai jimmei jiten*, II, 271.

55. Sakishiro Gakujin, "Genji no Shinatsū" (Present day China experts), in *Chūō Kōron*, Vol. 28, No. 12: 11–12 (1913).

56. Norman, "The Genyōsha," p. 280.

57. Arao's biography is in *TSSK*, III, 607–612, and in *Dai jimmei jiten*, I, p. 123. His exploits recur constantly through all literature on this subject.

58. *TSSK*, II, 186–199. The two were given consular protection, and then the Mitsui representative helped them get back to Japan. Yamada's biography is in *TSSK*, III, 454 and in *Dai jimmei jiten*, VI, 367.

59. It is worth noting that the *Jiyūtō* members tried to use commerce in developing Japan's position in Asia. In 1887 they formed an *Ajiya Bōeki Shōkai* (Asian Commercial Institute) dedicated to the development of Japanese trade, with a manifesto which held that trade was respectable and proper; "let us," they urged, "become known as the Yankees of the East." Since the party had almost no business connections in that early period, however, the organization disappeared without a trace. *Jiyūtō shi*, II, 389–406.

60. Nakajima Masao, ed., *Taishi kaiko roku* (Memoirs about China), a *Dōbunkai* publication compiled by the "Society for the compilation of writings about men who have rendered conspicuous service in regard to China" (Tokyo, 1936), I, 674–681, for the above and other cultural exchange activities. Sanetō Keishū, *Meiji nisshi bunka kōshō* (Cultural interchange between Japan and China in the Meiji Period), contains excerpts from diaries and writings of early Chinese ambassadors with accounts of meetings of early literary groups.

61. Inoue Masaji, *Shina ron* (Tokyo, 1930). This is his Waseda thesis. It contains a thirty-three page autobiographical preface. Among Inoue's other writings is a biography of Arao, *Kyojin Arao Kiyoshi* (The Great Arao Kiyoshi; Tokyo, 1930).

62. Watanabe, *gaikō shi,* pp. 301–306, who quotes the speech, and *Ōkuma Kō hachi-jū gonen shi* (The eighty-five year Life of Marquis Ōkuma; Tokyo, 1926), II, 672.

63. *Sanjū sannen no yume* (The thirty-three years' dream) was first published in 1902, the same year in which it was serialized in newspapers. In 1926 it was reissued, edited, indexed, and summarized by Yoshino Sakuzō. The third edition appeared in 1943.

64. See Chapter I. Ōtsu, *Kensei shi,* II, 83.

65. Newspaper editor, fiery nationalist, biographer of Yoshida Shōin and Yamagata Aritomo, author of *Kinsei Nippon kokumin shi* cited in Chapter I.

66. The 1943 edition of Miyazaki's book reflects the political conditions of its time. Yoshino Sakuzō's appendix summary is omitted, and the references to the heroism of Danton and the other revolutionaries are deleted. In the main, however, the editions are identical, and unless otherwise noted the 1943 edition has been used. The 1943 edition does add a valuable appendix by Miyazaki's wife and by his son.

67. Miyazaki's intensity extended to negative extremes, for he wrote a little work condemning the story of Abraham and Isaac as unfilial. *Kyōjin ron* (Madmen's arguments; Tokyo, 1902), 153 pp.

68. *Sanjū sannen no yume,* p. 64. Throughout the book, Miyazaki uses aliases for all the *shishi* mentioned:
Uchida Ryōhei — Koseki
Hirayama Shū — Nammanri
Kiyofuji Kōshichirō — Donu
Tōyama Mitsuru — Ūno
Miyazaki himself is usually referred to by his *gō,* Tōten.

CHAPTER 3. SUN YAT-SEN

1. During the revolution of 1911, Miyazaki wrote a series of feature articles for the Osaka *Mainichi* in which he described the background of the revolt. His account is of some interest, since it was derived not from secondary sources but from Sun himself. This is from the first of those articles, October 19, 1911. See also the

excellent history by Yoshino Sakuzō and Katō Shigeshi, *Shina kakumei shi* (A history of the Chinese revolution; Tokyo, 1922), p. 10. Hereafter cited as Yoshino-Katō.

2. There is some reason for thinking Sun was a Christian before going to Hawaii. In "My Reminiscences," *Strand Magazine* (London, 1912), XLIII, 301, he says, "I had led the life of any Chinese youth of my class, except that from my father's conversion to Christianity and his employment by the London Missionary Society I had greater opportunities of coming into contact with English and American missionaries in Canton." Few Western biographies follow this. Wittfogel, *Sun Yat-sen,* however, does so, p. 20. Georges Soulié de Morant, *Soun Iat-senn* (Paris, 1932), p. 15, adds to it by explaining that Sun's parents took refuge on Macao during the Taiping Rebellion. One of the most careful Japanese accounts, Hatano Ken'ichi, *Chūgoku Kokumintō tsūshi* (History of the Chinese Nationalist Party; Tokyo, 1943), p. 27, considers this quite dubious. Sun was frequently contradictory in his various memoirs. At any rate, there is no reason to doubt that he returned more conscious of his Christianity and aware of its meaning after attending a mission school.

3. Ō Su-shi (Wang Shu-chih), *Son Bun den* (Biography of Sun Wen; Tokyo, 1931), p. 99. Published under this pseudonym by Suzue Genichi, an employee of the South Manchurian Railways, who sought to avoid questioning on his Marxist leanings. See Itō Masao, "Suzue Genichi to sono jidai" ("Suzue Genichi and his times," *Sekai* (The World), No. 45: 52–58 (September 1949). Hereafter, cited as *Son Bun den.* A 1950 edition includes the article from *Sekai* (Tokyo, 1950), 554 pp.

4. Miyazaki, in *Mainichi,* October 21, 1911. This is the usual account. Sun, however, in *Memoirs of a Chinese Revolutionary* (London, n.d.), p. 186, says that he won Cheng over to the revolution.

5. *Son Bun den,* p. 103. Most books state that the organization was founded in Hawaii in 1894. Chou Lu, *Chung-kuo kuo-min-tang shih-kao* (Draft History of the Kuomintang; Shanghai, 1929), I, 28, prefers the earlier date. He bases his decision on Sun's *Kidnapped in London* (London, 1897), p. 13, "It was in Macao that I first learned of the existence of a political movement . . . the idea was to bring about a peaceful reformation." Hatano, *Kokumintō tsūshi,* pp. 43–45, after careful consideration of the evidence, concludes that Sun did join or form such an organization in Macao, but that his real revolutionary (as opposed to reformist) activities date from the Hawaii organization.

6. Kayano, *Chūka Minkoku kakumei hikyū* gives the full memorial in the official Japanese Foreign Office translation, pp. 15–34. Excerpts are to be found in Léon Wieger, S.J., *Chine Moderne,* I, "Prodromes" (Hsien Hsien, 1921), 216–219.

7. It should be noted that Sun did not attain undisputed leadership of the revolutionary movement until many groups like his *Hsing Chung Hui* united for a specific revolt in 1900, and for a broader program in 1905.

8. Yoshino-Katō, p. 24. This was in September 1895.

9. *Son Bun den,* p. 112.

10. "My Reminiscences," *Strand Magazine,* p. 301.

11. *Kidnapped in London* (London, 1897), p. 134.

12. Kita Ikki, *Shina kakumei gaishi* (Unofficial history of the Chinese Revolution; Tokyo, 1931), p. 12.

13. Mizuno Baigyō, "Son shi no kakumei to Nihon to no kankei," (Sun's revolution and its Japanese connections), *Gaikō Jihō* (Diplomatic Review), No. 588, p. 146 (June 1929). Feng Tzu-yu, *Chung-hua min-kuo k'ai-kuo ch'ien ko-ming shih*

(History of the revolution before the founding of the Republic) (Shanghai, 1928), p. 303.

14. Narita Yoshio, *Zōho kakyō shi* (Supplementary history of the overseas Chinese; Tokyo, 1941), p. 177. Lyon Sharman, *Sun Yat-sen: His Life and its Meaning* (New York, 1934), p. 60, gives the figure of 2500 Chinese for the year 1899 in the Yokohama area, and adds that most were Cantonese.

15. Miyazaki, *Sanjū-sannen no yume*, p. 132.

16. Sone's biography is given in *TSSK*, III, 316–317. He had a varied career. He worked for the General Staff, and became so well known as a China expert that he was granted an Imperial audience. He observed the French-Chinese war for the army, and wrote a little book in which he criticized the government's indifference to the fate of Annam. Later he worked with Kishida Kinkō, joined several of the Asia societies, and traveled in Formosa. Feng, *Chung-hua-min-kuo*, p. 303, considers him very pro-Chinese. He says that Sone frequently called himself a native of Shantung, that he read the *Analects* constantly, and that he wrote a history of the Taiping campaigns.

17. Miyazaki, *Sanjū-sannen*, pp. 131–135.

18. Miyazaki, in *Mainichi*, October 29, 1911.

19. Sun's choice of words is so close to the terminology the Japanese used (e.g., "a hero who should arouse China") that it probably reflects leading questions.

20. Mr. Miyazaki Ryūsuke, son of Torazō, still possesses these sheets of questions and answers, and he kindly allowed them to be photographed. Some are also reproduced in the appendix to *Sanjū-sannen no yume*, pp. 301–303. We find Sun and Miyazaki discussing the advantages of striking the Manchus in the southern provinces. Miyazaki suggests small islands off Formosa as bases, and running arms in by night. Sun prefers bolder descents. Sun asks about the attitude of the Japanese government, and Miyazaki assures him of Ōkuma's interest. Moreover, he explains, interest in Chinese problems has grown steadily since the Sino-Japanese war. Miyazaki also explains his mission for the Foreign Office.

21. *Inukai Bokudō den*, III, 722. From an article, "Reminiscences of Sun Yat-sen," which Inukai wrote for the Tokyo *Asahi* in August 1930.

22. Sun added to the register the character *Shō* (woodcutter), joking, "I'm just a Chinese woodchopper." Chung-shan (Nakayama) later became widely used for Sun's name in China, with the implication that Sun, as Central Mountain, towered over all others. In 1904, when he was becoming too well known as Nakayama, Sun changed to Takano for a time. Most leading Chinese exiles took Japanese names. Feng Tzu-yu, *Ko-ming i-shih* (Fragments of the history of the revolution; Chungking, 1944), III, 2. Feng, a participant in the revolution, spoke Japanese fluently. For his account of Sun's early friendships and status as language teacher, *Chunghua min-kuo k'ai-kuo*, p. 304.

23. Kayano, *kakumei hikyū*, p. 64, dates Sun's return in September 1897. Inukai's biographers agree. *Inukai Bokudō den*, III, 934. Miyazaki does not date this closely. There are many other dates given, the most persuasive argument for July 1898 being given by Yoshino Sakuzō, *Nikka kokkō ron* (Sino-Japanese relations; Tokyo, reprinted 1948), p. 35, who bases his argument upon the official positions of participants at that date. Inukai's biography shows that he had as much influence in September 1897 as in July 1898, however, and I have chosen to follow the date given by the participants.

24. This is Inukai's account. The consensus of the participants the author was able to interview in 1951, however, was that Sun's Japanese remained poor. These informants included Miyazaki's son and the supervisor of Sun's inn in Fukuoka. Inukai clearly felt that Sun was superior to most Chinese, and his pleasure in finding a clean Chinese, one who was fond of Japanese baths, is indicative of his opinion of Sun's countrymen. The only thing about Sun that distressed Inukai was his preference for tea over *sake*. *Inukai Bokudō den*, II, 722.

25. *Inukai Bokudō den*, II, 715. Itō held office from January to June 1898.

26. Oddly enough, Sun did not meet Itagaki Taisuke until 1905. Kayano, *kakumei hikyū*, p. 85.

27. Suenaga (b. 1869) is the son of a Tokugawa loyalist. A Fukuoka *shishi*, he was a colleague of the *Genyōsha* founders in many of their enterprises, served as editor for Hiraoka Kōtarō's Fukuoka newspaper (as did Kojima Kazuo), and traveled frequently to China. His last visit, in 1939, featured visits to Wu Pei-fu and Wang Ching-wei. Biography in *Zoku Taishi kaiko roku* (Supplement, Memoirs about China, Tokyo, 1941), II, 1217–1227. Akiyama was the publisher of a newspaper, *Niroku shimbun,* in which Miyazaki's book first appeared in serial form. His memoirs are cited below.

28. *TSSK*, I, 175.

29. Miyazaki, *Sanjū-sannen*, p. 150. In the *Mainichi* article of November 1, 1911, however, Miyazaki says that Hiraoka handed him five thousand yen for travel in China, assuring him that there were no *Gaimushō* strings attached. It will be remembered that Hiraoka contributed lavishly toward the formation of the *Kenseitō* (Ōkuma-Itagaki) Cabinet.

30. Hirayama Shū, "Shina kakumeitō oyobi himitsu kessha" (The Chinese revolutionary party and the secret societies), *Nihon oyobi Nihonjin* (Japan and the Japanese; Tokyo, November 1911), pp. 75–108. An unsigned article which is clearly Hirayama's on internal evidence. The article includes a parallel account of many activities he shared with Miyazaki as well as several letters addressed to Hirayama by Chinese. Hereafter, cited *Hirayama*. Hirayama (1870–1940) was from Fukuoka, and figured prominently in each enterprise related here. Biography in *Zoku Taishi kaiko roku*, II, 1207–1217.

31. The details of this incident disallow the interpretation of Wittfogel, *Sun Yat Sen,* who develops the theme that Sun became anti-imperialist only in his last stage of coöperation with Soviet advisers. Actually, Sun later approved American rule in the Philippines because it fitted in with his new ideas of tutelage.

32. *TSSK*, I, 631. *Inukai Bokudō den*, II, 788.

33. *Itō Hirobumi den* (Biography of Itō Hirobumi), issued by the "Prince Shumpo Eulogy Society" (Tokyo, 1940), III, 292–293.

34. Enrique J. Corpus, "Japan and the Philippine Revolution" (M. A. Thesis, University of the Philippines), *Philippine Social Science Review,* VI, 261 (Manila, October 1934).

35. Corpus, "Japan and the Philippine Revolution," p. 271.

36. *TSSK*, I, 627. Miyazaki, *Sanjū-sannen*, p. 151.

37. Corpus, "Japan and the Philippine Revolution," p. 277. Ponce arrived June 29, 1898.

38. Mariano Ponce, *Sun Yat-sen, El fundador de la Republica de China* (Manila, 1912), pp. 14, 30. This is a popular biography which contains virtually none of the activities recounted here. It is of value only for occasional personal touches.

39. Miyazaki, *Sanjū-sannen*, p. 183.

40. *Inukai Bokudō den*, II, 787.

41. Ponce, *Sun Yat-sen*, p. 3.

42. *TSSK*, I, 630. Corpus gives a different account. According to him, Aguinaldo and his men bought guns from American adventurers. (p. 287) Then, after the arrival of Ponce in Japan, various European firms competed for the business, so that Ponce had his choice of Mausers, Werndle, and the Japanese Murata. The latter were chosen because they were light, they had served well in the Chinese war, and "it would inject optimism and confidence in the ranks of the revolutionists to know that they were using guns from Japan which had proved to be a friend of the Filipinos." pp. 289–290.

43. All sub-rosa contracts were more expensive, since the contractor risked detection and had to bribe various officials. Nakamura had a guarantee of 20,000 yen, and he established a forfeit agreement for the same amount. Corpus, p. 291.

44. Corpus, "Japan and the Philippine Revolution," p. 293. *TSSK*, I, 630.

45. Hirayama, p. 80, says that Sun, Miyazaki, and he were each to draw ten thousand yen loans from a bank, but that police surveillance was so strict that they finally had Sun borrow it all himself. From Corpus' account, which is based on Ponce's letters to the Hong Kong *Junta*, it appears that all funds were Filipino, deposited to the Japanese account in the Hong Kong branch of the Yokohama Specie Bank. Sun was apparently on the expense account, as Corpus lists, among other expenses, "For transportation and secret expenses of Mr. Nakayama, R/July 19 . . . 1,300.00 (yen)." p. 293.

46. *Loc. cit.* Corpus erroneously gives the ship's name *Nonubiki Maru*. The ship's capacity was 1441 tons.

47. *TSSK*, I, 633. At this time Uchida was Hiraoka's son-in-law.

48. Corpus, "Japan and the Philippine Revolution," p. 291.

49. The letter, dated June 7, 1899, is given in *Inukai Bokudō den*, II, 782, and in Hirayama, p. 80.

50. Miyazaki, *Sanjū-sannen*, pp. 188–189.

51. Hirayama, p. 82.

52. Miyazaki, *Sanjū-sannen*, p. 192.

53. *TSSK*, I, 633–646. Hirayama, pp. 82–86.

54. Ponce, *Sun Yat-sen*, p. 60.

55. *Inukai Bokudō den*, II, 787–791. Kojima, "Ichi rō seijika," installment 4, *Chūō Kōron* (December 1950), is somewhat kinder to Nakamura, and implies that the Ōkura people were the villains of the piece. From Miyazaki's account, Kojima seems to act as mediator for Inukai. *Sanjū-sannen*, p. 268f.

56. Osaka *Mainichi*, December 17, 1900.

57. Hirano Yoshitarō, "Nisshi kōshō shi," in *Shina mondai jiten*, p. 594.

58. Joseph R. Levenson, *Liang Ch'i-Ch'ao and the Mind of Modern China* (Cambridge, 1953), p. 50.

59. Hirano, "Nisshi kōshō shi," p. 595. Lo (1866–1940) became one of the scholarly Confucians used by the Japanese to lend dignity and legitimacy to the puppet state of Manchukuo. Biography in *Tōyō rekishi daijiten*, IX: 112–113, date of death, Hummel, *Eminent Chinese of the Ch'ing Period* (Washington, 1943), I, 90.

60. Miyazaki, *Sanjū-sannen*, pp. 152–158.

61. *Itō Hirobumi den*, III, 394–402, cites Ito's intercession for another reformer, Chang Yin-huan, but makes no mention of help for K'ang Yu-wei.

62. Miyazaki, *Sanjū-sannen,* p. 164.

63. Miyazaki, *Sanjū-sannen,* p. 167. In the details of the correspondence admitting K'ang to Japan, p. 162, most names have been removed by censorship. The documents, however, can be found in the Library of Congress microfilms of Foreign Office Files, M.T.1.6.1.4.3.

64. *Ōkuma Kō hachijū-gonen shi,* II, 533–536. See also Feng, *Ko-ming i-shih,* I, 48. The *Kenseitō* (Ōkuma-Itagaki) Cabinet held office from June 30 to October 31, 1898.

65. Miyazaki, *Sanjū-sannen,* p. 170. Miyazaki almost missed the boat because of a boisterous farewell party. He usually managed to mix generous portions of *sake* with his idealism.

66. *Ōkuma Kō hachijū-gonen shi,* II, 678.

67. *Inukai Bokudō den,* II, 714. The *Kenseitō* Cabinet was succeeded by the cabinet headed by Yamagata Aritomo which lasted until the fall of 1900.

68. *Ōkuma Kō,* II, 536.

69. Miyazaki, *Sanjū-sannen,* p. 172.

70. Hirano, "*Nisshi kōshō shi,*" *Shina mondai jiten,* p. 595. Sun's "expulsion" in 1907 was similarly gentle.

71. Feng, *Chung-hua min-kuo k'ai-kuo-ch'ien ko-ming shih,* p. 43.

72. *North China Herald and Supreme Court and Consular Gazette,* LXXII, No. 1924 (June 24, 1904), translation of *Peking Gazette* of June 21: "The present year being the seventieth anniversary of my (i.e., Tz'u Hsi's) birth, . . . as a mark of my bounty . . . I now desire to bestow . . . a mark of the Imperial favor . . . and therefore command that, with the exception of the rebels K'ang Yu-wei, Liang Ch'i-ch'ao, and Sun Wun . . . whose crimes are of such magnitude that they do not deserve any pardon . . . all others who were implicated in 1898 shall be participants of the Imperial mercy . . . and shall be given the opportunity to reform their conduct."

73. Feng, *Chung-hua min-kuo,* p. 32.

74. Feng, p. 42.

75. Feng, p. 305.

76. Miyazaki, *Sanjū-sannen,* p. 171. Feng, p. 42.

77. *Inukai Bokudō den,* II, 726–727.

CHAPTER 4. *1900: WAICHOW AND AMOY*

1. Ōtsu, *Kensei shi,* V, 91–98.

2. Paul A. Varg, "The Foreign Policy of Japan and the Boxer Revolt," *Pacific Historical Review,* XV: 279f. (September 1946). This article, which is restricted to the events in North China, concludes that since Russia alone could gain by a partition of China, Japan held for coöperative action in China.

3. Yoshino-Katō, pp. 49–50.

4. Yoshino-Katō, p. 50. Miyazaki, in the *Mainichi* of November 17, 1911, however, gives the result as the *San-ha-ho-hui* (Triple Unity Society), and says that it was later changed to *Chung-ho-tang* (Loyal Coöperation Party).

5. Kiyofuji (1872–1931) was, like Miyazaki, from Kumamoto. He had a long period of coöperation with the Chinese revolutionaries. One of his last projects was to organize protest meetings against the China policy of the Tanaka cabinet. Biography in *Dai jimmei jiten,* II, 374.

6. Miyazaki identifies one donor as Nakano Tokujirō. *Sanjū-sannen no yume,* p. 205. Nakano, however, was an agent of the Kyushu mine operator, Yasukawa Keiichirō. See Kojima, "Ichi rō seijika," *Chūō Kōron,* February 1951, for the relation between prosperity in the coal industry and aid to the revolutionaries.

7. Miyazaki, *Sanjū-sannen,* pp. 206–207.

8. Feng, *Chung-hua min-kuo k'ai-kuo-ch'ien ko-ming shih,* p. 55.

9. Feng, *Chung-hua min-kuo,* p. 208. Liu had known Sun in earlier days in Canton. Feng, *I-shih,* I, 77. The Japanese accounts add that Liu's letter asked Sun Yat-sen to have K'ang Yu-wei assassinated in order to remove the main obstacle to union. Yoshino-Katō, pp. 54–55, and *TSSK,* I, 654.

10. It will be remembered that Kim Ok-kiun had been killed in this way. The Japanese always blamed Li Hung-chang for Kim's death.

11. Miyazaki, *Sanjū-sannen,* p. 208. Miyazaki waxes sentimental about his emotions on this trip; he did not expect to survive the revolution.

12. Miyazaki, *Sanjū-sannen,* p. 212.

13. According to Yoshino-Katō, pp. 55f., Miyazaki opened the meeting by declining to assassinate K'ang Yu-wei. Liu expressed pleasure at this, and explained that they had suggested it only because Li Hung-chang thought it would be the surest way to interest Sun Yat-sen. The *Kokuryūkai* account, *TSSK,* I, 656, is probably derived from Uchida. It becomes a cloak and dagger farce. Miyazaki demands for Sun a general amnesty, and sixty thousand *taels.* Liu promises to send half the money the next day, and does so. The amnesty, however, has to wait for word from Peking. This, of course, is shot through with inconsistencies, and can at best be interpreted as a play for time by Liu. In any case, the Japanese are said to have dismissed the whole idea once they had Liu's money. The Chinese accounts give no details of the meeting, but after all there were no Chinese revolutionaries present.

14. Miyazaki, *Sanjū-sannen,* pp. 213–218.

15. Miyazaki, *Sanjū-sannen,* p. 234. Miyazaki details each day's activities and emotions in some detail. He had never been in prison before, and he considered this rather scurvy treatment from K'ang in view of the help he had given him two years earlier. Singapore newspapers described the pair as "Japanese reporters" and "better class Japanese." Consul Ochi, who forwarded the clippings to Tokyo, was instructed by Foreign Minister Aoki to assure the British that, far from being assassins, the two were "reported to be friends of K'ang." Microfilms of Foreign Office Files, M.T. 1.6.1.4.3, Exp. 356, July 16, 1900.

16. Miyazaki, *Sanjū-sannen,* pp. 237–238. A. M. Pooley, *Japan's Foreign Policies* (London, 1920), gives a brief account of this in which he quotes Sun as explaining the money: "From Japan, where many great firms devote a percentage of their profits to the revolutionary movement, which represents to them the expansion of Japan." Consul Ochi, when he asked whether he should press for cancellation of the ban against the Japanese, was advised by Aoki to let the incident be forgotten. Foreign Office Files, Exp. 358, July 18, 1900.

17. Miyazaki, *Sanjū-sannen,* p. 245.

18. In Canton, United States Consul McWade reported that Li Hung-chang told him in conversation that wealthy Cantonese had begged him to stay. Some threatened to block the streets with their bodies if necessary to stop him from leaving. *United States Consular Dispatches,* Canton, Vol. 14, Jan. 2 to Dec. 31, 1900, No. 19, July 6, 1900. Record Group 59, National Archives.

19. Canton Consular Dispatches, Vol. 14, No. 24, July 18, 1900.

20. This is the conclusion drawn by Yoshino-Katō, p. 58. Their case is strengthened by Sun's appeal to the Hong Kong government, below, which they have not noted.

21. The Canton dispatches, with their emphasis on the terror of wealthy Chinese at the thought of Li's departure, support this view. One banker named Lao (possibly Liu?) is said to have contributed five million *taels* to Li Hung-chang, and a later dispatch reports that Cantonese have contributed over twenty million *taels* to Li in hope of maintaining order. Canton Dispatches, Vol. 14, Nos. 19 and 20, July 6 and 9, 1900.

22. The document is given by Hirayama, pp. 90–91, Feng, *Chung-hua min-kuo*, pp. 60–63, and Chou Lu, I, 34–35.

23. Miyazaki, *Sanjū-sannen*, p. 210.

24. Sun counted on defections in each of his revolts. If he had not, they would have been indefensible and irresponsible. The course of events in 1900, 1907, and 1911 showed that he was justified in this assumption. Yoshino-Katō, pp. 119–120.

25. Feng, *Chung-hua min-kuo*, p. 91, dates this conference June 21, 1900.

26. Fukumoto Nichinan (1857–1921) was a native of Fukuoka. After his China activities, he became successively a newspaper man and a historian. Biography in *Dai jimmei jiten*, V, 314. He and Ozaki Yukimasa (brother of Ozaki Yukio) joined Sun at Saigon on his way to Singapore. *TSSK*, I, 662.

27. Miyazaki, *Sanjū-sannen*, p. 247.

28. Kojima, *Ichi rō seijika* in *Chūō Kōron*, p. 212 (December 1950), identifies Hara as a major in the Japanese army.

29. The *Kokuryūkai* account, *TSSK*, I, 665, follows Hirayama, p. 89, and states that Hirayama was appointed to head the Foreign Office, Pi Yung-nien, the Home Office, Yang, the Treasury, and Hara, the General Staff. Feng, *Chung-hua min-kuo*, gives it still differently with Hirayama and Fukumoto as assistants in the Civil Administration. Chou Lu and Yoshino-Katō make no mention of this "cabinet."

30. In the earlier Hong Kong negotiations, Miyazaki assured the secret society men that if such plans had been in progress the Japanese would have heard of them.

31. Feng, *Chung-hua min-kuo*, pp. 90–100. The manifesto is also in Hirayama, p. 92. Yoshino-Katō, pp. 60–61, suggest that T'ang had been corresponding with Chang Chih-tung through Japanese intermediaries. They supposedly proposed to have Chang declare his provinces independent of Peking in the wake of the Boxer disturbances. But when Chang found out that their ultimate aim was to eliminate him, he struck first. This attempts to explain the delay between discovery and round-up of the conspirators. See also Feng, p. 306, for the help that T'ang received from Hirayama in the early stages of the revolt.

32. The Osaka *Mainichi* of September 10, 1900 gave a lengthy account of the revolt, and two weeks later it added a biographical account of T'ang as well as a description of his execution.

33. Li Hung-chang was in Shanghai on his way to Peking.

34. *TSSK*, I, 669–671. This is an interesting example of Japanese strategy. The three Viceroys were in high favor in the West at the time. Their assassination would have produced such hostility against Sun that he would have been cast completely upon Japanese favor.

35. Yamada's biography, *TSSK*, III, 454–456. This source credits Yamada with a role in the earlier negotiations with Liu Hsüeh-hsun. Yoshino-Katō, p. 69, say Yamada carried a letter from Hiraoka Kōtarō to Formosa.

36. Sun Yat-sen, *Memoirs of a Chinese Revolutionary*, pp. 196, 197.

37. Yoshino-Katō, pp. 62–63.

38. Canton Consular Dispatches, Vol. 14, Nos. 51–70. The last includes a translation of the acting Viceroy's report to Peking. Consul McWade accepts that official's conclusion that the rebels included partisans of Sun Yat-sen, K'ang Yu-wei, and several secret societies, and that the whole was coördinated with the earlier Hankow revolt. In later years, Homer Lea, who was then working for K'ang Yu-wei, claimed he was present. See Frederick L. Chapin, "Homer Lea and the Chinese Revolution" (Harvard University unpublished A.B. Honors Thesis, 1950), pp. 21f. The writings of Sun Yat-sen and the Japanese who were involved do not support this view.

39. Miyazaki, Sanjū-sannen, pp. 259–277, gives the letter.

40. Yoshino-Katō, p. 68.

41. Kayano, kakumei hikyū, p. 66, is the only writer who dates this. The Canton Consular Dispatches, No. 70, bear him out.

42. Yoshino-Katō, loc. cit.

43. Sun Yat-sen, Memoirs of a Chinese Revolutionary, p. 198. There is also a short eulogy by Sun, "Yamada Yoshimasa chun chien-pei chi-nien tz'u" (A word of homage at the tomb of Yamada Yoshimasa), in Tsung-li ch'üan-chi, I, Pt. 2, p. 1039. In 1913 Sun composed a memorial for Yamada. See Plate I.

44. Hirayama, p. 95.

45. Ōtsu, Kensei shi, V, 131. Actually, as will be seen below, Yamagata decided to resign several weeks before this.

46. See, for instance, Sharman, Sun Yat-sen, p. 65, "less than two weeks after the rising began, (Sun's) friends, the Japanese liberals, were out of power." This is probably the only time Yamagata was ever accused of being a liberal.

47. Yoshino-Katō, p. 69, use the phrase, "certain conditions." Yoshino's earlier Shina kakumei shōshi (A short history of the Chinese Revolution; Tokyo, 1917), p. 35, is more specific, and says that Sun reportedly promised Amoy to the Japanese.

48. Mainichi, October 4, 1900.

49. This lends strength to Consul McWade's interpretation noted above. But it will be remembered that Sun was the head of the coalition Miyazaki had engineered in Hong Kong.

50. Dispatches in the Mainichi on October 4, 8, 17, 19, 20, 21, 24, 26, 28, and 29, and for November 6, 8, and 23. On January 30, 1901, Sun was reported back in Yokohama, dissatisfied with his Japanese friends and their help, and planning to leave for Hawaii.

51. Mainichi, September 14, 1900.

52. Mainichi, September 12, 1900. The league was formally inaugurated later that month.

53. Loc. cit.

54. The report was written in 1896. Long excerpts from it are given in Tsurumi Yūsuke, Gotō Shimpei (Biography of Gotō Shimpei; Tokyo, 1937), II, 412-423.

55. Gotō Shimpei, pp. 423–426.

56. Gotō Shimpei, pp. 427–442.

57. Saigō, who led the punitive expedition to Formosa in 1874, ignored a last minute Tokyo decision against such a move.

58. Gotō Shimpei, pp. 443–450. Gotō encouraged the Chinese officials to ask for help in keeping order if they should require it.

59. Tsurumi's account of this is documented by the telegrams from Tokyo to Formosa, and his accounts of cabinet discussions are taken from an official and

unavailable transcript by a secretary named Yokozawa Jirō. I have drawn on these same sources in "Opportunists in South China During the Boxer Rebellion," *Pacific Historical Review*, XX, 3: 241–250 (August, 1951).

60. *Gotō Shimpei*, p. 457. Resistance in Peking ended August 14, so the time was growing short.

61. *Gotō Shimpei*, p. 458. Peking had now fallen.

62. *Gotō Shimpei*, p. 461.

63. This priest was a worthy in his own right. Takamatsu Sei (1856–1903) was from Fukuoka. He fought with Saigō Takamori, and thereafter decided to become a Buddhist missionary in order to counter Western imperialist and missionary aggression. He built temples on Formosa, founded the Honganji at Amoy, and spared no effort to further this branch of Japanese culture. Biography in *TSSK*, III, 290–291, details his collaboration with Kodama. The *Kokuryūkai* narrative, however, makes no mention of the abortive seizure of Amoy. I have found no mention of the incident in Japanese histories.

64. Amoy Consular Letters, Vol. 14, No. 85. Johnson to State, August 26, 1900.

65. Hirayama, p. 94.

66. Amoy Consular Letters, Vol. 14, No. 85, August 26, 1900.

67. *Gotō Shimpei*, p. 468. On August 27, Johnson wired Secretary of State Hay: "Situation critical. Japanese landing troops, guns. Consuls protesting. Chinese had kept faith, mob disproved. Thousands fleeing city." Amoy Consular Letters, No. 85. Although Johnson was well informed throughout, *United States Foreign Relations* for 1900 gives only three brief messages from Goodnow (at Shanghai) to Hay, relaying assurances from the Japanese Consul General at Shanghai that the temporary landing of troops had been done "solely to protect consulate and foreign residents." p. 266.

68. This was not done without some difficulty. The transports were not equipped with wireless, and they had to be flagged by the warships when they arrived off the coast. Two days later, the situation was still critical. Johnson wired Hay on August 30, "Panic increases; no demonstrations against foreigners; officials request if annexation unintended, conduct Japanese unjustifiable, shops closed, looting general, 50,000 fled, native troops withdrawn prevent conflict Japanese." That same day, in a longer dispatch: "The entire city was moved with but one impulse and that was to remove their families and save them from a fate worse than death." Amoy Consular Letters, Dispatches 86, 87.

69. Amoy Consular Letters, Dispatch 88, September 5, 1900. Three days later, the foreign consuls in Amoy dined with their Japanese colleague, making every effort "to allay any feeling the Japanese might have entertained that their action was in any way resented by those present." September 8, Dispatch 89.

70. *Gotō Shimpei*, pp. 478–482.

71. *Mainichi*, September 9, 14, and 16, 1900.

72. *Mainichi*, September 17, 1900.

73. *Mainichi*, September 27 and October 17, 1900.

74. *Gotō Shimpei*, p. 482.

75. Ōtsu, *Kensei shi*, V, 131, attributes the resignation to political pressure from the *Seiyūkai*. The Yamagata *Life*, Tokutomi Iichirō (Miyazaki's old school teacher), *Kōshaku Yamagata Aritomo den* (Tokyo, 1935), III, 426f., ignores the Amoy story, and states simply that Yamagata, who had planned to resign earlier, stayed on to steer the ship of state through the Boxer crisis. *Itō Hirobumi den*, III, 463–466, says

that Itō had assured Yamagata of the support of the *Seiyūkai* in the Diet. But despite a written pledge of support dated September 9, Itō wrote his close friend Inoue Kaoru on the next day that Kodama's complaints and Gotō's activities in Tokyo were putting the cabinet in a very difficult position; a resignation could be expected shortly. These official biographies tend to give only information which lends luster to their heroes. Gotō's is naturally most complete in this instance. Kodama's has not been available.

76. Sun Yat-sen, *Memoirs of a Chinese Revolutionary,* p. 196. Italics mine.

77. Sun, *loc. cit.,* says of Kodama, "a man who sympathized a great deal with the Chinese Revolution, as he considered that the North was entirely in the grip of anarchy." Sun continued to think highly of Kodama. The *Mainichi* for February 17, 1913, reported that Sun had decorated the general's tomb with a wreath.

CHAPTER 5. THE T'UNG-MENG-HUI

1. *TSSK,* I, 704. Nezu (1860–1927), army trained, had been one of the original members of the China Trade Research Bureau. Biography in *Dai jimmei jiten,* V, 62, and in *Taishi kaiko roku,* II, 554–561.

2. *TSSK,* I, 707. Ōtsu, *Kensei shi,* V, 355.

3. The full platform of the League called for eternal equality of all Asiatic nations, unity of public opinion, and a firm stand in China. Konoe's speeches were backed by a Reporters' Association headed by Inukai. *Mainichi,* September 19, 20, and 25, 1900.

4. *TSSK,* I, 709–712. Ōtsu, *Kensei shi,* V, 358–360.

5. *TSSK,* I, 705.

6. Ōtsu, *Kensei shi,* V, 377. See also Tatsuji Takeuchi, *War and Diplomacy in the Japanese Empire* (New York, 1935), pp. 135–137.

7. *TSSK,* I, 688.

8. *TSSK,* I, 692.

9. According to O. Tanin and E. Yohan, *Militarism and Fascism in Japan* (New York: International Publishers, 1934), pp. 44–45, the firm of Yasuda contributed to the societies. Later, when General Kodama headed the War Ministry, he paid the expansionist groups.

10. *Ibid.,* pp. 42–43.

11. *TSSK,* I, 651.

12. Sugiyama Hirosuke, "Shakai" (Society), in *Gendai Nihon shi kenkyū* (Studies in Recent Japanese History; Tokyo, 1938), p. 26.

13. Preface to *Sanjū-sannen no yume,* pp. 8, 9; last chapter, p. 291, and an appendix reprint of an interview with Miyazaki's widow at the time of the funeral ceremonies for Sun Yat-sen in 1929, pp. 308–309. Mrs. Miyazaki told the reporters that when she came to tell Sun·that her husband was sick and that the family needed his help, Sun tried to dissuade her from taking her husband home with her by showing her pictures of his own family, who were also in financial straits. Miyazaki then startled them both by announcing his decision to enter a ballad school of *naniwa bushi* run by one Tōchūken Kumo-emon, a ballad reciter and Bushidō booster. For the latter, see *Heibonsha Hyakkajiten* (Heibonsha Encyclopedia; Tokyo, 1940), XVIII, 643.

14. Figures from Roger F. Hackett, "Chinese Students in Japan, 1900–1910," in

Papers on China, Vol. 3 (Harvard Regional Studies, mimeographed, 1948), p. 142. They are based on an analysis of the *Japan Weekly Mail.*

15. Japan's opportunity was not limited to China. She encouraged Korean students too, setting up special organizations to encourage them. In 1900 there were 68 Korean students, of whom 21 were at military schools. *Mainichi,* September 24, 1900, and February 12, 1901. In 1906 there were also Japanese teachers in Siam and Siamese students in Tokyo. In that same year, 50 Indian students got special attention from Ōkuma, who assured them that Japan regarded India as the Holy Land and was eager to repay her cultural debt. See the summary in *Bulletin de l'École Française d'Extreme-Orient,* pp. 481f. (Hanoi, 1906).

16. Hirakawa Seifū, *Shina kyōwa shi* (History of the Chinese Republic; Shanghai, 1920), pp. 30, 31.

17. Hirakawa, *Shina kyōwa shi,* p. 38, says that while it took students returning from Japan only a week or so to set up a newspaper in China, those coming from Europe would need several months.

18. Kita Ikki, *Shina kakumei gaishi,* p. 56.

19. For a contemporary view, see J. O. P. Bland, *Recent Events and Present Policies in China* (London, 1912), p. 84. "Few Chinese stayed longer than three months . . . the Japanese started worthless schools, and sold diplomas . . . and when the Japanese government investigated these 'schools' in 1906, over half of the students left Japan."

20. Yoshino-Katō, p. 75.

21. Feng, *Chung-hua min-kuo,* etc., p. 116; Yoshino-Katō, p. 76.

22. This diary, by a youth who wrote his name in Japanese kana as So Ko-man (Sokauman) is given in Sanetō, *Meiji Nisshi bunka kōshō,* pp. 277–336.

23. The best general study of the student movement is to be found in Sanetō Keishū, *Chūgokujin Nihon ryūgaku shikō* (Draft history of the Chinese students in Japan; Tokyo, 1939), p. 368.

24. George Lynch, "Two Westernized Orientals" (Sun and Ōkuma), in *Outlook,* 67. 12: 671–674 (1912). Sun was never discouraged by failure. In speaking of his 1895 revolt, he told a Japanese friend that it all hinged on dynamiting part of Canton. "Had I been a little more cruel hearted," he said, "I feel sure my revolutionary scheme must have succeeded." Told by N. Kato, "Reminiscences of Dr. Sun," English *Mainichi* (March 13, 1925).

25. *Inukai Bokudō den,* II, 724. Inukai considered Sun a "real *shishi.*" So did Kayano when Sun told him his three favorite occupations, in order, were revolutions, reading, and women. *kakumei hikyū,* p. 348. Elsewhere, however, Kayano stresses Sun's deeply religious motivation. p. 48.

26. Georges Soulié de Morant, *Soun Iat-senn,* pp. 112–117. The author, a French official at Shanghai, issued Sun's visa to Indochina for this trip.

27. Feng, *I-shih,* I, 132, and *Chung-hua min-kuo,* p. 146. Chou Lu, *Kuo-min-tang shih-kao,* I, 74.

28. Sharman, *Sun Yat-sen,* p. 91, gives the impressions of Dr. Hager, an old friend of Sun's.

29. Shirayanagi Shuko, *Meiji Taishō kokumin shi* (History of Meiji, Taisho; Tokyo, 1938), V, 64. See also Hyman Kublin, "The Japanese Socialists and the Russo-Japanese War," *Journal of Modern History,* XXII. 4: 322–339 (December 1950).

30. Takeuchi Zensaku, "Meiji makki ni okeru Chū-Nichi kakumei undō no

kōryū" (Cross currents of the Chinese and Japanese revolutionary movements at the end of the Meiji Period), *Chūgoku kenkyū* (China Studies), No. 5, p. 80. (1948).

31. After plans for an attack against the Ch'angsha garrison were discovered, Huang had escaped the city by slipping through the gate in disguise. Later the gate was renamed for him. *TSSK*, II, 369.

32. Fujimoto, *Kyojin Tōyama Mitsuru Ō*, p. 516.

33. Miyazaki Ryūsuke, appendix to *Sanjū-sannen no yume* (1926 edition), p. 3.

34. From Sun's last speech in Japan, at Kobe, November 27, 1924. Given in *Mainichi*, November 28, 1924, and in Sun Yat-sen, *China and Japan: Natural Friends–Unnatural Enemies* (Shanghai, 1941), p. 143. This booklet was issued, with a foreword, by Wang Ching-wei to justify his own defection. Chinese original in *Tsung-li ch'üan-chi*, II, 542.

35. Fujimoto, *Kyojin Tōyama*, p. 509, and *TSSK*, II, 375. Miyazaki was present at the meetings, but could follow little of what was said.

36. According to Kayano's account of a meeting between Sun and Huang, the latter's first question was, "Have you got any money?" In answer Sun showed him his suitcase contents, thereby sealing the alliance. *kakumei hikyū*, p. 382. Kayano and Miyazaki were apparently rivals for Sun's confidence, and each is inclined to be reticent about the other's contributions. In this case, neither mentions the other's presence at the meeting between Sun and Huang. Kayano, who died during the recent war, was born in 1873. A samurai from Tosa, he worked for a time as reporter in China. His biographers point out that his work for liberalism in China was a natural corollary to the struggle of the Tosa leaders for constitutionalism in Japan. *Zoku Taishi kaiko roku*, II, 1185–1207.

37. Chou Lu, *Kuo-min-tang shih-kao*, I, 38.

38. *TSSK*, II, 375–377; Chou Lu, p. 40.

39. Sakamoto (1865–1923) was a member of the Diet, helped publish *Min Pao*, and had interests in coal mines in China. *Dai jimmei jiten*, III, 114. For the ritual designed to keep the society secret, see Hatano, *Kokumintō tsūshi*, p. 70.

40. The rules are given in Chou Lu, *Kuo-min-tang shih-kao*, I, 86. Feng, *Chunghua min-kuo*, p. 309, says that when, in addition to Hirayama Shū and Kayano Chōchi, two Japanese socialists were proposed for membership and office, Miyazaki and Hirayama advised against it, "since the Japanese government was helping Sun."

41. Hirano, "Nisshi kōshō shi," *Shina mondai jiten*, p. 598, feels that this may be the source of Sun's views. The book in question, "Tochi kinkō, jinrui no taiken" (Fair share of land, the right of mankind), is in Yoshino Sakuzō, ed., *Meiji bunka zenshū*, XXI, 299–329. Henry George was much in vogue in Japan after the Russo-Japanese War, and several journals published his book serially.

42. Yoshino-Katō, p. 88.

43. Chou Lu, I, 44–104, gives these in full.

44. Hatano, *Kokumintō tsūshi*, p. 75. Soulié, *Soun Iat-sen*, p. 127, gives November 26, 1905, as the date of the first number.

45. Kayano, *kakumei hikyū*, p. 60, tells of a concentrated police search for sources of support for *Min Pao* which ended with the embarrassing discovery that a police official, Koga, was furnishing the house in which it was printed.

46. Shirayanagi, *Meiji Taishō shi*, p. 83.

47. *Japan Weekly Mail*, October 26, 1907.

48. It is perhaps worth noting that the statement called, not for an alliance, but for coöperation among the two *kuo-min*, or peoples.

49. *Wang Ching-wei wen-tze* (Writings of Wang Ching-wei; Canton, 1926), pp. 95, 127, 137.

50. For Sun's statement, Kayano, *kakumei hikyū*, p. 2.

51. Article in Chou Lu, I, 442–451.

52. Kayano, *kakumei hikyū*, p. 387, tells of an editorial battle Hu waged with Liang Ch'i-ch'ao's adherents on this point, and, pp. 293–298, gives a letter Hu wrote the *Kokumin shimbun* in 1907 to straighten them out on the same matter.

53. Chou Lu, I, 442f., and Kayano, p. 303.

54. Feng, *Chung-hua min-kuo*, etc., p. 198.

55. Muramatsu Shōfu, *Akiyama Teisuke wa kataru: Kane, Koi, Hotoke* (Akiyama Teisuke talking: Money, Love, Buddha; Tokyo, 1948), p. 260.

56. *Ibid.*, p. 16.

57. From other sources it would appear that Akiyama was capable of taking care of his finances. In 1904 he was impeached by his fellow Diet members for a sensational "Extra" of his *Niroku Shimbun* which announced a new issue of government bonds, and thereby implied financial stringency in the conduct of the war. Midoro Shōichi, ed., *Meiji Taishō shi*, Vol. I, *Genron* (Press), (Tokyo: Asahi, 1930), p. 207.

58. Muramatsu, *Akiyama*, p. 22–23.

59. Kayano, *kakumei hikyū*, p. 83.

60. Hirano, "Nisshi kōshō shi," p. 600.

61. *TSSK*, II, 435–436. Hirano, *loc. cit.*

62. Feng, *Chung-hua min-kuo*, p. 199.

63. Kuzuu, *Nikkan gappō hishi*, I, Appendix history of the *Kokuryūkai*, p. 12. But Sun was not officially readmitted before 1911.

64. *TSSK*, II, 437. Feng, *Chung-hua min-kuo*, p. 201.

65. *TSSK*, II, 382–392. Kayano, *kakumei hikyū*, pp. 49–55 and 85f., gives the best account of the Nagasaki meetings.

66. Also involved in the project: two young socialists (Kita Ikki and Wada Saburō), Kiyofuji Koshichirō, and Ike Kyōkichi.

67. Takeuchi Zensaku, "Meiji makki ni okeru Chū-Nichi kakumei undō no kōryū," p. 78.

68. *Son Bun shugi* (Sun-ism; Tokyo: Gaimushō, 1935), II, 590. A collection of Sun's papers and letters. For the document giving Miyazaki power of attorney, see Plate II.

69. Soulié de Morant, *Soun Iat-senn*, pp. 128f., implies that this help was largely planned by military adventurers without the approval or knowledge of Paris.

70. Kayano and Inukai had helped in an earlier attack scheduled for Swatow in 1906. Their ship with arms was almost captured, and in the resulting mix-up the conspirators dumped the guns into the sea to keep out of trouble with their own government. Kayano, *kakumei hikyū*, pp. 109–110.

71. Yoshino-Katō, pp. 119–120.

72. Ike's book, *Shina kakumei sen jikkenki* (A First Hand Account of the Revolutionary War in China), was published serially in the Osaka *Asahi*, but has not been available for this study. Yoshino quotes from it at length. Sun added an introduction to the book which can be found in *Son Bun shugi*, II, 388–389.

73. Mr. Miyazaki lent me six such letters, and others can be found in *Son Bun shugi*, pp. 589, 591, 639, 702.

74. Narita, *Zōho Kakyō*, pp. 168–170, and *Son Bun den*, p. 150. "Citizenship" refers to one of three types which were to be stratified according to whether one

had joined the movement before the revolution, during the revolution, or after its success.

75. According to figures given by Narita, *Zōho Kakyō*, pp. 172–173, the proportion of funds supplied by overseas Chinese rose steadily in each of Sun's *putsches*.

76. In Sun's correspondence with Japanese friends, Japanese in America also served as intermediaries. Kayano reproduces a note from Sun to Tarō Ōtsuka, in Chicago, thanking him for forwarding Kayano's telegram to him in October 1911. A letter from Sun to Kayano refers to Ōtsuka as "your relative." *Son Bun shugi*, II, 640.

77. F. L. Chapin, "Homer Lea," p. 96. The Japanese edition of Lea's diatribe against Japanese militarism sold very well. It had introductions by Generals Togo, Terauchi, Nogi, and Kuroki. The publisher of a pirate edition was forced to apologize to Ike by Mayor Ozaki Yukio, friend of Inukai, and whose brother was among the *shishi*.

78. The *Tatsu Maru* Incident is described by Hayashi, *Waga shichi jūnen o kataru* (The Story of my Seventy Years; Tokyo, 1939), pp. 273f. At the request of Count Ishii, Uchida Ryōhei had Sun Yat-sen do what he could to stop the boycott. *TSSK*, II, 435. Fullest coverage is found in Wang Yün-sheng, *Liu-shih-nien-lai Chung-kuo yü Jih-pen*, V, 175–198.

79. Proudly recounted by the *Kokuryūkai* in *TSSK*, II, 25–50, and *Nikkan gappō hishi*, 2 vols.

80. The files have been microfilmed by the Library of Congress. *Kakumeitō kankei* (Documents relating to the Revolutionary Party), begins February 1910. M.T. 1.6.1.4.1, Reel 101.
For Miyazaki's son's account, Appendix to *Sanjū-sannen no yume*, pp. 323f.

81. *Ibid.*, exposures 132, 136f.

82. Kayano, *kakumei hikyū*, p. 83. Apparently the agents were particularly anxious to keep track of Kita Ikki. For many of such "subversives," *Gaimushō* agents and their reports were probably duplicated or supplemented by Army and/or police surveillance.

83. Foreign Office Files, Reel 101, exposure 59, dated May 29, 1910. The agents reported Miyazaki was frequently ill and that he vomited blood. Agent 1091, on June 3, allowed admiration to creep into his report: "This man's body is weak," he wrote, "but his spirit is strong." Exposure 94.

84. *Ibid.*, Exposure 423, Clipping dated November 3.

85. One such, Makino Hankai, was a source of a good deal of information to agents in Hong Kong. Makino, a Fukuoka man and charter member of the *Genyōsha*, also participated in the Osaka Incident, wrote an admiring biography of the man who tried to kill Ōkuma in 1889, agitated for war with China and Russia, represented Fukuoka in the Diet, and then travelled in Southeast Asia as secretary of an organization which sought to keep contacts alive with overseas Japanese. *TSSK*, III, 491–493. Exposures 376–399, Reel 101.

86. John G. Reid, *The Manchu Abdication and the Powers, 1908–1912* (Berkeley: Univ. of California Press, 1935), p. 17. For diplomatic correspondence relating to Yuan's dismissal, Foreign Office Files, Reel 111, Exposure 1130f.

87. Thus Wang Ching-wei denied the applicability of Japanese institutions to his Manchu captors in 1909. Kayano, *kakumei hikyū*, pp. 116f.

88. Tokutomi Iichirō, *Kōshaku Katsura Tarō den* (Biography of Prince Katsura; Tokyo, 1917), II, 395–414, gives a good account of these negotiations.

CHAPTER 6. THE 1911 REVOLUTION

1. This is evident from the Foreign Office Files, Separate Volume 6, "The Dismissal of Yuan Shih-k'ai," Reel 111, M.T.1.6.1.4.3, Exposures 1197f. The volumes devoted to the revolutionary party do not include the months of revolutionary activity. No doubt the confusion was too great for even the *Gaimushō* agents.

2. For instance, the *Mainichi* of November 24, 1900, carried a signed editorial by Hara Kei announcing that he was leaving the paper for the *Seiyūkai*. He assured readers that he would continue to represent business interests as he had previously.

3. Kuzuu Yoshihisa, *Nisshi kōshō gaishi* (Unofficial History of Sino-Japanese Relations; Tokyo, 1939), II, 14. This is a *Kokuryūkai* publication.

4. Kinoshita Hanji, *Nihon kokka shugi undō shi* (A History of the Japanese Nationalist Movement; Tokyo, 1940), p. 10.

5. A news story of November 23 seemed in partial contradiction to the warning that trade was languishing. It reported that exports in clothing to China had increased greatly since the start of the revolution. Chinese were buying Japanese hats to replace their pigtails, and Japanese suits to go with the hats.

6. *The China Yearbook of 1912* (London, 1912) has a convenient twenty page preface detailing the confusion of the first month of the revolution. For a longer and better account, see Yoshino-Katō, pp. 177–265.

7. *TSSK*, II, 318–320.

8. For Kawashima's early life, *TSSK*, II, 212–250. His Peking activities are treated in pages 272–279. Biography in *Zoku Taishi kaiko roku*, II: 198–205.

9. Wu Lu-chen and Tsai Ao were generals trained in Japan who became very important in the revolutionary movement since they were in command of troops. Tsai Ao later led the 1916 revolt against Yuan Shih-k'ai. Yoshino Sakuzō, *Shina kakumei shōshi*, p. 52. For a more detailed account of the maneuvering that resulted in Wu's death, see Yoshino-Katō, pp. 277f.

10. The army officers were Colonel Takayama, Major Taga, and Captain Matsui.

11. The Mongol Princes were K'e-la and Pa-lin. *TSSK*, II, 327.

12. There were, however, rumors that Japan was arming bandits in the South Manchurian Railroad zone. See Shu Pu, "The Consortium Loan to China, 1911–1914" (Unpublished Doctoral Dissertation, Univ. of Michigan, 1950), p. 72.

13. *TSSK*, II: 250–338, *passim*. Prince Su (1866–1922) was an important Manchu functionary. In 1901, he was emissary to England to congratulate Edward VII on his accession. *Mainichi*, February 5, 1901. He used his influence to prevent Wang Ching-wei's execution after the assassination attempt of 1909. Kita Ikki wrote of the Prince that he was like the French emigrees, seeking help from former enemies. *Shina kakumei gaishi*, p. 21. Biography in *Tōyō rekishi daijiten*, IV, 257.

14. *TSSK*, II, 469.

15. Kita's later bitterness at the failure of Japanese aims must be read against his own contradictory motives. As a socialist, he wanted to oppose the "bourgeois" Saionji cabinet, and yet he also wanted to further Japan's continental expansion. This brought about simultaneous membership in the *T'ung-meng-hui* and the *Kokuryūkai*. There is a good biography by Tanaka Sōgorō, *Nihon Fascism no genryū: Kita Ikki no shōgai to shisō* (Tokyo, 1948).

16. *Genyōsha shashi*, p. 581.

17. Kita, *Shina kakumei gaishi*, pp. 77–80. Kita was in close touch with Ch'en Chi-mei, head of the Shanghai *T'ung-meng-hui* group. Their joint efforts to import arms from Japan failed.

18. Tōyama and his men sponsored Kojima as a candidate who specialized in sincerity and Japanese ideals. Not a cent was spent for the election or for bribery, and the papers hailed the victory as a triumph for virtue. See Fujimoto, *Kyojin Tōyama Ō*, pp. 551–554, and Kojima's personal account, in *Chūō Kōron*, pp. 168f. (January 1951).

19. *TSSK*, II, 403.

20. The *Japan Weekly Chronicle*, December 21, 1911, described a parade of Chinese "determined to die" units in Nagasaki. Japanese and Chinese lined the route cheering wildly. The Chinese consulate, which still flew the Dragon Flag, was shunned. Hereafter, cited as *JWC*.

21. *TSSK*, II, 463–464.

22. Fujimoto, *Kyojin Tōyama*, pp. 512–513.

23. Sharman, *Sun Yat-sen*, p. 130. Sun Yat-sen, "Tzu ch'uan," in *Tsung-li ch'üan-chi*, I, Part 1, pp. 16, 17.

24. This concern is further evidenced by a letter Sun wrote Miyazaki from England, asking about Saionji's attitude. *Tsung-li ch'üan-chi*, III, 209.

25. Chapin, "Homer Lea," Appendix, p. 140, letter dated March 24, 1910; "I think it is the most valuable thing that any rivalry [*sic*] Power could get. Would you try to find out whether the War Department of this country would avail this opportunity of obtaining these secret documents?"

26. Chapin, "Homer Lea," p. 102. From Penang Consular File 893/00, December 18, enclosure, article from Penang Gazette, December 14, 1911.

27. Chapin, "Homer Lea," p. 105. Dispatch dated December 22, 1911.

28. Miyazaki had trouble getting there because of financial difficulties. He probably went as a reporter. Appendix to *Sanjū-sannen no yume*, p. 326.

29. Kita, *Shina kakumei gaishi*, p. 112, says that the Japanese went to meet Sun partly out of fear that he might be assassinated.

30. "Saggitarius," *The Strange Apotheosis of Sun Yat-sen* (London, 1939), p. 42.

31. Kita, *Shina kakumei gaishi*, p. 109.

32. *JWC*, May 16, 1912. Terao was dismissed from his position when he went to Nanking, for the government was afraid of showing sympathy for the revolutionaries. Kita, *Shina kakumei gaishi*, pp. 104–105, points out that the revolutionaries, far from possessing good Japanese arms, had to use old museum pieces that would not turn sideways. They had hardly learned to use such relics in Japan.

33. For an account of his doings, *Genyōsha shashi*, pp. 581–583. Tōyama's expenses were paid by his Kyushu mine operator friends. Fujimoto, *Kyojin Tōyama*, p. 531.

34. *TSSK*, II, 467.

35. *Inukai Bokudō den*, II, 735–741, gives a day-by-day account by Soejima Giichi of the group's activities. Inukai tried to go incognito, but he disclosed his identity at Nagasaki during an argument with the station master. *JWC*, December 29, 1911.

36. *Inukai Bokudō den*, II, 716.

37. For extended treatment of the Hanyehping problem, Marius B. Jansen, "Yawata, Hanyehping, and the Twenty-one Demands," *Pacific Historical Review*, XXIII, No. 1: 31–48 (February 1954). Accounts somewhat at variance with each other can be found in *Segai Inoue Kō den*, V: 296–318, and in *Tōa shintaisei no senku: Mori Kaku* (Forerunner of the New Order in Asia: Mori Kaku; Tokyo, 1940), pp. 381–402. Inoue was a Mitsui adviser, and Mori (1883–1932) was an architect of the Mitsui empire in China.

38. Kayano, *kakumei hikyū*, p. 159. *Mori Kaku*, p. 384. Mori was hurriedly sum-

moned from New York by Mitsui's Tokyo headquarters when the Chinese revolution broke out. Yamada's account of his conversation with Sun goes as follows: "You're in with the Mitsui money bags; get me some money." "About how much?" "The more the better." "What's the most you would want?" "One or two hundred million yen would do." *Mori Kaku*, p. 382.

39. *TSSK*, II, 428, 440–446; *Mori Kaku*, p. 378, gives the contract. Uchida is designated as representative of the Chinese Republic, and interest is to be 8¼% annually. The Mitsui men who compiled Mori's biography complain of lack of clear proof that this larger loan was ever fully made or repaid. John V. MacMurray, ed., *Treaties and Agreements with and concerning China, 1894–1919*, II, 1077–1083, indicates that three million yen were handed over at this time. For further discussion, see Yoshino Sakuzō, *Nikka kokkō ron*, pp. 108–110.

40. For the terms of the contract and Sheng's letters, *Mori Kaku*, pp. 392–402. The Japanese press also reported that Inukai purchased land in Hankow for Mitsubishi. *JWC*, February 8, 1912. Other stories intimated that Sun offered the China Merchants Steam Navigation Company as security as well. If so, the revolutionaries were rather free with their assets, for German reports had it that the same interests had been used to tempt British bankers. *Die Grösse Politik der Europäeischen Kabinette* (Berlin, 1926), XXXII, 205. Hereafter, *GP*.

41. Kita, *Shina kakumei gaishi*, pp. 136–137.

42. *TSSK*, II, 445.

43. *TSSK*, II, 468.

44. Kita, *Shina kakumei gaishi*, pp. 132–136.

45. Sun, "My Reminiscences," *Strand Magazine*.

46. Shu Pu, "The Consortium Loan," p. 79, quotes the Shanghai *Shih Pao* of November 4, 1911.

47. *TSSK*, II, 447.

48. Fujimoto, *Kyojin Tōyama Ō*, p. 538. Sun, no doubt, was not trying very hard to understand, so the Japanese took the convenient excuse of blaming the interpreter, confident that their eloquence would have sufficed if it had been transmitted.

49. As will be noted below, there was a joint Russo-Japanese policy in regard to Manchuria.

50. *TSSK*, II, 459.

51. Kita, *Shina kakumei gaishi*, pp. 108–150, *passim*.

52. Andō Norikata, *Saionji Kimmochi* (Tokyo, 1928), p. 45. *Kōshaku Yamagata Aritomo den*, III, 779.

53. Kuzuu, *Nisshi kōshō gaishi*, pp. 14, 15.

54. Foreign Office Files, "The Dismissal of Yuan Shih-k'ai." See Note 1, above.

55. Shu Pu, "The Consortium Loan," pp. 49, 51.

56. *The Foreign Relations of the United States* (1911), p. 52. Hereafter, *FR*.

57. *FR* (1911), pp. 56, 57.

58. Reports of Japanese aid to the revolutionaries had been countered by Japanese charges of German aid to the Manchus. See *GP*, XXXII, 244. The *Kokuryūkai* account says there were so many Japanese and Germans active that some foreigners thought the revolution was a German-Japanese war. *TSSK*, II, 412.

59. *FR* (1911), p. 108.

60. *FR* (1911), p. 67. Sun told the secretary of the American legation of this offer. He must have meant the negotiations for the Hanyehping loan mentioned above.

61. *FR* (1911), p. 50.

CHAPTER 7. THE REVOLUTION OF 1913

1. *Inukai Bokudō den,* II, 717. Sakishiro Gakujin, "Genji no Shinatsū" (Present day China experts), in *Chūō Kōron,* Vol. 28, No. 12, 14 (1913).
2. *Ōkuma Kō,* II, 674. Similarly, when Nezu Hajime arrived in Nagasaki in July 1912, he said that the situation in China was promising; good, young men were running the government, and no counter-revolution was in sight. *JWC,* July 18, 1912.
3. Ōtsu, *Kensei shi,* VII, 747.
4. Fujimoto, *Kyojin Tōyama Ō,* pp. 555–559.
5. Tokutomi, *Kōshaku Katsura Kō den,* II, 630–664; Shinobu Seisaburō, *Taishō seiji shi* (Political History of Taishō; Tokyo, 1951), I, 141–180.
6. Ōtsu, *Kensei shi,* VII, 210–279.
7. Shu Pu, "The Consortium Loan," p. 521.
8. Li Chien-nung, *Chung-kuo chin-pai-nien cheng-chih-shih* (Political history of China during the last hundred years; Shanghai, 1947), II, 372–382.
9. Sharman, *Sun Yat-sen,* pp. 147–154.
10. Li, *cheng-chih-shih,* pp. 382–390.
11. On November 9 and 10, the *Mainichi* announced that Sun had already sailed. The next day's news put a halt to preparations for his welcome. See also *JWC,* November 21, 1912.
12. Muramatsu, *Akiyama Teisuke,* pp. 49–68. Mori's biographers state that Mori persuaded Sun to come to Japan instead of going to America. *Mori Kaku,* p. 203.
13. For the resignation, *Mainichi,* February 13, 1913.
14. Muramatsu, *Akiyama Teisuke,* pp. 100–102.
15. Tai T'ien-ch'ou (Tai Chi-t'ao), *Jih-pen-lun* (Discussion of Japan; Shanghai, 1928), p. 176, introduction by Hu Han-min. Pages 90–98 contain the talks with Katsura. The author cites these and the opinions of General Tanaka Giichi and Admiral Akiyama Masano to show what cordial Sino-Japanese relations might have ensued had these men directed Japanese policy. Mori Kaku reported that Katsura had obtained from Sun Yat-sen promises of Manchuria in these talks. On his death-bed, Katsura is said to have exclaimed, "I must get power once more in order to carry out my plans." *Mori Kaku,* p. 405. There is also a discussion of the Sun-Katsura talks (based on Tai) in Hosokawa Karoku, *Ajiya minzoku seisaku ron* (Discussion of the policy of the peoples of Asia; Tokyo, 1940), pp. 12–14.
16. See the discussion of Sun's *Chung-kuo ts'un-wang wen-ti* (1917) in Chapter IX, below.
17. *JWC,* March 6, 1913.
18. *JWC,* February 27, 1913.
19. *Mainichi,* February 17, 1913.
20. *JWC,* February 27, 1913. From a speech Sun gave at a banquet given in his honor by the *Dōbunkai* in Tokyo.
21. *JWC,* March 13, 20, 1913. In considering this value-laden phraseology, it should be remembered that the *Chronicle* readers were at the mercy of two translators.
22. *TSSK,* II, 508. Sharman, *Sun Yat-sen,* p. 156, however, implies that Sun left Japan on March 18. The Foreign Office Files are no help on this point, but Tai, *Jih-pen-lun,* p. 91, says they were in Japan some sixty days. This would make the *Kokuryūkai* date possible; Japanese newspapers, although they are not explicit, support the *Kokuryūkai* account. For a photograph taken during the visit to Fukuoka, see Plate III.

23. *Mori Kaku*, pp. 205–212, includes the documents of agreement. See also *JWC*, June 5, 1913. Among Japanese officials was the financier Shibusawa Eiichi. See Obata, *An Interpretation of the Life of Viscount Shibusawa*, pp. 177f.

24. *JWC*, April 3, 1913.

25. *TSSK*, II, 462.

26. *GP*, XXXII, 396.

27. Ōkuma changed his mind as early as August 1912. *JWC*, August 22, 1912.

28. *JWC*, May 15, 1913.

29. *JWC*, June 12, 1913.

30. *JWC*, June 14, 1913.

31. *Ōkuma Kō*, III, 81, 85.

32. "En Sōtō to Nihon" (President Yuan and Japan), *Gaikō Jihō*, Vol. 18, No. 209, July 15, 1913. This article consists of translations from the Chinese press. See also *JWC*, June 26, 1913.

33. Wang Yün-sheng, *Liu-shih-nien lai Chung-kuo yü Jih-pen*, VI, 19.

34. Kuzuu, *Nisshi kōshō gaishi*, II, 61.

35. *JWC*, August 7, 1913.

36. Shu Pu, "The Consortium Loan," p. 522.

37. Shu Pu, "The Consortium Loan," pp. 522, 571.

38. For instance, Admiral Akiyama (praised in Tai's *Jih-pen-lun*) was sent on an inspection trip of Manchuria and China in the summer of 1913. He encouraged Tanaka Giichi and others to give weapons to the revolutionaries. See the brief biography in *Taishi kaiko roku*, II, 755–756.

39. *JWC*, July 24 and August 7, 28, 1913. German reports considered the revolt entirely Japanese inspired, and expressed satisfaction with Germany's improved status in China as a result of the exit of "(der) ganz unter Japanischen Inspirationen stehenden Sun-Yat-Sen." *GP*, XXXII, 282.

40. This gentleman was a friend of Miyazaki's. *Mori Kaku*, p. 411.

41. *Mori Kaku*, pp. 403–406.

42. *Inukai Bokudō den*, II, 718; Fujimoto, *Kyojin Tōyama Ō*, pp. 860–862; Foreign Office Files, *Kakumei tō kankei*, "Bōmei sho o fukumu" (Refugees), M.T.1.6.1.4.1, August 14, Exposure 1347.

43. Nakano Kōdō, "Bōmei no kyaku ni taishite inujini no setsu o tsugu" (Counseling our refugee guests about a useless death), *Chūō Kōron*, 28. 11: 58–59 (1913).

44. *Mori Kaku*, pp. 213–219. For a December 1913 loan which gave Japan considerable control over the Hanyehping Company see my article, "Yawata Hanyehping and the Twenty-one Demands," p. 42.

45. Kuzuu, *Nisshi kōshō gaishi*, II, 33–34. Ōtsu, *Kensei shi*, VII, 114, lists several additional anti-Japanese outrages.

46. *TSSK*, II, 552–560.

47. Abe, in trying to calm the agitation over insults to the flag, had remonstrated with the patriots that the flag was, after all, only a tool. Several of the *shishi* thought this might be a misquotation and called upon him to give him an opportunity to recant. When he stuck by his statement, a youth named Okada, after taking *hara-kiri* lessons from an army captain, struck Abe down. The patriots then held a ceremony for Okada at the tomb of Arao Kiyoshi. *TSSK*, II, 560–562.

48. Despite further arrests, riots continued for several days thereafter. The

Kokuryūkai reports that police were so unpopular that their children were shunned at school until they begged their fathers to quit the force. *TSSK*, II, 566.

49. For Yuan's telegram, *JWC*, September 18, 1913. As a gesture of government favor Abe was posthumously promoted Ambassador to Belgium. *JWC*, September 11, 1913.

50. Shu Pu, "The Consortium Loan," pp. 594f.

51. See the letter from Ch'en Chi-mei to a comrade in Sun, *Memoirs of a Chinese Revolutionary*, "Who Was Right?," pp. 147–160.

52. Foreign Office Files, Exposure 2861, December 21, 1913, Agent 1788.

53. Miyazaki or Kayano visited Huang almost daily.

54. Chiang arrived September 1, and left for Tokyo a week later, but visited Sun very seldom. Foreign Office Files, Exposures 1813, 1915, 4847.

55. Ch'en (uncle of Ch'en Kuo-fu and Ch'en Li-fu) is second only to Tai among those in constant attendance on Sun.

56. Foreign Office Files, Exp. 1243, enclosed *Asahi* clipping, August 11, 1913.

57. Foreign Office Files, Exp. 2775f, December 8, 1913.

58. Foreign Office Files, Exp. 2859, December 21, 1913, quoting Tōyama.

59. Foreign Office Files, Exp. 3345f, report by Yamaza from Peking, January 14, 1914.

60. Foreign Office Files, Exp. 3725, 5219, Feb. 3 and July 9, 1914.

61. Foreign Office Files, Exp. 3594, 3613, February 3, 1914.

62. Foreign Office Files, Exp. 1836, with clippings from Shanghai papers.

63. Foreign Office Files, Exp. 2477, October 28, 1913.

64. Foreign Office Files, Exp. 2761–2775, complete with documentation of Chinese protests and diplomatic assurances.

65. Foreign Office Files, Exp. 3228, January 13, 14, 1914.

66. Foreign Office Files, Exp. 3228f, contain protest from Wai-chiao-pu dated November 26, 1913.

67. Foreign Office Files, Exp. 3051, January 12, 1914. Actually, the poison expert remained at work in Peking until Yuan's death, on Mori's payroll. *Mori Kaku*, 411.

68. Foreign Office Files, Exp. 5425, August 4, 1914.

69. *Ten Letters of Sun Yat-sen: 1914–1916* (limited edition of 100, Stanford University Libraries, 1942), p. 6, dated August 14, 1914.

70. *Ibid.*, p. 14, October 12, 1914.

71. *Ibid.*, p. 14.

72. *Ibid.*, pp. 25, 40; December 19, 1914, and May 27, 1916.

73. Foreign Office Files, Exp. 4467f, February 1914, Prospectus and Catalogue of school as enclosures.

CHAPTER 8. *1915: GUIDANCE BY FORCE*

1. Observers often commented upon the increasing age of Japan's leaders. Katō Kōmei, on returning from a trip to China in 1913, remarked that on a previous visit, in 1899, he had found Chinese leaders older than those in Japan. Now, however, Chinese officials were in their thirties, while Japan was ruled by old men. Itō Masanori, *Katō Kōmei den* (Biography of Katō Kōmei; Tokyo, 1929), I, 737.

2. *Inukai Bokudō den*, II, 222–232. *Ōkuma Kō*, III, 111.

3. Shinobu, *Taishō seiji shi*, pp. 191f., 288.

4. *Segai Inoue Kō den*, V, 352f. Inoue also wanted the government to make Yuan Shih-k'ai stop putting pressure on Sheng Hsüan-huai. *Segai Inoue Kō den*, V, 307.

5. For the treaties, E. B. Price, *The Russo-Japanese Treaties of 1907–1916 Concerning Manchuria and Mongolia* (Baltimore, 1933), Chapters 2, 4, 5; for Russian activities in Mongolia, Gerard M. Friters, *Outer Mongolia and its International Position* (Baltimore, 1949), Chapter II.

6. Shinobu, pp. 44, 136, points out that most Japanese investments in China had been made with borrowed money, and that the total Japanese investment there was still relatively small.

7. *Segai Inoue Kō den*, V, 369.

8. Tokutomi Iichirō, ed. *Kōshaku Matsukata Masayoshi den* (Biography of Prince Matsukata Masayoshi; Tokyo, 1935), II, 910f.

9. *Kōshaku Yamagata Aritomo den*, III, 920–927.

10. *Segai Inoue Kō den*, V, 375. See also Shinobu, pp. 234–237.

11. For the uncertain Western reactions to the document, see P. Weale (B. Lennox Simpson), *The Fight for the Republic in China* (New York, 1917), who gives a translation, pp. 126–128, and Sharman, *Sun Yat-sen*, pp. 193–195. American Minister Reinsch forwarded a copy to Washington; *FR* (1915), pp. 131–137. The Memorandum is given in its entirety by Ōtsu, *Kensei shi*, VII, 491–503, and it is mentioned with pardonable pride in the official *Kokuryūkai* chronology in Kuzuu, *Nikkan gappō hishi*, I, 21.

12. Weale's translation is adequate, although he does not list the Royalist party by name, grouping all dissidents as "malcontents." Cf. Ōtsu, VII, 496.

13. The memorandum was prepared in fifty copies. One got to Peking, into Chinese hands. It was soon translated into Chinese and English and caused a great deal of embarrassment to the Japanese. *TSSK*, II, 572.

14. Ōtsu, *Kensei shi*, VII, 504–505. *Ōkuma Kō*, III, 259. Among the members were Inukai's old friends Kashiwara and Professors Terao and Soejima.

15. *Ōkuma Kō*, III, 260.

16. Mario Toscano, *Guerra diplomatica in Estremo Oriente (1914–1931)* (Torino, 1950), 2 vols., is by far the best work in Western languages. Unfortunately it does not make full use of the *genrō* biographies or of Wang Yün-sheng's *Liu-shih-nien-lai Chung-kuo yü Jih-pen*. Theodore H. White, "The Twenty-One Demands" (Harvard University, A.B. Honors Thesis, 1938), is based almost exclusively upon Wang. Thomas E. LaFargue, *China and the World War* (Stanford University Press, 1937), and Takeuchi, *War and Diplomacy in the Japanese Empire* are also helpful.

17. Wang Yün-sheng, *Liu-shih-nien-lai Chung-kuo yü Jih-pen*, VI, 270. *Katō Kōmei den*, II, 162, however, slights Ariga's importance. No doubt the *genrō* were quick to indignation.

18. *Katō Kōmei den*, I, 23–28.

19. The official biographies occasionally cancel each other out. *Katō Kōmei den* blames the harshness of the demands on the *genrō* and cites Katō's liberal policy in 1925 as proof of this. Matsukata's biographer credits Katō's change of heart to a stern reprimand by Matsukata in 1915. *Matsukata den*, II, 920.

20. Hara Kei noted in his diary that the *genrō* were being censorious without having any alternate policies to suggest. *Hara Kei Nikki* (Tokyo, 1951), Vol. 6, May 5, 1915; p. 246.

21. The low estimate of Hioki's ability given by Toscano, *Guerra Diplomatica*,

I, 374, however, suggests that Inoue's objections to Katō's agents were probably justified.

22. For *genrō* insistence on his departure, *Ōkuma Kō*, III, 322.

23. For the adroit manner in which Ōkuma's recommendation of Katō to become his successor was sidestepped, see Shinobu, *Taishō seiji shi*, I, 268f.

24. Takeuchi, *War and Diplomacy*, p. 191.

25. *Mori Kaku*, p. 371.

26. Kuzuu, *Nikkan gappō hishi*, I, appendix, p. 21.

27. Osaka *Mainichi*, April 27, 1915.

28. *TSSK*, II: 349–353. "Actually Ariga was merely obeying the instructions of the Japanese government which had sent him to China." Ariga is honored with a biography in the ranks of pioneer *shishi*. *TSSK*, III, 594–595.

29. *TSSK*, II, 578.

30. Uchida's biography in *Dai jimmei jiten*, VI, appendix, p. 17.

31. *TSSK*, II, 578–579.

32. Ōtsu, VII, 507.

33. *Mainichi*, May 10, 1915. *Ōkuma Kō*, III, 293f., also insists that the demands achieved a great deal. Certainly they did give the Japanese new opportunities in Manchuria.

34. *Inukai Bokudō den*, II, 285–303.

35. *Mainichi*, May 18, 1915.

36. Watanabe Ikujirō, *Ōkuma Shigenobu* (Tokyo, 1943), p. 228. See also his *Kinsei Nihon gaikō shi*, p. 480, for his conclusion that Inukai's grievance with the Foreign Office was that it had erred in its assessment of the international atmosphere, which was antithetical to imperialism. Professor Watanabe is also writing a new apologia for Ōkuma. Part I, "Ōkuma Shigenobu to taika gaikō" (Ōkuma and the China Policy), *Ōkuma Kenkyū* (Tokyo, 1952), pp. 117–163.

37. Watanabe, who found the document among Ōkuma's papers, reprints the letter, *Ōkuma Shigenobu*, pp. 194–198. Wang Yün-sheng, *Liu-shih-nien-lai Chung-kuo yü Jih-pen*, VI, 34–38, also gives the letter. Wang Ching-wei included it in the collection of Sun's pro-Japanese writings which he circulated under the title *China and Japan: Natural Friends — Unnatural Enemies* (Shanghai, 1941), pp. 1–7. Sharman, *Sun Yat-sen*, pp. 187–189, uses a version which found its way into the English language press in China. She doubts that Sun wrote all of it, since it includes a request for reforming "religion." Actually the original need not be construed to mean more than "culture." "Saggitarius," p. 56, refers to a discussion of the letter by T. F. Tsiang in *China Critic*, July 5, 1934, which has not been available for this study.

38. Wang Yün-sheng, VI, 38. Toscano, *Guerra Diplomatica*, I, 119.

39. To an *Asahi* reporter in 1914, Sun was critical of Japan's occupation of Shantung. *Son Bun shugi*, II, 747–752.

40. *Mainichi*, January 23, 1915.

41. Foreign Office Files, M.T.1.6.4.1, Exposure 5491, August 3, 1914.

42. *Mainichi*, January 27, 1915.

43. *Mainichi*, February 28, 1915. See also a memorandum from the Governor of Nagasaki to the Foreign Office on the numbers of Chinese returning to China; Foreign Office Files, Exp. 5532, March 9, 1915.

44. Clipping, dated March 12, in Foreign Office Files, Exp. 5541.

45. *Mainichi*, February 18, 1915.

46. *Mainichi*, March 13, 1915. The editors naturally applauded Sun's sentiments. Cartoonists depicted Huang Hsing and others carrying Yuan's litter. But actually Huang never went over to Yuan's side.

47. Letter in *Tsung-li ch'üan-chi*, II, 273–274, and in *Son Bun shugi*, pp. 775–780.

48. The document was in a dossier with the Uchida memorandum which was sent to B. L. Simpson by an anonymous informant in 1915. See Weale, *Fight for the Republic*, pp. 140–144. The document also found its way into the *North China Daily Herald*, a journal glad to believe the worst of Sun.

49. Sharman, *Sun Yat-sen*, p. 197.

50. Koike (1873–1921) later entered the business world. Biography in *Taishi kaiko roku*, II, 1268–1270. Hara Kei noted in his diary on November 29, 1915, that Koike was scheming with the China *rōnin*. *Hara Kei nikki*, VI, 340.

51. Foreign Office Files, Exposures 5546–5553. The letter is written in Japanese, but the signature is Sun's. The card of Wang T'ung-i is stapled to the letter.

52. *TSSK*, II, 591–595.

53. *TSSK*, II, 594–595.

54. For a treatment of Yuan's attempt at taking the throne and its collapse, see Li, *cheng-chih shih*, II, 412–473.

55. Kayano, *kakumei hikyū*, p. 355.

56. *Ibid.*, pp. 356–357.

57. *North China Daily Herald*, December 11, 1915. See also *TSSK*, II, 598–601.

58. *The North China Herald*, December 11, reported that Viceroy Sheng Yun of Shansi was in Tokyo representing Prince Su in negotiations with Sun Yat-sen and Huang Hsing. The same day readers were told of the discovery of a thousand sticks of explosives in the baggage of some Japanese passengers at Shanghai.

59. *TSSK*, II, 631. Liu Yen, *Chung-Jih chiao-she shih* (A history of Sino-Japanese negotiations; Shanghai, 1921), p. 62, credits Ōkura with one million and Prince Su himself with 300,000 *yuan*.

60. *TSSK*, II, 625–648.

61. For the Terauchi Cabinet and its loan policy, see Shinobu Seisaburō, *Taishō seiji shi*, II, 330–397, "Nishihara Loans," and Frank C. Langdon, "The Japanese Policy of Expansion in China, 1917–1928" (Unpublished Doctoral Dissertation, University of California, Berkeley, 1953). Under Terauchi loans totalling approximately two hundred million yen were furnished to the Peking government for a variety of purposes, but most of the money was used for administrative and military expenses, and little of it was ever repaid.

62. Although the Tokyo government deplored Sun's Russian ties, it should be noted that the middle twenties were in general a period of rapprochement between Japan and the Soviets. Japan obtained a favorable treaty with the Soviet Union in 1925 and at the same time guarded against Soviet influence in Japan through the Peace Preservation Law with its checks on dangerous thoughts. At the same time Communist propaganda, which played an important part in the Chinese nationalist united front, was much more anti-British than it was anti-Japanese. Japan's Pan-Asian doctrines were, by definition, anti-Western, and if they promoted the colonial revolutions they also promoted, ultimately, the world proletarian revolution. See, on this point, B. Nicolaevsky, "Russia, Japan, and the Pan-Asiatic Movement to 1925," *Far Eastern Quarterly*, VIII. 3: 259–295 (May 1949).

63. *TSSK*, II, 683–727. After the "restoration," it seemed likely that Peking would be beseiged by troops of Tuan Chih-jui. Minister Hayashi, through Mitsui agents,

dispensed enough bribes to make possible the reoccupation of the city without blood-shed. See Hayashi's Memoirs, *Waga shichi-jūnen o kataru* (The story of my seventy years; Tokyo, 1939). Chang Hsün fled to the Netherlands legation for sanctuary. To J. J. L. Duyvendak, who visited him daily, he denied any suggestion of Japanese complicity in his attempt. See Duyvendak's "De laaste dienaar der Mandsjoes" (The last servant of the Manchus) in *China Tegen de Westerkim* (Haarlem, 1927), a lengthy biographical account of Chang. Prince Su, involved in Kawashima Naniwa's earlier restoration attempt, lived under Japanese protection thereafter, and his daughter, who was brought up as the adopted daughter of Kawashima, was executed by the Chinese as a collaborator after World War II. See the bitter account of the execution of Kawashima Yoshiko in Masanobu Tsuji, *Underground Escape* (Tokyo, 1952), pp. 233–234.

64. Muramatsu, *Akiyama Teisuke*, p. 125.

65. *TSSK*, II, 768–769.

66. Kayano, *kakumei hikyū*, pp. 350–351.

67. *TSSK*, II, 795–802.

68. *Transcript of the Record*, International Military Tribunal for the Far East, Testimony of Inukai Takashi, pp. 1478–1522. (Inukai Takashi, son of Inukai Ki, was adviser to Wang Ching-wei at Nanking, and, in 1953, Minister of Justice in Tokyo.) See also Paul Elmquist, "The Sino-Japanese Undeclared War of 1932 at Shanghai," *Papers on China*, Vol. 5 (Harvard University Regional Studies, mimeographed, 1950), pp. 64–65.

69. Higashi-Kuni Naruhiko, *Watakushi no kiroku* (My Memoirs; Tokyo, 1947), pp. 59–60. Tōjō vetoed the proposal.

CHAPTER 9. SUN YAT-SEN AND JAPANESE AID

1. See D. C. Holtom, *Modern Japan and Shinto Nationalism* (Chicago, 1947), p. 19. "Indeed, the doctrine that her state structure is the strongest and most excellent of all the world must have as its corollary the idea that non-Japanese peoples can benefit only by being brought under its sway."

2. The preface appears in Chinese in the 1926 edition of *Sanjū-sannen no yume*, and it is translated into Japanese in the 1943 edition. Also in *Tsung-li ch'üan-chi*, I, Pt. 2, p. 1049. Sun's reference is to a T'ang novel, the *Ch'iu Jan k'e-ch'uan*, by Chang Shuo (667–730). Cf. *Tōyō rekishi daijiten*, II, 219.

3. Bernard Martin, *Strange Vigour: A Biography of Sun Yat-sen* (London, 1944), p. 177, quotes a letter written to Mrs. Cantlie March 19, 1915, from Tokyo: "Yuan Shih-k'ai is the exact prototype of the Kaiser . . . he is pro-German through and through, and if Germany comes out victorious . . . China will surely become Germany's dependency." The same letter says that the Japanese government "fears to show us friendliness" because of the "intervention and the conservative influence of the English government."

4. *Ibid.*, p. 179, letter to Mrs. Cantlie dated January 18, 1916.

5. *Inukai Bokudō den*, II, 725. See also B. Nicolaevsky, "Russia, Japan, and the Pan-Asiatic Movement to 1925," in *Far Eastern Quarterly*, VIII. 3, 274 (May 1949).

6. K. K. Kawakami, "Sun Yat-sen's Greater Asia Doctrine," *Contemporary Japan*, p. 242 (September 1935).

7. *Chung-kuo ts'un-wang wen-ti; Tsung-li ch'üan-chi*, I, Pt. 2, 936–1007. *China and Japan: Natural Friends — Unnatural Enemies*, pp. 9–124.

8. *China and Japan*, p. 101.

9. *Ibid.*, p. 116.

10. *Memoirs of a Chinese Revolutionary*, p. 136.

11. *Tsung-li ch'üan-chi*, III, 337.

12. R. d'Auxion de Ruffe, *Is China Mad?* (Shanghai, 1928), p. 136. This diatribe is a translation and revision of the author's earlier *Chine et Chinois d'Aujourd'hui*.

13. Quoted in *Is China Mad?*, p. 139. Sun delivered an answering blast; "If, therefore, foreigners should dare to oppose or obstruct my presence in Shanghai, I, with the support of my countrymen, am determined to take some drastic steps. . . We, Chinese people, are not to be trifled with so long as we dwell in our own territories."

14. Muramatsu, *Akiyama Teisuke*, p. 124.

15. See the interview Sun granted the English edition of the Osaka *Mainichi* on November 28, 1924. "Dr. Sun Yat-sen expressed intense hatred for the doings of Britishers in the Far East. To his mind, Americans and other foreigners are not entirely undeserving of censure, but the Britishers are the worst lot imaginable. It is the British in China who are always creating trouble there, Dr. Sun indignantly remarked. . . Dr. Sun said he does not hate every Britisher, but in Shanghai and in Kobe he has refused to see British or American newspapermen because from past experience he knows only too well how these newspaper workers maliciously distort facts. Individually speaking, Dr. Sun said, he has many British and American friends . . . but Britishers are a curse to China. . . Dr. Sun said that to the Britishers in China he is an eyesore. They hate him and he hates them more than they him. In every possible underhanded way, these Britishers carry on a campaign against him, on the pretext that he is a trouble maker, utterly forgetting that they themselves are the real trouble makers in China."

16. *Loc. cit.*

17. English *Mainichi*, November 29, 1924. The speech can be found in *Tsung-li ch'üan-chi*, II, 539–549, and in *China and Japan*, pp. 141–151. Extracts were given in the English *Mainichi* of November 29, and the *Mainichi* carried serially a translation by Tai T'ien-ch'ou under the title "The Kingly Way"; December 3, 4, 5, and 6, 1924. Kayano also gives the speech, pp. 331–345, but his censor deleted all references to Russia.

18. *China and Japan*, p. 151. These closing phrases were omitted from the *Mainichi* accounts.

19. Kawakami, "Sun Yat-sen's Greater East Asia Doctrine," p. 240.

20. Kayano, *kakumei hikyū*, p. 351.

21. *Ibid.*, Introduction, p. 8.

INDEX

INDEX